A Summer Bright and Terrible

Also by David E. Fisher

NOVELS

Crisis
Compartments
A Fearful Symmetry
Grace for the Dead
The Last Flying Tiger
The Man You Sleep With
Variation on a Theme
Katie's Terror
Hostage One
The Wrong Man

NONFICTION

The Creation of the Universe
The Creation of Atoms and Stars
The Ideas of Einstein
The Third Experiment
The Birth of the Earth
A Race on the Edge of Time
The Origin and Evolution of Our Own Particular Universe
Fire and Ice
Across the Top of the World
The Scariest Place on Earth
Tube (with Marshall Jon Fisher)
Strangers in the Night (with Marshall Jon Fisher)
Mysteries of the Past (with Marshall Jon Fisher)

A Summer Bright and Terrible

Winston Churchill, Lord Dowding,

Radar, and the Impossible Triumph

of the Battle of Britain

David E. Fisher

 Shoemaker & Hoard

Library of Congress Cataloging-in-Publication Data
Fischer, David E., 1932–
A summer bright and terrible : Winston Churchill, Lord Dowding, Radar, and the impossible triumph of the Battle of Britain / David E. Fisher.
p. cm.
Includes bibliographical references.
ISBN (10) 1-59376-047-7 (alk. paper)
ISBN (13) 978-1-59376-047-2
1. Britain, Battle of, Great Britain, 1940. 2. Air warfare—History—20th century. 3. Dowding, Hugh Caswall Tremenheere Dowding, Baron, 1882–1970. 4. Churchill, Winston, Sir, 1874–1965. I. Title.
D756.5.B7F57 2005
940.54'211—dc22
2005003765

Gallery illustrations: map by Mike Morgenfeld; Spitfire from postcard by Valentine & Sons, Ltd.; the Hurricane courtesy of British Aerospace, Military Aircraft Division; radar towers courtesy of Gordon Kinsey, author of *Bawdsey* (Terence Dalton Limited); Douglas Bader courtesy of Royal Air Force Benevolent Fund; Keith Park from the collection of the Walsh Memorial Library, MOTAT, New Zealand, also courtesy of Dr. Vincent Orange; the Bristol Beaufighter courtesy of British Aerospace, Bristol Division; Dowding statue photo by Lisabeth DiLalla. Every attempt has been made to secure permissions. We regret any inadvertent omission.

Book design and composition by Mark McGarry
Set in Fairfield

Printed in the United States of America

Shoemaker S&H Hoard
An Imprint of Avalon Publishing Group, Inc.
Distributed by Publishers Group West

10 9 8 7 6 5 4 3 2 1

This book is for
Satchel Rhain
and
Bram Jakob

I was simply frightened that we should lose. It was a perfectly straightforward fear, instinctive and direct. The summer of 1940 was an agony for me: I thought that the betting was 5:1 against us. . . . I felt that, as long as I lived, I should remember walking along Whitehall in the pitiless and taunting sun . . . in the bright and terrible summer of 1940.

LEWIS ELIOT,
in *The Light and the Dark,* by C. P. Snow

Contents

Preface

In England the summer of 1940 was the sunniest, driest, most glorious summer in living memory. In that bright and terrible summer Hitler's Germany lay spread like a galloping cancer across Europe. Austria and Czechoslovakia had been swallowed, Poland destroyed, Belgium, Holland, and France enveloped and subjugated in a new form of warfare, the Blitzkrieg. Twenty-five years earlier, the German and French armies had lain supine in trenches for four years, gaining or losing yards at a time. Now suddenly the armored Panzer Korps came thundering through the French lines with dive-bombing Stukas blasting a path for them, and within a few weeks, the continental bastion of democracy had fallen.

The British army escaped at Dunkirk, but the soldiers who returned to England were no longer an army. They were a rabble without guns or ammunition. They had left their tanks, their mortars, their machine guns and their cannon behind on the bloody beaches of France. As the summer blossomed, their future wilted.

Winston Churchill was appointed prime minister on the day France was invaded, and now he stood like a lion roaring. "We shall fight them on the beaches . . . we shall fight in the fields and in the streets. . . . We shall *never* surrender."

It was an empty boast. If once the Wehrmacht crossed the

English Channel, there was nothing in England to fight them with. Old men and young boys were parading around in the Home Guard with broomsticks for weapons, prompting Noël Coward to write his clever ditty ending with the refrain "If you can't provide us with a Bren gun, the Home Guard might as well go home." It was tuneful, it was clever, it was pathetic.

There were no Bren guns.

There was only the Royal Air Force.

All Hitler's hordes had to do in order to rule all of Europe was cross twenty miles of seawater, but there's the rub. For as soon as they clambered onto their invasion barges, which were piling up along the French coast, and set sail, the Royal Navy would come steaming out of its port on the northwest of Scotland and sweep them aside, shattering the barges and tossing the army into the waters of the English Channel.

But wait. Why was the Royal Navy huddled in the west in the first place? Its normal home port was Scapa Flow, in the northeastern Orkney Islands, positioned perfectly to disgorge the battleships that would sink the Wehrmacht. The answer to this embarrassing question was the Luftwaffe.

In the First World War, the battleship had been the lord of the sea. In this new conflict, it was already apparent that the lord had abdicated: The airplane was the definitive weapon. Afraid of the German bombers, the navy had deserted its bastion and retreated west, beyond the range of the Nazi planes. If the invasion began, the Royal Navy would indeed come steaming forth in all its bravery and majesty, but they would come steaming forth to their deaths. It would be the Charge of the Light Brigade all over again, an outmoded force gallantly but uselessly falling to modern technology. Just as the horse-mounted officers of the Light Brigade were mowed down in their tracks by machine guns and cannon, the battleships and cruisers of the navy would sink under the bombs of the Stukas.

Unless, of course, the Royal Air Force could clear the skies of those Stukas.

And so it came down to this: If the Luftwaffe could destroy the Royal Air Force, the German bombers could destroy the Royal Navy and nothing could stop the invasion. Once ashore in England, the Wehrmacht would roll through the country more easily than it had in France, where it had been opposed by a well-armed army. Churchill might roar and bellow, but the British would not fight them on the beaches and in the streets, for they had nothing left to fight them with. The story that as Churchill sat down in the House of Commons after his famous rodomontade, he muttered, "We'll beat them over the heads with beer bottles, because that's all we've bloody got left," is probably untrue but it does reflect the truth of the moment.

As the days of that terrible summer rolled on, America's eyes turned with a growing anxiety to the tumult in the skies over England. Americans had long thought of the Atlantic Ocean as an invincible barrier between themselves and Europe, but if Hitler defeated England and gained control of the world's strongest navy, the Atlantic would become an open highway to the U.S. eastern seaboard.

And to most observers, Hitler's victory seemed certain. JFK's father, Joseph Kennedy, ambassador to England, came home with his family and proclaimed that England was finished. (The joke going the rounds in London: "I used to think that pansies were yellow until I met Joe Kennedy.") At America First rallies around the United States, Charles Lindbergh was singing the praises of the German Luftwaffe, calling it invincible, anointing its fighter planes as the world's best by far. Hitler could not be defeated, he shouted, and Congress listened. (And a Hitler victory wasn't a bad thing, he went on. The Nazis were clean, efficient, and moral, aside from that little business with the Jews. And you couldn't really blame them for that, he whispered.)

Even as Lindbergh was arguing that Germany's air force was unstoppable, President Franklin D. Roosevelt announced that Luftwaffe bombers would soon be able to fly from bases in West Africa to attack cities as far west as Omaha, Nebraska. Though this technical accomplishment was a fantasy, something developing in the Peenemunde laboratory of Werner von Braun was not. It was an engineering feat no one yet knew about: an improved version of the as-yet-unveiled V-2 rocket. Named the V-10, it would be a true intercontinental ballistic missile, which could reach anywhere in America. And just the year before, nuclear fission had been discovered—in Berlin.

So the stage was set. In July of that summer, when the vaunted German air force began its aerial assault as a prelude to a cross-Channel invasion, the Allies' only hope lay in the few fighter pilots of the Royal Air Force and in the resolute, embattled man who led them: not Churchill, but the man who had fought Churchill and nearly every other minister and general in a series of increasingly bitter battles through the prewar years; who without scientific training directed the energies of England's vast scientific aerial establishment; who had defied the fierce arguments of Churchill's own scientific adviser and instead backed and promoted the single technical device—radar—that would provide the backbone of Britain's aerial defense and the slim margin of victory.

Rather incredibly, this was also a man whose mind broke from the strain at the height of the battle, who talked to the ghosts of his dead pilots, but who nevertheless was able to keep another part of his mind clear enough to continue making the daily life-and-death decisions that saved England. The man whose name today is practically unknown: Hugh Caswall Tremenheere Dowding, Air Chief Marshal of the Royal Air Force, Commander in Chief of Fighter Command. Lord Dowding, First Baron of Bentley Priory.

part one

The Winter of Discontent

IT IS WEDNESDAY, September 6, 1939, three days after the declaration of war. On the crest of a hill overlooking the London suburb of Stanmore, amid a forest of cedar trees and blossoming vegetable gardens, stands one of the lesser stately homes of England, Bentley Priory. The site goes back in history to the year A.D. 63, when Queen Boadicea, defeated after a furious struggle against the invading Romans, took poison and was buried there. In the twelfth century the priory was established, but today the prayers of Air Marshal Dowding, aka "Stuffy," head of the Royal Air Force's Fighter Command, are to a different God as he stands above a different kind of altar. He is in an underground bunker, seated on a balcony next to King George VI, looking down at the main room and at the altar: a twenty-foot square table on which is etched a map of the southeast corner of England.

Just after ten o'clock that morning, a black marker was placed on the table, indicating a radar warning of incoming aircraft, and a flight of Hurricanes was scrambled. A red marker, indicating the British fighters, was placed in position. Dowding nodded to His Majesty; this was how the system worked.

He explained that a chain of radar stations had been set up along the southern and eastern coasts of England. (He actually used the words "radio direction finding stations" since the acronym *radar*—for *ra*dio *d*etecting *a*nd *r*anging—was a later American invention.) These could spot incoming airplanes while they were still out of sight over the Channel, or even still over France. The information was passed by a newly constructed series of telephone lines directly here to Bentley Priory, and simultaneously to the pertinent Group Sector commands.

The entire air defense of Great Britain had been organized into four Fighter Groups. No. 11 Group covered the southeastern corner, with No. 12 Group to its immediate north. Bombers coming from Germany would enter No. 12 Group's jurisdiction, which was expected to be the primary battleground. But now with France fallen to the enemy, the French aerodromes were available to the Luftwaffe. These were closer to England and so would be the primary bases for the German attacks. Because a direct line from the French airfields to London would bring them into No. 11 Group, No. 12 Group would now be expected to provide mostly backup. To the west, No. 10 Group would provide more reinforcements, while No. 13 Group in the far north would guard against surprise attacks and provide training for replacements.

The system had received its first test just moments after the declaration of war. On Sunday, September 3, 1939, Prime Minister Neville Chamberlain addressed the nation by radio: "I am speaking to you from the Cabinet Room at Number 10, Downing Street. This morning the British Ambassador in Berlin handed the German Government a final Note stating that, unless we heard from them by 11 o'clock that they were prepared at once to withdraw their troops from Poland, a state of war would exist between us. I have to tell you now that no such undertaking has been received, and that consequently this country is at war with Germany."

He spoke at 11:15 A.M. Ten minutes later, the air-raid sirens sounded over London.

The nation was dumbfounded. For the past six or seven years, they had been warned that the next war would be decided in the space of a few hours as bombers would blast cities into smithereens, but they hadn't believed it. Now they streamed into the basements of the largest buildings, which displayed hastily printed signs, AIR RAID SHELTER, as uniformed bobbies on bicycles raced down the streets with large placards hanging from their necks: AIR RAID! TAKE SHELTER!

In the Operations Room at Bentley Priory, a single black marker was placed on the table, and at Biggin Hill aerodrome, a telephone rang. The airman on duty yanked it from its cradle, listened for a moment, and then yelled out the window, "Scramble! Blue section, scramble!"

Three pilots raced across the grass to their planes as the mechanics started the engines. In less than a minute, the Hurricanes were tearing across the aerodrome and screeching into the air.

Fifteen minutes later, they came floating back to earth without having fired their guns. The blip on the radar screens turned out to be a small civilian airplane in which an assistant French military attaché, Captain de Brantes, was flying back to London from a weekend of partying in Paris. Well, some things are more important than a declaration of war, and he hadn't been paying attention. Nor had he bothered to file a flight plan. The radar beams saw him coming, the Controllers listed him as "unidentified," and the air-raid sirens went off.

Dowding hadn't been annoyed. In fact, he was rather pleased. The incident had provided an excellent surprise test of the system. And the system had worked. Earlier that year, someone had asked him if he was prepared for war. What would he do when it came, was the question, "Pray to God, and trust in radar?" Dowding had answered, in his stuffy manner, "I would rather pray for radar, and trust in God." Now it seemed that his prayers had been answered.

At least it seemed that way until that night, when, as the *Times* of London reported, "Air raid warnings were sounded in the early hours of the morning over a wide area embracing London and the Midlands."

And yet, again, no bombs were dropped. The *Times* went on to say that "the air-raid warnings were due to the passage of unidentified aircraft. Fighter aircraft went up and satisfactory identification was established."

But this account was not only wrong; it was total nonsense. In 1939, it was impossible even to locate aircraft at night, let alone identify them. The daytime "raid" had pleased Dowding; the nighttime raid worried him. Well, actually, it scared the hell out of him. Because nothing had happened.

There were no German aircraft flying over England that night. There were no aircraft of any kind up there. Yet just before 2:30 A.M., the radar station at Ventnor picked up a plot coming in over the waters toward the coast. At Tangmere aerodrome, No. 1 Squadron was at readiness when the telephone rang. Three Hurricane fighters were sent off to intercept. They searched until their fuel ran low, and then other sections were sent off. None of them found anything.

It wasn't that Dowding wanted the Germans to bomb England, but when his system said there were bombers there, he desperately wanted the bombers to be there! Nothing was worse than nothing. Nothing in the air when radar said something was there—that was frightening. If he couldn't trust radar, there wasn't much use in praying to God for anything else.

There wasn't anything else.

Now, three days later, a new blip on the radar screen is observed: More enemy aircraft, and another black marker is added to the table. The Bentley Priory Controller scrambles a whole squadron to deal with it. But no sooner are they airborne when another blip appears on the screen. More squadrons are scrambled.

And still more. Each squadron of Spitfires or Hurricanes seems to be followed by another formation of German bombers. One by one, more and more squadrons are sent up. Dowding begins to look distinctly worried. On the wall are lists of the RAF squadrons headed by green or red lights: On Reserve, or Committed. As another red marker is placed on the table, the last green light changes to red.

By this time, every single squadron east of London has been scrambled, and the system is overloaded: The Controllers have too many aircraft aloft, and neither the Controllers nor the radio telecommunications link to the aircraft nor the telephone lines from the radar stations can handle the traffic. The king of England is accustomed to embarrassing situations; he says nothing, merely watches as the system Dowding had carefully explained to him slips into chaos. The monarch glances at the wall, sees that all the lights are now red, and understands that every British fighter is now in the air. He remembers the warnings of Armageddon from the air, the prophecies that the coming war will be won or lost on the first day.

He wonders if this will be the last day for poor England.

The battle rages for an hour as blips fill the radar screens, from midchannel up to London and down again throughout Kent. Fighter contrails fill the sky, punctuated by the black puffs of antiaircraft bursts. A squadron of Spitfires dives on a formation of Messerschmitts (Me's) and shoots down two as the British planes zoom past and climb back up into the sun. When the Brits look back, the Me's are gone.

There is no letup on the radar screens, but after an hour of fighting on emergency boost, the British planes are running low on fuel and, despite pleas from the Controllers, who are trying to direct them onto new plots, the pilots are forced to return to their aerodromes. At Bentley Priory the Controllers turn one by one to Dowding, but there is nothing he can say, nothing he can do. Any further raids will sweep in unattacked to catch all his forces on the ground.

When war was first declared, Dowding had gone on the radio to promise the people he would protect England from aerial attack.

It looks like he was wrong.

But no further raids materialize. As the fighters return to base, the enemy plots fade away too, and soon the skies are clear and the radar scopes empty. The WAAFs (Women's Auxiliary Air Force members), emotionally and physically exhausted, take off their headphone sets and lean wearily against the map tables. The Controllers sit quietly by their silent telephones, the king scratches his ear, and Dowding begins to breathe again.

Army units quickly disperse throughout the battle area, searching for bomb damage and for airplane wrecks, trying to assess the damage done by and to the Luftwaffe. Meanwhile, back at the aerodromes, the Squadron Intelligence Officers interview the returning pilots.

At first there is jubilation. The fighters of the Royal Air Force seem to have won a decisive victory. No factories or airfields have been bombed. No houses have been destroyed. In fact, no bomb craters are found.

The jubilation turns to wonder. No bomb craters at all? Strange...

Stranger still, no German airplane wrecks are found. Although the antiaircraft batteries are sending in report after report of sightings on which they had fired, in all of England only two planes seem to have been shot down, and both of these are British Hurricanes. Of the RAF fighters, only one Spitfire formation reports attacking anyone, and only one squadron of Hurricanes was attacked. The Spitfires report shooting down two of the enemy.

The Intelligence Officers begin to feel a bit uneasy. One of the downed Hurricane pilots reports that the German Messerschmitts that attacked him were painted, not with swastikas or crosses, but with roundels similar to those the RAF uses. The crews in the field call in that the two wrecks are riddled with machine-gun bullets. Air Vice-Marshal C. H. N. Bilney asks them to look again. While the British fighters have only machine guns, the Messerschmitts have cannon as well. The report comes back quickly: Small holes only, no large cannon holes are seen. Bilney drives out to take a look at one of the wreckages. It is true: The downed Hurricane shows only small holes. "Knowing that German bullets had steel cores as opposed to the lead cores of ours," he reports to Dowding, "I got a piece of wood, put some glue on one end and fished around in the wing for bullet fragments. I soon found quite a lot of lead."

And the jubilation turns to consternation. What the bloody hell happened up there in the sky?

What happened was confusion amid the catastrophic collapse of the entire defense system, due to a fault that had been previously recognized but not totally assimilated. The radar transmitting antennae radiated their radio signals both forward and backward simultaneously, and couldn't tell from which signal—forward or backward—any received echoes were obtained. That is, an aircraft directly east or directly west of a radar station would give exactly the same blip. The only solution was to try to electronically black out the backward emissions. The radar wizards thought they had done that.

They hadn't. Somewhere to the west, behind the coastal radar towers, a British airplane had taken off. The radar operators thought the towers were looking eastward, over the Channel, but somehow the towers picked up the airplane behind them. Naturally it was reported as an unidentified aircraft coming in toward England, and a section of Hurricanes was sent off to intercept it. But as they rose into the air from their aerodrome *behind* the coastal radar towers, they were picked up on the scopes and plotted as more incoming aircraft *in front of* the towers—as enemy aircraft coming in across the sea.

A whole squadron of Hurricanes was scrambled to meet this new "threat." And this squadron was also picked up on radar as an enemy formation, a bigger one this time. Two squadrons of Spitfires were scrambled, which were in turn identified as more Germans . . .

None of the British pilots were experienced in war. When the rear section of No. 74 Squadron of Spitfires broke through a cloud and saw fighters below, they instinctively attacked, diving into them at well over three hundred miles an hour. At that speed and with their adrenaline pumping and the *tally-ho* ringing in their ears, they weren't about to think in terms of aircraft identification. They simply pushed the red button and opened fire. As the tracers flashed past them, the Hurricanes broke and scattered, most of them never even seeing their attackers, and naturally reported being bounced by Me's.

As the reports drift back in to Bentley Priory—no bomb damage, no German planes shot down, no cannon holes in the Hurricanes— as the sun begins to sink over the west counties, as a disturbing quiet envelops the land, King George solemnly bids good-bye to Dowding and his staff. He drives away, and Dowding is left to sift through the reports and to reflect on what it means.

"I shall pray for radar, and trust in God," he had said.

But there was an old saying in Scotland, where he was born, which he had never before understood: "Beware of answered prayers."

A cold chill began to settle deep in his spine.

two

BRITAIN'S VULNERABILITY to aerial attack had been anticipated some thirty years earlier. It all began with a headstrong newspaper publisher and a swimmer cutting through the waters of the English Channel.

The year was 1904, and the idea came from the fertile imaginings of a young Englishman named Alfred Harmsworth, who at the age of thirty-nine was publisher of the *Daily Mail,* one of the many penny papers in England. He had the strangest notion of offering a hundred-guinea prize for the first person to swim the English Channel, hoping that when he publicized this in his paper, people would begin to buy it.

And so he did, and so they did. Soon he had built the *Daily Mail* into one of the largest-circulation papers in the world, topping the million-reader mark, and Harmsworth looked around for another prize contender.

It took him a couple of years, but in 1906, he found it: Aviation was the thing. While most people regarded the Wright brothers' flight of a few years earlier as little more than a stunt, Harmsworth thought otherwise. He offered a prize of ten thousand pounds for the first aviator to fly from London to Manchester.

The idea was ridiculous. The distance between London and

Manchester was 185 miles, and the European record for distance was 220 *yards*. The prize was quite properly ridiculed by *Punch* magazine, which offered the same amount of money for the first man to swim the Atlantic and for the first flight to Mars.

No one attempted to win either the *Daily Mail*'s or *Punch*'s prize. Lord Northcliffe, as Harmsworth now was, realized he had bitten off more than anyone could chew, and two years later, in 1908, he found a more promising possibility. If it had excited people to read about someone swimming across the Channel, how about someone flying over it? He announced a prize of one thousand pounds for the first flight from France to England.

Unlike Northcliffe's previous offer, this was a well-thought-out proposal. At first it sounded sensational, the stuff of science fiction—actually to fly through the air from the Continent across the wild waters to England. But it was clearly doable: The Channel was twenty-two miles wide at its narrowest point, between Calais and Dover, and by 1908, some airplanes, like the Wright Flyer, could fly for an hour and a half and could cover the twenty-two miles in less than an hour. Everyone expected Wilbur Wright to try for the prize, but Wilbur declined to risk the only airplane he had in Europe on a flight across water. It wasn't until the following summer that a young man named Hubert Latham announced his intention of taking home the prize.

Latham was a twenty-six-year-old Englishman who lived in Paris. He was rich, he was handsome, he was suave and sophisticated. The man was famous not only for his ivory cigarette holder and charming smile but for his society affairs, his big-game hunting in Africa, and his skill at racing motorboats at Monaco. Within three months of learning to fly, "Le Tham" (as he was known to the French newspaper-reading public) had established a world endurance record of one hour, thirty-seven minutes, landing only when it began to rain.

Now he was on the cliffs near Calais with his streamlined monoplane, the Antoinette IV. A French cruiser waited in the Channel to rescue him if he failed. On July 19, 1909, he took off cleanly, circled around the field to gain height, and then sailed out over the cliffs, disappearing across the water to the cheers of the crowds who saw him off.

But airplane engines in those days were not reliable. The same engine that had previously kept him in the air for an hour and a half now decided to sputter to a halt in fifteen minutes, and he was forced to glide down and splash into the sea six miles from the French coast. Luckily the Antoinette floated until the cruiser steamed by to find Le Tham perched patiently on its wing, smoking a cigarette in his famous ivory holder.

He immediately sent to Paris for a new machine, but as the days slipped by, another Frenchman, Louis Bleriot, appeared on the scene. He had made a fortune manufacturing headlamps for the newly burgeoning automobile industry, and then, inspired by the Wright brothers, he began designing airplanes—without, however, the Wrights' success. One after another of his designs crashed and burned, and with each one went a sizable piece of his fortune.

But by 1909, when his eleventh design, the Bleriot XI, had made several flights of up to twenty minutes, he decided to enter it in the race for Lord Northcliffe's prize. The trouble was that the Channel crossing would take at least half an hour, ten minutes longer than his longest flight. Another problem was that he had badly burned his foot on the exhaust pipe that ran through the cockpit, so he could hardly walk. And most troubling of all, he was out of money. By now he had spent all his headlamp fortune and his wife's substantial dowry; he was not only crippled, he was bankrupt. He could no more buy enough fuel to fly the Channel than he could buy eggs for breakfast.

But on July 1, 1909, his wife was visiting some wealthy Parisian friends in a second-story apartment in Paris. Nobody noticed that their little girl had climbed up onto the windowsill and was leaning out, until with a cry Bleriot's wife sprang out of her chair and seized the child just as she slipped. In gratitude for saving their daughter's life, the friends insisted on financing Bleriot's attempt across the Channel.

Meanwhile, Hubert Latham's new airplane had arrived. Several days of clouds and strong winds prevented him from attempting the flight, but on the night of July 24, the winds began to show signs of possibly weakening and the clouds began to break. Latham went to bed, leaving word to be awakened at dawn if the weather continued to improve. By 2:00 A.M., the air was calm and the sky clear—but no one woke him. His mechanics were asleep, and so Latham slept on.

In the Bleriot camp, however, the mechanics were alert. When they saw the stars coming out, they ran to wake Bleriot. The plane was wheeled out of the hangar and checked quickly, for there wasn't much to check: The little airplane had no instruments, not even a compass.

Bleriot was close enough to Latham's camp to see it through his binoculars. To his amazement—and relief—it was quiet and dark. At 4:41 A.M., the sun began to rise. Bleriot took off with the sun, swerved out over the cold waters of the Channel—quite alone, with no escorting French naval vessel in case he crashed—and steered as best he could for England.

In the dim light of the rising dawn, the weather held clear and somehow the engine continued its steady beat. In less than half an hour, he could make out a darkening along the horizon: England! But the famous white cliffs of Dover were nowhere to be seen.

He had no idea where he was, and the prize had specified that the flight be from Calais to Dover. Then he spotted three ships all going in the same direction. Reasoning that they might be headed for a port, and that the port might be Dover, he turned around and flew in that direction. Luckily, he was right: Just as the winds began to pick up and bounce him around, he saw the famous white cliffs.

"The wind was fighting me now worse than ever. Suddenly at the edge of an opening that appeared in the cliff, I saw a man desperately waving a tricolor flag, out alone in the middle of a field, shouting 'Bravo! Bravo!' I attempt a landing, but the wind catches me and whirls me round two or three times. At once I stop my motor, and instantly my machine falls straight upon the land. I am safe on your shore."

The man was a French newsman who was waiting for Latham, but who welcomed Bleriot just as effusively, wrapping him in the French flag and kissing him soundly on both cheeks. Bleriot had flown for thirty-seven minutes and had covered twenty-four miles. Many others had flown for greater distances but, as we all know, symbolism is greater than reality. "England is no longer an island," Lord Northcliffe exclaimed as the crowds went wild. "England is no longer an island!"

Winston Churchill soon saw what he meant, lamenting that "England came into big things as an accident of naval power when she was an island. Through an accident of airpower she will proba- bly cease to exist."

The first hints of the power of air had come as early as 1911, when the Italians used primitive airplanes to bomb the Senussi tribes in Africa. The Italians' action broke all the rules of civilized warfare, as they weren't able to distinguish between spear-carrying warriors and baby-carrying women, but no one in Europe or America seemed to care. Actions taken against African blacks had little to do with civi- lized peoples.

But then on Christmas Eve of 1914, in the first year of World War I, a single German airplane ventured over England and dropped one tiny bomb into the garden of a suburban home outside Dover. The Kaiser was horrified; honorable men did not conduct warfare against helpless women and children, though Italians might, nor could such cowardly actions have any conceivable effect on the battlefields, where the real decisions of victory or defeat would be made. He absolutely forbade any further such adventures.

And yet . . .

Others began to think about it. True, that lone bomb had done nothing to help Germany's cause. On the other hand, could the British do anything to stop more airplanes from dropping more bombs? The German naval staff, in particular, was intrigued. War had begun, the army had invaded France, but the U-boats were not yet seen as an effective weapon and the Kriegsmarine was not part of the war; they were irrelevant. How could they get into the action? Searching for some way to justify their existence, the admirals hit on a unique development. Count Ferdinand von Zeppelin had perfected gigantic, lighter-than-air dirigibles that, the admirals suggested to Kaiser Wilhelm, could carry bombs over England and drop them, not on civilians—not on women and children, certainly—but on military targets. The admirals pointed to the London docks as suitable for attack.

Still the Kaiser refused. The accuracy of bombs dropped from a height sufficient to keep the zeppelins safe from ground fire was clearly insufficient to safeguard the homes of families living near the docks.

But the months began to slip by without the anticipated successes in the trenches of France, and increasingly the admirals suggested, proposed, and finally promised that they could hit the docks and not the houses. Finally the Kaiser relented. Permission was granted to attack the docks, but the resulting bomb raids did not turn out as anticipated. The admirals were wrong: The docks were largely undamaged, while the houses nearby were demolished and civilians were killed.

The Kaiser was appalled, but the German newspapers were ecstatic. They reported the raids jubilantly, and the German people responded with an enthusiasm they had lost when the army's advance stagnated. The outcries of the outraged British served only to stimulate morale in Germany. The navy urged further attacks. Suddenly, the bombing of women and children looked like an effective way to wage war after all.

The German army staff could not let the navy claim this new war for themselves. They ordered their own airships to bomb London, seeking not only the docks—which the navy could argue belonged to *them*—but any "targets of opportunity." Again the Kaiser protested, but the arguments were too strong, the chances of success too high, the airships both too expensive to waste and unsuitable for any other military operations, and on May 30, 1915, he capitulated to the extent of authorizing the aerial bombing of targets east of the Tower of London. The only civilians in the East End lived in slums, and no one was expected to care much about them.

The German Admiralty quickly responded by proposing to attack military targets "of interest to Naval strategy" throughout the city of London. These would include the British Admiralty offices, the railways (which brought goods to the docks), and the Bank of England (which provided the financial support for all naval operations). Once this concept was approved, the next step was inevitable: They began to bomb *all* railways, all offices, all administrative and logistical support facilities. Since these were scattered through the city, interspersed with truly civilian offices and residences, the necessity of civilian casualties simply had to be accepted.

Again—for the last time—the Kaiser balked. But English aircraft by now had retaliated against Karlsruhe, and even though that single raid had been more ineffective than the airship attempts to hit the docks of London, the future was clear. The enemy would build bigger airplanes and more destructive bombs, and the only defense was to rain destruction on them so dramatically that they would not dare to challenge warfare in this new realm. The Kaiser conceded, and unrestricted aerial bombing of London began.

And, of course, it escalated. Soon the airships were wandering all over the southeast of England, and the German army responded by developing giant Gotha bombers that could carry a heavier bombload than the zeppelins could. By 1917, these airplanes were dropping hundreds of pounds of bombs each, traveling at heights and speeds too high and fast to be reached by the Royal Flying Corps fighters or antiaircraft cannon. In June, a force of twenty Gothas attacked London in daylight, dropping two tons of bombs directly onto the Liverpool Street railway station and one 110-pound bomb directly onto a nursery school, killing sixteen babies and severely injuring a score more. On February 16, 1918, a squadron formed specifically for the purpose of bombing England dropped a specially designed one-ton bomb on Chelsea. It hit nothing significant and did little damage. But one month before, the same commander had attacked London with then-standard 660-pound bombs. Aiming for the Admiralty, he had hit instead the Odham Printing Works, which had been designated an air-raid shelter because of its heavy construction, designed to hold the gigantic printing presses, beneath which five hundred Londoners huddled in the basement. The bomb shattered the foundations of the building, the printing presses collapsed, and the upper floors came crashing down into the basement and onto the masses sheltering there. Thirty-eight people died and a hundred others were injured. Had the bomber carried the one-ton bomb that night, all of them would have been killed.

The future looked promising.

three

The First World War ended when the German U-boats were defeated, America came into the war, and the British tanks overran the trenches and crushed the German machine-gun nests. The airplane had not been a decisive weapon; the air raids on Britain had killed fewer than two thousand people during the entire course of the war, in a country that killed seven thousand in traffic accidents every single year. But those air raids had shown the future, and it was terrifying.

In 1921 an Italian general, Giulio Douhet, wrote in *Command of the Air* that future wars would not be fought by armies on the ground, but by fleets of bombers sailing over their enemy's defenses. They would be able to drop unimaginable terror on the home population, destroying the people's will to resist. Within two days, he wrote, thousands of civilians would flee the cities. Nothing could stop the bombers, and no population could withstand them.

His argument was heard loud and clear in both England and America. England's Major General J. F. "Boney" Fuller wrote in 1923 that a fleet of five hundred bombers could cause two hundred thousand casualties "and throw the whole city into panic within half an hour." There would be "complete industrial paralysis," a rebellion against any government that could not provide protection—and none could—and the war would be lost within a couple of days. Lord Balfour, heading the Committee on Imperial Defence, estimated that an enemy could drop a daily seventy-five tons day after day, and that London could not endure this. The Air Ministry revealed the results of a statistical analysis showing that England's traditional enemy, France, could produce seven thousand deaths and an additional twelve thousand severe casualties within the first week.

In America, General Billy Mitchell wrote that the only possible defense was offense: "The hostile nation's power to make wars must be destroyed. . . . [This included] factories, food producers, farms, and homes, the places where people live and carry on their daily lives."

In other words, terror bombing.

The message was too horrible for Americans to hear, and so they tuned him out and retreated behind their oceans. If those dreadful Europeans wanted to bomb each other, let them and be damned!

Those dreadful Europeans, it seemed, had little choice. Aside from building bigger fleets of bombers as a deterrent, what could they do? Well, there was always the League of Nations and mutual disarmament, of course.

But there were problems with the League, aside from the fact that the United States had turned its back on it. In 1923, the League proposed a disarmament conference, which was finally convened in 1932, to little avail. Germany opened the proceedings with the indisputable point that the Treaty of Versailles, which had ended the Great War, was manifestly unfair; they wanted to be treated equally with the other great nations of the world. The British were willing to do so, but the French would not accept Germany as an equal partner unless Britain would guarantee to join France if Germany again initiated a war, and this Britain would not do. It had had enough of foreign commitments. The Japanese brought up the issue of racial equality, which the Europeans thought was in quite poor taste and with this regard the currents of the conference were turned awry, and lost the name of action.

Its defeat was inevitable. Of all the nations, Britain was the most vulnerable to aerial attack and therefore should have argued most strenuously for disarmament—which would mean primarily the abolition of the airplane as a weapon of war. But how could they, when they were making such effective use of it?

They had agreed with all the other nations in the League on the proposal to banish poison gas, but that was an easy one. People were terrified of gas, so the ban was popular among the populace. What's more, it had never been an effective military weapon, so the ban didn't bother the people in charge. The airplane, though, was a different matter: It definitely had its uses, particularly to the British, for whom the subcontinent of India and the vast deserts of Arabia constituted a tremendous burden—the white man's burden, as Kipling so famously put it. There were enormous profits to be garnered there, but there was also considerable expense in the form of standing armies to keep the peace along the Northwest Frontier of India and wherever the Bedouin tribes gathered in Arabia. The natives were understandably restless, feeling that the white man was a burden too heavy to be borne, and so the British were forced to keep armies permanently garrisoned, clothed, fed, and housed throughout their recalcitrant empire.

But no longer were these armed masses necessary, not since the British had discovered that a few squadrons of bombers could take the place of these large, expensive armies. If a tribe along the Northwest Frontier or far up the Nile began attacking its neighbors or the local missionaries, a couple of bombers would fly up from Bombay or Cairo and, within a few hours, would destroy the offending village from the air. The marauding tribesmen could do nothing but prance around helplessly on their horses and fire ineffective bullets into the air while their homes, wives, and children were blown to bits. If the very next day another rebellion were to take place hundreds of miles away, the same squadron could deal with it. A minuscule number of men and machines could keep the king's peace throughout the Mid- and Far East.

So when the League of Nations was presented with a resolution prohibiting the use of military airplanes to bomb civilians, in the manner that poison gas had been prohibited, the Colonial Secretary and the Chancellor of the Exchequer of England hesitated to embrace it. The British army battalions that had earlier policed the Empire had been largely disbanded in an effort to satisfy the budget that had been ruined during the war, and it would be prohibitively expensive to bring them back again under arms and ship them out. No, the bombing of civilians was here to stay; it was simple economics.

What the British began to whisper in the back rooms of the League was something a bit subtler. They suggested the civilized nations should ban airpower against each other, but should not interfere in each nation's internal affairs. To put it bluntly, which they tried desperately not to do, it was a regrettable but stern necessity to keep the peace among benighted natives by bombing them, though it would be morally reprehensible to use those same airplanes to bomb the people of Berlin or London.

The ban on poison gas was simple and straightforward; the proposed British ban on airplanes was cluttered with subordinate clauses, winks, and tongues firmly in cheeks. It did not have the clear moral suasion of the ban on gas.

There was yet another problem with the proposed ban. Despite having one of the world's smallest armies, Britain had become the most powerful nation in the world, because of its navy. If any country should go to war against this island nation, Britain's first course of action was to use the navy to blockade the offender. The effect of the blockade—to starve the country into submission—was essentially a weapon against the civilian population. How then could the British argue for the abolition of the airplane on the grounds that it attacked civilians, when their own basic strategy was just as guilty? They could not press for an international agreement against air forces unless they were prepared to give up their navy's most effective weapon. And this they were not about to do.

There were still more problems. Airliners and bombers alike are designed for the best possible speed, range, and carrying capacities, which meant that civilian airplanes could be modified overnight to carry bombs instead of passengers, which in turn meant that the only way to ban military airplanes would be to ban all airplanes. The Secretary of the Air Ministry pointed out that even small biplanes intended for pleasure flying could be modified overnight to carry 350 pounds of bombs over distances of hundreds of miles (and we have recently seen how terrible a weapon even unarmed jet airliners can be).

The arguments were irrefutable. It was impossible to ban airplane design, airplane production, and even the use of airplanes to bomb civilians. The only possible recourse was to pursue the exact opposite: for each nation to build for itself an air force capable of deterring attack by imposing always the threat of instant and massive retaliation by fleets of bombers.

The idea of bombing civilian populations from the air goes back an incredible three hundred years, to the year 1650, when an Italian priest, Francisco Lana, published a book describing an aerial ship. Lift was to be provided by four evacuated copper globes, each twenty-five feet in diameter. Because we live at the bottom of an ocean of air, he reasoned, propulsion was to be by oars and sails. But he never tried to build it, because "God would surely never allow such a machine to be successful since it would create many disturbances in the civil and political governments of mankind. Where is the man that can fail to see that no city would be proof against surprise when the ship could at any time be steered over its squares or even over courtyards of houses and brought to earth for the landing of its crews? Iron weights could be hurled to wreck ships at sea, or they could be set on fire by fireballs and bombs, nor ships alone but houses, fortresses and cities could thus be destroyed with the certainty that the airship could come to no harm, as the missiles could be hurled from a great height."

Needless to say, the idea languished for a while. The first military use of the air was for observation rather than bombing. The strategy sounds rather passive, but if the concept had been followed faithfully, Napoleon would have ruled the world.

It was balloons rather than airplanes, but the concept was the same. Balloon flight had been pioneered in France in the mid-1700s, and so the Committee of Public Safety, set up in Paris after the French Revolution, decided to use observation balloons to help France's armies. In 1793 they built the world's first military observation balloon. Filled with hydrogen and tethered to the ground, the balloon carried a hanging basket for two people, one to handle the balloon and the other to act as observer and to communicate with the ground by dropping messages in sandbags. At its extreme height, the observer equipped with a telescope could see nearly twenty miles; in other words, he could see the whole of that era's battlefields. It was so brilliant an idea that it led to the establishment of the world's first air force, the Compagnie d'Aéronautiers, in 1794.

That year, during his conflict with Austria, Napoleon became the first military commander to use the advantages of the air for reconnaissance. The balloon successfully spied on Dutch and Austrian troops from high above its own armies, providing detailed reports of the location and composition of enemy troops and directing artillery fire against them. The Austrians protested that this was a violation of the rules of war, but Napoleon laughed off the charge. They then attempted to shoot it down, but the balloon floated too high for their bullets.

Its success led to the building of three more balloons, which were used during all of Napoleon's battles for the next two years. Then, in 1797, he brought the aéronautiers with him to Egypt, and when the British successfully shot them down, he lost faith, disbanded the group, and abandoned the concept. He did so to his everlasting regret, for in 1815, the balloons could have reversed the final decision at Waterloo.

Let's reconstruct the situation. After returning from Elba, Napoleon has roused the French people to his side and is now ensconced in Paris. Here comes the Duke of Wellington and the Prussian general, Gebhard Leberecht von Blücher, leading two prongs of armies. Blücher is defeated by one of Napoleon's lieutenants and retreats. Wellington sets up on a hill near the village of Waterloo.

What should Napoleon do? He can remain in Paris and await siege, or he can attack Wellington. Two questions arise: First, how strong is Wellington? His forces are visible on the slope of the hill, but he has a reputation for hiding more forces on the back slope. Second, where is Blücher? Is he retreating back to Prussia, or has he regrouped and headed to Waterloo to help Wellington?

Napoleon feels that Wellington is bluffing, that he hopes Napoleon will think he has more troops behind the hill since he's done that before, and so Napoleon will hide in Paris. Then, when more British troops arise, Wellington will attack. Also, Napoleon's intuition and understanding of psychology lead him to believe that Blücher doesn't have the heart for more war and is on his way back to Prussia.

So he attacks the British troops on the hill at Waterloo. But Wellington did have more troops hidden, and as they arise from the back slope of the hill, Blücher suddenly emerges from the woods with his Prussian army to roll up Napoleon's flank, and Waterloo is lost.

Balloons would have been able to look over the hill and find the hidden British troops, and would also have seen Blücher long before he made his disastrous appearance. The course of history would have been quite different.

But now, in the early years of the twentieth century, Napoleon is long gone and so is the idea of any military use of the air, despite the success of the Wright brothers. The British army has bought a few of these flimsy airplanes, but it cannot find any use for them.

Until, that is, a young staff officer steps outside the constricting box of military thinking . . .

four

WE DON'T KNOW very much about Dowding's early life, except that it seems to have been a normal one for a soldier of his generation. But, of course, what was normal for his generation is not quite that for ours.

Though the two world wars brought us into the modern era, their roots lay far back in the dim mists of Victorian times. Dowding, who like most of the war's commanders was born at the height of Queen Victoria's reign, grew up in that mixture of naive credulity and scientific optimism that characterized the times. During the thirty-two years from his birth to the outbreak of the First World War, the world was an exciting place to a person of inquisitive mind. Science had broken out of its bottle like a wild genie, and the universe had become, incredibly, both more understandable and more mystifying. Nothing, it seemed, was beyond the promise of science to understand and control—but not quite yet. Radio waves had sprung out of the aether—indeed, Dowding was the first person in the world to communicate directly from an airplane to a ground station—and X-rays had appeared out of nowhere, leading to the even more mysterious emanations of radioactivity. Einstein proclaimed that space and time did not absolutely exist, and the world was shown to be immeasurably older than the biblical term of six thousand years.

But other scientific investigations led to mysteries as yet unfathomable. Television was promised but proved elusive. N-rays were discovered and then lost again. Evolution went off on myriad tracks that dwindled to dead ends. Malthus showed that the world could not survive the next hundred years; Marconi received radio messages from Mars; Matthews invented the death ray; and Sir William Crookes, president of the most respected organization of scientists in the world, the British Association, published a series of investigations into the spirit world. Nothing, it seemed, lay beyond the reach—if not the grasp—of science. Nothing was impossible, though much remained mysterious, only dimly glimpsed, going bump, bump, bump in the forests of the night.

As a child growing into a young man, Hugh Dowding was a normal product of those times; that is, he ignored them. Neither scientifically nor psychically acute, he displayed little interest in all these revolutionary thoughts swirling in the wind. Though at a later and crucial period in his life the atmosphere he had unconsciously absorbed in his youth would surface, at the time he was concerned solely with his own life, with finding his own way, which was as difficult for him as it is for most of us.

Often described as a typical dour Scotsman, he was nothing of the kind unless environment tops heredity. He came from a long line of Englishmen who would seem right at home in the classic villages described by Agatha Christie. On both sides his forebears were mostly clerics, earning small but regular livings in various English parishes, with one great-grandfather who won and lost a fortune, a maternal grandfather who was a general, and an eccentric uncle, nicknamed "Beelzebub," who retired from the navy as an admiral and left for South America to catch insects. His father was an English schoolteacher who bought his own preparatory school in Scotland, and so Hugh was born there, in Moffat, in 1882. Growing up as the son of the headmaster, Hugh decided that the only thing he didn't want to be in life was a schoolteacher. But then what was one to do? The usual choices for the son of a poor professional were the Church, law, medicine, or the army or navy.

Hugh chose the army for a reason that any schoolchild could understand: All the other professions required the study of Greek.

And so, upon graduation from Winchester, he gained enrollment in a one-year army course that would guarantee him a commission in the Royal Engineers. All he had to do was complete the course successfully. Unfortunately, the impetus of not having to learn Greek wasn't sufficient to induce him to take the course seriously, and he failed. "I would have got the commission if I had kept my place, but I failed through laziness," he admitted. He wasn't tossed out of the army completely, but he was forced to take a lower position, as a subaltern gunner in the artillery.

Which wasn't at all bad. The year was 1900, he was eighteen years old, and life as a subaltern in an army at peace was rather pleasant. He was soon sent to India, where he enthusiastically took up horse racing and polo. The other traditional occupations of the young officers, drinking, carousing, and fornicating, didn't interest him as much, and so it was here that he earned his nickname, "Stuffy." But he thought it was the others who were the stuffy ones; they were the ones who weren't open to new ideas, as he soon discovered.

Aside from the pleasant life he led, several episodes confirmed his opinion of the closed-mindedness of others. This assessment would replay itself later, in more important times. In one of the ongoing army exercises, Dowding was given command of one section, while the opposing group of Ghurkas was to be led by one of his contemporaries, another subaltern, named Cyril Newall. The exercise was scheduled to begin at six A.M., but Dowding roused his troops and had them on the march by four o'clock. He caught the Ghurkas at their breakfast, and routed them. This was the beginning

of a long rivalry with Newall, which would have serious consequences in 1940.

At other times his initiative served only to get him in trouble.
The first time he took his turn as garrison orderly officer, he found
that one of his duties was to inspect the daily meat ration. Not
knowing anything about what to look for in such an inspection, he
bought a manual that warned that sometimes old animals were
foisted off on the military, and that an inspector could determine the
age by noting that the vertebral spaces should be at least a quarter
inch wide. When he took a look and found no visible spaces at all,
he decided that the animal was too old and so rejected it.

Which meant that the garrison had no meat that day. When the
commanding officer was served his vegetarian meal, he glowered at
Dowding "in a most unchristian temper," as Dowding recalled,
telling him that the next time he held the duty, to mind his own
bloody business.

This lesson was reinforced when he held the duty of range officer. His job was to take the artillery's target out to sea, to a distance
of roughly three miles. At that point a flag flying from a hill beside
the station would be lowered, and he was then to drop the target,
move comfortably away, and record the accuracy with which the
cannons bombarded the target.

Since it was Dowding's first time as range officer, the Colonel of
the Regiment accompanied him. They sailed away the requisite
three miles, and Dowding proposed to stop and drop the target. But
the Colonel pointed out that the flag had not yet dropped, and
ordered him to keep going. And going, and going...

Despite Dowding's protestations that the cannon had a range of
only five miles, they kept going. Finally, when they were close to fifteen miles out at sea, the flag dropped. Dowding stopped the
launch, released the target, and watched as the cannon fire didn't
come close to reaching it.

As they returned, Dowding remarked that he expected to catch hell for this. The Colonel didn't see why, since Dowding had followed his orders perfectly, but agreed to test the situation. When they reached headquarters, the Colonel waited outside while Dowding went in alone. Immediately, the sound of loud shouts was heard, asking why he had sailed so totally out of range, if his entire family were imbeciles or was it only him, did he have any idea what the range of a cannon was, and, if he did, did he care or did he think he had been dispatched on the launch to enjoy a leisurely sea voyage?

Whereupon the Colonel made his entrance.

Dowding was beginning to realize that following the manual, obeying instructions as they were written, wasn't all that it was cracked up to be.

After six years in India, he got back to England to attend the Staff College at Camberley, a necessary step in a military career. There he discovered that the military tendency to walk about with blinkers on and to keep a rigid mind was not confined to the lower rank of officers. In current terminology, the staff talked the talk but didn't walk the walk. "I was always hurt by the lip service the staff paid to freedom of thought," he later said, "contrasted with an actual tendency to repress all but conventional ideas."

This lack of imagination and initiative was exemplified at the college. Every student took turns being commanding officer of a military exercise, but since he was the youngest and most junior, Dowding was the last one. It was 1913 when he got his chance. When he did, he found that he had six aircraft, or aeroplanes, as they were then called, at his disposal. No one ever made any use of these aircraft, because no one had the slightest idea what to do with them.

It had been only a few years previously, in 1907, when the Wright brothers, rebuffed by the United States, had offered their invention to the British. Lord Tweedsmuir replied on behalf of their Lordships: "I have consulted my expert advisers with regard to your suggestion as to the employment of aeroplanes. I regret to have to tell you, after the careful consideration of my Board, that the Admiralty, while thanking you for so kindly bringing the proposals to their notice, are of opinion that they would not be of any practical value to the Naval Service."

The army was no more impressed. A member of its council, on being urged to consider airplanes as suitable reconnaissance machines, replied that "aircraft could not fly at less than forty miles per hour, and it would be impossible for anyone to see anything of value at that rather high speed."

A major problem in any military operation is to know exactly where the enemy are and how strong they are. Dowding decided to use his six aircraft to fly around and find them. The instructor overseeing the operation of the exercise told him that the plan was ridiculous; aside from the obvious impossibility of seeing anything clearly at "that rather high speed," the aeroplanes would never be able to find their way around. That is, he said, they might fly from point A to point B, but they couldn't simply get up there and fly around in circles looking for the enemy, and, if they should find them, have any idea where they were or how to get home again to make their report.

Dowding replied that they could simply follow the railway lines that crisscrossed England in those days. The instructor laughed: If they all tried to follow the same line, they'd crash into each other.

Nevertheless it was Dowding's prerogative to ignore the instructor's advice, although this would be putting his future career in peril. And so he did use the aircraft, and they did find the enemy and observed them clearly. With this information, he won the exercise overwhelmingly since he now knew exactly where the enemy was whereas they had no idea where he was.

Considering the result, and comparing it to the instructor's ignorance, Dowding had decided that "the army might as well have some staff officers who knew something about flying," so he decided to learn to fly. Official policy was that the Central Flying School of the Royal Flying Corps (RFC), which had been established just the previous year, would accept only officers who already knew how to fly; they had to get a civilian license at their own expense. So Dowding got his civilian ticket by taking lessons at daybreak, before his official duties began. He passed the RFC flying test on the day of his graduation from the Staff College.

"My original intention in learning to fly was to increase my value as a staff officer," he explained. He never had any thought, at the start, of actually flying with the RFC, but by now flying had gotten into his blood and he saw that the future of the army lay in the air as well as on the ground.

He decided on a career in the RFC, only to have his calling halted before it began: His father simply forbade it. The senior Dowding thought flying was too dangerous, and that was that. Dowding was thirty-two years old, but it never occurred to him to go against his father's wishes. He later said that "the only thing in my life that I held against my father was that he wouldn't let me go into the Royal Flying Corps as soon as I got my ticket, because he thought flying was much too dangerous an occupation."

But it was 1914, and in August, the Great War broke out. While that too made life more dangerous for an army officer, even for one in the artillery, "my father could not do a thing about it." Although Dowding was officially in the artillery, he was also a reservist in the RFC, which called him up within a few hours of the outbreak of war. He was sent to join a new squadron at a station commanded by Hugh "Boom" Trenchard, and it was there that he and Trenchard had their first run-in.

Trenchard was the first commander of the RFC, and its architect. He built it from scratch, and like any good architect, he had his own ideas. His nickname, "Boom," came from the observation by his comrades that the telephone seemed redundant when he used it. Speaking from headquarters to the front lines, he could supposedly be heard clearly if he just opened the window. The volume of his voice was a measure of the clarity of his vision; he knew what he wanted and he didn't want to be bothered by anyone who had his own ideas. And here came Dowding . . .

"We thought that the war would be over before we crossed the Channel," Dowding said. "I used to go and worry Trenchard about twice a week about being posted to France." Trenchard was not the kind of commander who enjoyed being hassled by a junior, even if it was due to his enthusiasm, and after several weeks of this, he sent Dowding to France—but as an observer rather than as a pilot.

The airplanes in France carried no guns or bombs and were used solely for observation (in the manner Dowding had pioneered the previous year at the Staff College). The crew consisted of a pilot and an observer, the latter being largely untrained. "It was by way of being a fearful insult to send out a qualified pilot as an observer, but I was well enough content."

At first the pilots, both German and English, used to wave to each other as they flew past on their missions, but soon someone threw a rock instead of waving, and from there it quickly escalated to shooting at each other. Dowding was one of the first. "I had a Mauser pistol with a shoulder stump. It was quite a good weapon for the purpose, but I never hit anything." Nor did anyone else in those early days.

With two aircraft zooming in different directions, it was nearly impossible to hit anything. It quickly became apparent that the best way would be to point the airplane at the opponent and fire straight ahead, but in that case, the bullets would hit your own propeller. A Frenchman named Roland Garros took the first step when he fit his propeller blades with steel deflectors, so that the bullets that didn't slip through the whirling blades would just be knocked away. This worked beautifully for a while, but eventually the constant battering weakened the blades. When one of them shattered, Garros was forced down behind German lines. Anthony Fokker, a Dutch airplane designer working for the Germans, was shown Garros's setup and quickly improved it by installing an interrupter gear.

With this installed, the machine gun fired only when the path between the spinning propeller blades was clear. Fokker's new monoplane quickly initiated the "Fokker scourge," sweeping the skies clear of British and French aircraft until one of the Fokkers crashed behind the Allied lines and they were able to copy the system and restore the balance of power.

But now the war in the air had been irrevocably changed. With the realization of the utility of their own observation planes came the concomitant knowledge that the enemy's were just as useful to them. The solution was obvious: Shoot them down. The air became a killing ground.

five

THE OBSERVATION planes were being shot down like flies, which didn't bother the generals too much. After all, they were losing a thousand men a day in the trenches; war is hell, and that's just the way it is. But what did bother them was that for the observation planes to bring back their observations, the observers had to return home, land, and hand over their notes. So an observation plane shot down was a plane that didn't bring back any information.

By 1914, ships at sea were just beginning to be equipped with radio sets. Eventually, it dawned on the Royal Flying Corps that if they could fit radios into their airplanes the information could be sent back while the observers were still up in the air, perhaps even over enemy lines. Then, even if the plane were lost, the information would still be received. In 1915, a year after being sent to France as an observer, Dowding was posted as Flight Commander to the newly formed Wireless Squadron, which was established to investigate the possible use of radio as a means of communication between airplanes and the ground.

After several months of hard work, he determined that the system would work. Dowding himself was the first person in England—perhaps in the world—to sit in an airplane several thousand feet high and talk to someone on the ground. But there were snags to be hammered out, as in any new technology, and the brass hats grew impatient. The War Office, ignoring Dowding's progress reports, finally informed the squadron that they had determined that "radio-telephonic communication between air and ground was not practical," and that was the end of that.

After the Wireless Squadron was disbanded, Dowding was sent to command No. 16 Squadron, part of the wing commanded by Trenchard, who was now a Lieutenant Colonel and who hadn't forgotten his earlier annoyance with Dowding. Unfortunately, Dowding had barely taken up his new position when a problem surfaced: The squadron was shipped the wrong replacement propellers for their airplanes. He complained to Trenchard, who impatiently reminded him that there was a war on and that he should improvise, as any good commander in the field must. Dowding replied that in this case it was impossible; the propellers simply didn't fit. Trenchard retorted that he had been informed on good authority that they could make the propellers fit by simply drilling a larger central hole for the spinner. Dowding argued that drilling would weaken the wooden shaft. Trenchard turned to his adjutant, who had operated an automobile sales and repair agency in civilian life. The aide smiled and said that this was nonsense, implying that Dowding was being unreasonably obstructive. Banging his fist on the desk, Trenchard boomed out at Dowding, telling him not to be so damned persnickety and to just get on with it!

Airmen didn't wear parachutes in those days. If Trenchard was wrong and one of the propeller blades broke off in flight, the unbalanced propeller would probably throw the plane into an uncontrollable spin and the pilot would be killed. But there comes a time when you can no longer argue with your superior officer. So Dowding returned to his aerodrome and had the larger hole drilled. The mechanics then fit the modified propeller on his plane, and Dowding, unwilling to risk the life of one of his pilots, took the plane up himself to see if the propeller would break off. It didn't, and he landed in one piece, not quite sure if he was relieved to be alive or irritated to be wrong.

No sooner had he landed than the telephone rang. It was Trenchard, with as close to an apology as Boom was able to make, telling him that he had been misinformed. Realizing after Dowding left his office that he should talk to someone with more engineering background than his adjutant, he had called in his engineering officer and asked his opinion. The engineer had said that Dowding was right, the propeller would probably fall off in flight. Brusquely, now, Trenchard told Dowding to forget about drilling the hole; he would arrange for new propellers to be shipped. Understandably miffed but less than diplomatic, Dowding expressed his regret that Trenchard had preferred "to take the word of some half-baked motor salesman against mine." After a moment's silence, Trenchard said that new propellers would be sent and hung up.

By 1916, Dowding was himself a Lieutenant Colonel and in command of a frontline fighter squadron. A poignant description of him at that time is found in the autobiography of one of the fliers he commanded. Attempting to disguise any real names, he refers to Stuffy Dowding as "the Starched Shirt," and describes their first meeting as the youngster joined the squadron and was introduced to him in the mess: "The Starched Shirt gave me a limp hand together with a tired smile, and if I had not been so nervous myself I should have seen at once that, amongst other things, he was cursed with shyness. After I had returned to my place dead silence reigned which he attempted to break by speaking to everyone in turn. But it was always with that same tired little smile, in a quiet, rather nasal voice, his eyes half-veiled like a coy maiden's, ready to turn hastily away from embarrassing talkativeness. . . . And yet he was in many ways a good man. In the long run I came to esteem him as much as any member of the squadron. He was efficient, strict and calm; he had a sense of duty . . . and my heart warmed to him."

The pilot, Duncan Grinnell-Milne, toward the end of the book gives an ironic prophecy when he tells an even younger fighter pilot Dowding's name: "'Never heard of him,' murmured Shutters. And somehow I found his answer full of meaning: the Starched Shirt was a General now, in charge of training or something, a successful senior officer, not a bad fellow at heart. . . . Yet the younger generation of war pilots had 'never heard of him'; his name would not be remembered when the far-off days of peace brought airmen together to talk over old exploits, his name would never figure upon the honours roll of any squadron."

Ironic, indeed, or perhaps merely an illustration of how vaguely we can read the future. Neither Grinnell-Milne nor the anonymous Shutters is remembered now, but wherever fighter pilots gather today a toast is raised to the memory of the Starched Shirt, old Stuffy Dowding.

His fame, however, would come later. In 1916 he was still serving under Trenchard, who was now a major general and in command of the entire RFC in France. During the battle of the Somme, Dowding's squadron was decimated, and after the battle was over, he requested rest leave for the battered survivors. Trenchard immediately said no.

Dowding renewed his request, although he was by now well aware of Trenchard's contumely. The classic film *Dawn Patrol* and an updated Second World War version, *Twelve O'clock High*, were based on what happened next. The story is that of a commanding officer ordered to send his men to their deaths day after day, of his attempts to give them a rest, and of the relentless orders from his superiors to keep on going, day after day after day.

Dowding's request was denied. Again Dowding repeated himself, and then again and again. Continually he badgered Trenchard, protesting against the practice of sending new replacements directly into battle, and demanding that his squadron be pulled out of the line for a rest. The strain was growing too much for his men, whose life expectancy was measured in weeks for the veterans and quite literally in mere minutes for the fledglings, who were sent out from England with insufficient training and only a few hours in the air. As they desperately strove to stay in formation while simultaneously keeping their nose on the horizon, the wings level, and the ball-and-needle balanced, they were usually shot down in flames by the first wave of attackers, whom they never even saw.

Dowding saw no sense in such madness. He did not want to be one of those who, in Siegfried Sassoon's words of 1918, "speed glum heroes up the line to death." Trenchard was not impressed by the poetry. "He grew very angry," Dowding said, "though our casualty rate was 100% a month." As one of Dowding's junior officers later wrote, "It was out of his anxiety over the severity of those losses that there developed in Dowding's mind the intense feelings that he came to have about casualties; and that, in part, was the cause of the rift between him and Trenchard that came to perplex so many of us."

Angry is not a strong enough word for Trenchard's reaction. He stormed about his headquarters and, as soon as he could, got Dowding promoted out of his hair and sent home in charge of a training command.

In France the slaughter went on. Dowding no longer had to give the daily orders to send men to their deaths, but he was removed from that horror only on the surface. As commander of the Southern Training Brigade back in England, he was continually ordered by Trenchard to send more pilots to replace those being lost over the trenches of France. Dowding replied that it took time to train a pilot properly. Trenchard replied that he would have to forget the word *properly*. "There's a war going on over here!" he bellowed. "I need more pilots!" He ordered Dowding to cut the training period and send him pilots, half-trained if necessary, but pilots of whatever caliber, to fill the empty cockpits.

Dowding refused. New pilots, even with a full period of training, were no match for experienced aviators in their Fokkers. To cut the training program, to send them over without the best training he could give them, would be tantamount to murder. He would not do it. Trenchard's answer came booming back across the Channel: "If you won't give me the bloody recruits, give me their instructors!" Dowding refused angrily. To do so would destroy even the possibility of giving the chicks a decent chance of life over there. He was in command of training, and he would run the command in his own way! He very quickly then learned the facts of life, as an immediate order came in from Headquarters, Royal Flying Corps, transferring nearly all his instructors to the front. He was left with just one for each training squadron.

This was disastrous, Dowding railed. The instructors would soon be killed in France, and with only one instructor per squadron, the flow of new pilots would be so drastically curtailed that the RFC would soon cease to exist. But Trenchard was the power in the new service, and the order was repeated. So Dowding made one last effort, writing to Trenchard's Senior Personnel Staff Officer (SPSO) and asking him to intercede, to explain that the training brigade simply couldn't afford to lose its instructors. But the SPSO hadn't reached his exalted position by being blind and deaf. He knew better than to try to explain to Trenchard anything that the boss didn't want to hear explained. Instead, he showed him Dowding's letter, and the resulting boom was heard clear across the Channel, frightening the gulls from Dover to Brighton and unborn children in their mothers' wombs. "That finished me with Trenchard," Dowding realized.

six

IN THE SUMMER OF 1940, all the hopes of the free world would hang by the threads strung together by Dowding to frustrate and foil the Nazi Huns. During the late 1930s, first as director of research and then as head of Fighter Command, he would form the technical weapons, the support facilities, the new generation of fighters, and the interlocking operational support to make possible a defense against the bomber—a defense that everyone else thought was impossible. Alone among his colleagues, he would fight and argue and somehow put it all together, barely in the nick of time. Looking back today at all the other senior commanders of the Royal Air Force and His Majesty's government, it is impossible to identify anyone else who could have done it.

He was, as a contemporary general put it, "a difficult man, a self opinionated man, a most determined man, and a man who knew more than anybody about all aspects of aerial warfare."

Some twenty years earlier, when the First World War ended in 1918, he had very nearly been drummed out of the service.

As the War to End All Wars came to its flawed conclusion, the impetus to close down the armed forces was strong. Boom Trenchard emerged as the strongman of the Royal Flying Corps. Taking office as Chief of Air Staff when it was reformed as the Royal Air Force (RAF), he saved it from a bewildering array of parliamentary cost cuts, and he did so by considering who was essential and who was not.

And of all the nonessential officers in that war just ended, Hugh "Stuffy" Dowding was high on his list of those to be discarded. Kicked out of France by Trenchard, he had at least survived the war, while most of his contemporaries had not. In consequence, by 1918 he was one of Trenchard's most senior officers, but soon after the cessation of hostilities, he was informed by mail that "your services will no longer be required in the Royal Air Force." He was dismissed from the RAF, with orders to return to the Garrison Artillery.

In light of his steadily worsening relationship with Trenchard, he had not been expecting promotion, but this sudden dismissal was an unexpected and most serious blow. The officers of the Garrison Artillery, with whom he had trained in the early years, had served in that service throughout the war and had gained experience and reputation there, while Dowding had been away playing with airplanes. So although he had seniority in the RAF, he had none in the artillery. Luckily for him, despite Trenchard's animosity, there were a few highly placed RAF officers who took up the battle on his behalf—though he didn't make it easy, as for example in the case of the court-martial of one of the officers under his command.

Dowding was then commanding No. 1 Group when he received orders from the Air Ministry to bring court-martial charges against the young officer, a fighter pilot named Sholto Douglas. A fatal accident had occurred at the Flying Training School, which was part of Dowding's group, and the Court of Inquiry found that it was due to faulty maintenance of the aircraft. Because the commanding officer of the school had been off base at the time, the Air Ministry decided that the Chief Flying Instructor, Douglas, was to be held responsible.

Instead of immediately convening the court-martial, Dowding

investigated the situation himself. Quickly concluding that Douglas had done nothing wrong, he refused to proceed with the court-martial. The Air Ministry, he said, "were being stupid." His stubborn stand prevailed, and the future Marshal of the Royal Air Force Lord Douglas of Kirtleside had his career saved. (On an interesting note, when Dowding was summarily fired after he won the Battle of Britain, it was largely Sholto Douglas's doing. What goes around comes around, they say, but sometimes it comes back with reverse spin.)

Despite this perfect example of Dowding's stubbornness and the animosity it naturally begat in the Air Ministry, his friends eventually prevailed on Trenchard to recognize that his stubbornness always manifested itself as concern for those serving under him, never for his own advantage. Furthermore, they argued, he had demonstrated a devotion to duty and a level of competence far above the usual, and finally, with Trenchard's grudging acceptance, he was granted a permanent commission as Group Captain in the Royal Air Force.

He settled down again into the comfortable life of a peacetime officer, and at the age of thirty-six, Stuffy Dowding fell in love. Clarice Vancourt was a gentle and caring soul, a nurse, and a cousin to one of his brother officers. Somehow she saw in this inarticulate, reserved officer a shared gentleness, a soul longing to care for and to be cared for, and she managed to communicate with him in a manner beyond words. They married soon after, had a son the first year, and in the second year she suddenly took sick. Before anyone had time to realize how serious it was, she died. She was with him so suddenly, coming at a time when he had begun to think that such things were not for him, and then just as suddenly she was gone. His unmarried sister Hilda moved in with him to take care of the child, and Stuffy buried himself in work.

There are those for whom the life of romance is not intended. For Dowding it had been a brief excursion into another world. His son would grow up to be a fighter pilot under his command; his wife, so soon lost, would return to comfort him in his worst time of need. But he knew nothing of that as yet. He breathed a prayer of thanks for having been briefly blessed, a sigh of regret for the necessities of his fate, and returned to the austere life of a bachelor in His Majesty's service.

His stubbornness never abated, for he never recognized it as stubbornness. Unlike most of his fellows and superiors, he was always open to new ideas; he took great pleasure in catching a glimpse of possibilities dimly seen. But it never occurred to him to defer to those who outranked him, simply because of their rank. It never occurred to him to give up, or indeed to compromise in the face of an official decision that he felt was wrong.

Despite this, his integrity and competence shone through, and year by year he advanced through the ranks. Though Trenchard continued to regard him with suspicion for a while, he finally began to recognize the hard work and clear thinking that Stuffy showed, and once he came around he came completely. "I don't often make mistakes," he told Dowding, "but I made one with you." By 1930, with Trenchard's blessing, he had been knighted, promoted to Air Marshal, and given a place on the Air Council as the Member for Supply and Research.

It could not have been a more suitable appointment. Throughout the 1920s, the prevailing view among both members of the government and senior commanders of the RAF was that all available funds should be used to build more and more bombers since no defense against them was possible. Alone in the corridors of power, Dowding began to wonder if that were true. Alone among his peers, he decided that it wasn't necessarily so.

It was a ridiculous position to take, and if you or I had been there at the time, we would have regarded him—as so many did—as a fruitcake. At least I would have, for that was the reaction I had to a remarkably similar situation: the silliness of President Reagan some fifty years later in the matter of Star Wars.

The first I heard of Star Wars was in 1983, when the great physicist Edward Teller visited the physics department at the University of Miami. In the course of his seminar, he mentioned that we no longer had to worry about Soviet intercontinental ballistic missiles. Afterward, at lunch, I asked him what he meant. He said that he and several other scientists had worked out a defense against the missiles, but that it was a secret that President Reagan would soon announce. Teller was a physicist of renown and I tended to trust him, so you can imagine my shock when Reagan made his public announcement a couple of months later.

Consider the Star Wars situation during those Cold War days. The (Soviet) enemy has intercontinental ballistic missiles capable of delivering multiple nuclear warheads to any spot on earth. These missiles are released from remote Siberian outposts or from submarines anywhere in the world's oceans; rocket-propelled, the missiles climb vertically into the stratosphere and then arc over, traveling well above the altitude and beyond the speed of any defending fighter planes. Arriving over enemy (American) territory, they release their multiple warheads, which then plunge down at speeds of many thousands of miles per hour, far beyond the capabilities of our defenders to catch up to them and destroy them.

Enter Star Wars. We position satellites overhead in continuous position to monitor the sky. They are equipped with laser guns; the laser energy, traveling at the speed of light, is fast enough to easily catch the missiles and destroy them.

What's the catch? First, we do not have the technology to put satellites up there and keep them serviced for years, perhaps decades, to be ready to react within seconds when a missile launch is detected. Second, we cannot put up enough satellites to react to the thousands of warheads the Soviets are capable of sending at us in hundreds of missiles. Third, a laser must lock on to its target for a finite time to deliver enough energy to destroy it, and this our lasers cannot do. Nor do we have any other weapon capable of knocking out the missiles. Finally, even if we could someday solve all these problems, the Star Wars system by its very conception is designed to destroy weapons zooming through the stratosphere. The Soviets could then simply use low-flying cruise missiles to zip under our defenses, while any terrorist nation could use even simpler, cheaper means of delivering nukes: suitcases lugged by people on foot, perhaps, or automobiles crossing our infinitely long and easily penetrable borders.

The system just could not work, and to this day, it hasn't, despite the continuous inflow of governmental moneys. Nor, in the 1930s, could Dowding's. First, the British fighters couldn't catch the German bombers, which could speed along at upward of 250 miles an hour, faster than the fastest British fighters. Second, even if the fighters could manage to reach and fly above the bombers, so as to use the speed of a dive to catch them, the fighter planes carried only two machine guns, which fire low-caliber ammunition intermittently through the propeller. The fighters wouldn't be able to hold a bomber in their sights long enough to deliver enough bullets to bring it down. Third, they couldn't manage to be above the bombers when arriving in the first place, because the bombers wouldn't be sighted until they crossed the coast. At that point, the enemy's primary target, London, would only be ten minutes' flying time away, whereas it would take the British fighters nearly twenty minutes to reach the operational altitude of the bombers.

So every other RAF staff officer's belief that, as Stanley Baldwin put it in a 1932 radio address to the nation, "the bomber will always get through," is not only understandable but correct. The only defense against being bombed is to have enough bombers to rain even greater destruction on the enemy, and so to deter them.

Why on earth can't Dowding see that?

Well, there is one difference in the two situations. In the 1930s, bombers are the only threat. Dowding doesn't have to worry about cruise missiles or spies sneaking nuclear bombs into the country, since neither cruise missiles nor nuclear weapons have yet been invented. His only enemy is the bomber. He is free to concentrate on stopping the bombers, and his powers of concentration are enormous. For "powers of concentration," read "stubbornness," and you have the opinion of everyone else in the Royal Air Force.

seven

In the scheme of things, the bombing of England in the First World War was little more than a nuisance. The economic damage, far from crippling the nation as the German leaders had hoped, was less than that done by rats every year. People were killed, yes, and every death is a tragedy, but they were not killed in sufficient numbers to affect the outcome of the war in the slightest.

Nevertheless, the bombing was an ill omen of things to come. Particularly fearsome was the specter of the wholesale gassing of civilian populations from the air. The use of poison gas in artillery shells had been outlawed by international agreement early in the century, but the Germans had found a loophole. Instead of shooting gas shells at the Allies, they brought gas canisters into the frontline trenches and just opened the valves, letting the gas drift over into the British and French trenches. There was nothing in the letter of the law to prohibit this; the tactic's only flaw was that the dispersal of the gas depended on the uncontrollable wind, and as it turned out, the prevailing winds were west to east, blowing most of the gas back onto their own troops.

So gas, horrible as it was, turned out to be rather useless in trench warfare. Dropping it on cities, however, was a different matter. Fleets of bombers loaded with gas canisters would sow untold horror in the crowded streets of London. Of course it would seem to have been a simple matter for the League of Nations to remove the loophole and simply ban poison gas, no matter how it was delivered, by artillery shell or windblown or aerial bomb. But the League— deprived of the world's most powerful nation, the United States— was proving to be incapable of any real action.

The outlook was indeed terrible. In February 1918, a dozen German Gothas bombed London on three consecutive nights, dropping three hundred tons of explosives and killing thirty-eight people. Reporting on this, an air commodore wrote that "the foreign folk in the crowded East End district were singularly liable to an unreasoning panic. . . . In the shelter of the tube stations the distress of Jewish mothers and children was very difficult to soothe. They would scream loudly . . . while bands, shedding every vestige of manhood, would behave like animals of the wild, sometimes brutally trampling people to death in a mad, insensate rush for safety."

A dozen bombers, three hundred tons of bombs, and insensate panic. Imagine the impact of hundreds of bombers dropping poison gas and incendiary bombs as well as high explosives: It was a Dantean vision of hell on earth. The prospect was so horrible that it led to a push for world disarmament, which, given the helplessness of the League of Nations, was a retreat from reality. At any event, events themselves were moving in a different direction.

In England the pivotal events were connected with the far-flung empire. In 1920 Winston Churchill was Colonial Secretary when a rebellion against British occupation suddenly erupted in the Euphrates valley. A bomber squadron was sent from Egypt, and the rain of bombs from the air soon squelched the rebellion. Churchill was so impressed that he asked Trenchard if the air force couldn't all by themselves keep the peace in Iraq, a traditional trouble spot then as it is now. Trenchard sent four squadrons to Baghdad under the command of Dowding to replace the British ground troops there, and they were immediately successful.

Dowding initiated a strict but workable plan. As soon as any trouble developed, he would warn the offending villages first, and then, if they didn't surrender, he would send a few planes and drop a few bombs, which served to clear things up. The British were able to maintain order there for the next fifteen years, at a considerable savings in both money and lives over the previous strategy of maintaining infantry and cavalry to wage full-scale war against the rebellious tribes.

In Germany the impetus was the failure of the Weimar Republic—a democracy forced on the people by the conquering powers of the First World War and bitterly resented. It could not bring the people together under the disheartening restrictions of the Treaty of Versailles, and conditions disintegrated into armed conflict between the forces of the left and the right, the communists and the Nazis. When Hitler won out, the possibility of universal disarmament was no longer viable. The question then became, in England and France, which of the armed services should form the fulcrum of defense, and in Germany, which should form the fulcrum of offense.

France reined itself in behind the Maginot Line, as America did behind its oceans. In neither case was this a fortunate course of action. Germany decided on mechanized ground warfare, with tanks replacing horses and with small bombers acting as mobile artillery in support of the tanks. England embraced the Douhet theory, fearing the bombardment of its cities, and in consequence established Bomber Command of the RAF as its prime deterrent throughout the 1920s and early 1930s.

In 1929, Dowding came back from the Near East and within a year assumed the role of Air Member for Research and Development, and everything began to change.

So. Here comes Dowding, and naturally he views his new position as having to do with the research and development of better bombers. He's just come back from bombing the Iraqis and he knows how effective that was. What's more, the general mind-set among the Air Staff is based on Trenchard's view that the bomber is the backbone of the air force. This is reinforced by all the research developments of the past two decades, for since the Great War, the bomber has become faster than the biplane fighters. It is better armed since its machine guns don't have to fire through propellers and therefore are not restricted to fire only intermittently, and it is now capable of carrying several thousand pounds of bombs. It is truly an awesome weapon.

In a sense, this is good news; if the bomber is terrible enough, perhaps no one will ever want to start a war. On the other hand, over there in Germany, Hitler doesn't look as if he's worrying too much about bombing women and children. So Dowding, who always takes his job quite seriously, begins to wonder if perhaps there isn't some way to defend against the bomber.

There were three problems. First, the new bombers were faster than the fighters, so how could they be caught? Second, the fighters' armament was limited to two machine guns firing through the propeller, and this wasn't enough to shoot down a bomber, even if by some chance the fighter caught up to it. And third, the bombers flew so high that they would reach their target before the fighters could even climb up to their altitude.

But the possibilities of new technologies were hanging in the wind. If you could detect the bombers before they reached England, you might be able to have the fighters waiting for them. Detection by sound, that was the key. Dowding was not talking of sneak attacks by individual aircraft, but large masses of them, aerial armadas crossing the Channel to lay waste the cities of England. Hundreds and hundreds of two- and four-engine monsters, filling the very sky with their noise.

Indeed, if you see an old war movie, one made in the early stages of the battle, you're likely to see searchlights daubing the sky and soldiers seated below a group of immense horns, turning wheels to rotate the horns, earpieces affixed, searching the sky for the noise of the invaders. This was thought to be the very picture of modern technology, and for a time, people thought that something like it might work.

In southeast England they built a large wall, into which they placed a multitude of sensitive microphones. This was much less sophisticated than the Hollywood version, for the wall was fixed in place and could "look" in only one direction. But in 1934 it was the best they could do. Those building it faced it toward England's traditional enemy, France, rather than the more modern threat, Germany—just another instance of how far behind the times they were. And when it was completed, they invited the Air Member for Research and Development to view a test.

Again the similarity to Star Wars: When the first Star Wars test was undertaken—and subsequently triumphantly announced as a success—the incoming missile's path was known to the defenders, and it was just one missile instead of hundreds. In 1934, a bomber was to come in conveniently on a line leading directly to the wall, and Dowding was told that they would hear it long before it came into view.

They sat down to wait, but before any aircraft engines could be heard over the loudspeakers, there came instead a weird sort of jingle-jangling. Those in attendance looked around, puzzled, until suddenly one of them saw the problem and jumped up to race off and fix it. He had seen in the distance a milkman making his early-morning rounds, and the clanking of his bottles was overwhelming the sound of the incoming bomber.

And that was that, Dowding thought. Conceivably, with further research funds, they might construct a movable wall to detect aircraft coming in from any direction, but how to quiet the ambient sounds of the country? The technique was bound to pick up any sounds—motorcars as well as milkmen, birds twittering and cows mooing, the rumble of distant thunder. There was no way to distinguish the sounds of airplane engines from any other noise.

Dowding marked down a large X on the group's request for further research funds, and turned his attention reluctantly to the death ray.

A death ray? Well, why not? The death ray was a staple of scientific and horror fiction during the 1920s and 1930s, and wasn't fact stranger than fiction? It had been only a few decades since Heinrich Hertz had discovered radio waves, which turned out to be electromagnetic radiation invisible to the human eye. Since then, X-rays and radioactivity, with its alpha, beta, and gamma rays (the last of which can penetrate human skin and concrete walls), had sprung out of nowhere within the lifetimes of most people, and so it was easy to imagine even deadlier forms of radiation as yet undetected and even more powerful. Of course, it was all nonsense, although it is amusing to recollect that an unnoticed paper by Einstein had already shown the realities of laser technology, which could lead to a real sort of death ray. But at the time it was all smoke and mirrors.

At which Grindell Matthews was an expert.

In 1924, he claimed to have developed an electromagnetic beam that could "kill vermin at a distance of 64 feet, explode dynamite, and stop internal combustion engines." The press descended on him for proof and came away with a bit less; a reporter from the *London Daily Mail* asked the inventor whether he could verify the claims. "Matthews smiled, and I found confirmation in that," he wrote. Apparently, a knowing smile was enough, and the subsequent *Daily Mail* story was reprinted around the world, each reprint adding something new, until the War Office was forced to ask for a demonstration.

There being neither vermin nor dynamite in Matthews's laboratory on the specified day, he announced that he would put out an electric light with his deadly ray. And indeed he did: He switched on the ray, and the light died out. But when he turned to discuss the matter with the attendees, one of them quickly darted in the path of the supposed death-ray beam and stood there, unharmed and grinning ferociously.

The death ray was a hoax, but neither Matthews nor the press gave up, and for the next twenty years, there was a succession of such devices loudly heralded in the papers. As Dowding took up the post of Air Member for Research, he was forced to evaluate a number of—shall we say, creative—proposals: a device to firm up clouds for use as floating aerodromes, liquid nitrogen to freeze the waters of the Channel to trap an invading armada, and, of course, death rays of every conceivable and inconceivable type. They all had to be carefully looked into, for no one was forgetting the history of the tank, which had been submitted to the War Office in 1914 and dismissed with the scribbled comment: "The man's mad!"

The War Office, hounded by the press, offered a reward of one thousand pounds—double what the average man earned in a year—for a real death ray, one that could be shown to kill a sheep at a distance of a mile. This, of course, brought out every nut case and con man in the kingdom, each of whom had to be honestly evaluated. Dowding was kept busy working nights and weekends without respite, for with Germany rearming, the pressure was building to do something, anything that would provide some hope. The death ray, as it turned out, offered none.

Nor did anything else. Although Trenchard tried to reassure Parliament that his bomber force would deter any attack, it was becoming clear that England was particularly susceptible to this new kind of warfare. In reply to Trenchard, one parliamentarian pointed out the simple observation that the Thames River provided a beacon for bombers, shining in the dark by moonlight and leading them directly from the Channel into the heart of London. Another member of Parliament focused on the incendiary bombs that had been developed since the last war, and described data indicating that even a small force of bombers could turn Britain's cities into raging infernos.

When Trenchard replied that it was within England's power to visit the same destruction on any enemy who dared to attack, both Parliament and the general population winced. It was England alone that had all its population crammed into a small island with no place of escape. London epitomized the problem. The capital was the center of England's political, shipping, trading, economic, cultural, and historical life. London was the very soul of the country, and there it was, stuck at the southeastern corner of the island. Placed there as if inviting attack from any continental power, the city was too close to the coast for any effective defense to be mounted. It was "the greatest target in the world, a kind of tremendous fat cow, a valuable fat cow tied up to attract the beasts of prey," as Winston Churchill sadly described the capital.

England's traditional strength had been its navy, but now it was becoming increasingly evident that even the greatest warships were vulnerable to aerial attack. Churchill grumbled ominously, telling England that "war, which used to be cruel and magnificent, has now become cruel and squalid. In fact it has been completely spoilt. I wish flying had never been invented. The world has shrunk since the Wrights got into the air; it was an evil hour for poor England."

He was not alone. A. P. Rowe, a rather obscure staff member of the Directorate of Scientific Research of the Air Ministry, undertook a search through the ministry files for all scientific proposals to improve air defense since the Great War. Among the many thousands of files, he found only fifty-three, none of which had the slightest use. He failed to find a single suggestion that would provide the slightest answer to Baldwin's pronouncement "The bomber will always get through."

Rowe felt alone and lost. Although Churchill was rumbling on, the politician was a political outcast whom no one paid attention to, his speeches described as "an old man farting in the wind." And although a few members of Parliament echoed Churchill's warnings in that chamber, no one listened. So Rowe packed his clothes and went off on vacation after writing a memo to his superior, H. E. Wimperis, Director of Scientific Research, telling him that the directorate was spending its time on useless endeavors while the world was falling down around them. He asked Wimperis to tell his superior, the Secretary of State for Air, that "unless science can find some way to come to the rescue, any war within the next ten years is bound to be lost."

He received no reply.

eight

Perhaps Trenchard was right that there was no defense against the bomber, and perhaps Rowe was right that any war within the next ten years was bound to be lost. With Hitler rearming Germany so rapidly, war certainly looked imminent within less than ten years, and here was London, Churchill's "tremendous fat cow," waiting helplessly to be bombed and gassed and set on fire. The problems seemed insoluble. And yet...

What was it Rowe had said? "Unless science can find some way to come to the rescue..." So doom was looming, but not yet inevitable. Sound detection didn't work and the death ray didn't work, but what else might we have? The trick was not to despair because of the three insoluble problems, but to tackle them one by one. Looking around, Dowding's attention was drawn to the Schneider Trophy races and the genius of a rather nondescript man named Reginald Mitchell.

In the 1920s, airplane races and their aviators were the darlings of public entertainment, and the races sponsored by M. Schneider were the premier event. The rules had been set by the French founder back in the 1910s, when the future of aviation lay obviously with seaplanes, which could land on, and take off from, lakes and harbors, obviating the necessity of constructing costly airfields all over the world. For these races, hundreds of thousands of spectators would show up, lining the shore and filling the waters around the course with hundreds of yachts, sailboats, rowboats, and barges. At the appointed time, they would hear a gunshot, and the first plane would take off. From a distance, they would see at first only a plume of water advancing faster and faster, and then it would suddenly cease and instead a small gnat would emerge from it and would claw itself into the air, roaring over their heads, turning and coming back around the course. Again and again the gunshot would sound, and one after the other, the competitors would flash around, bewildering the senses as they flew at very nearly two hundred miles an hour!

Though the competition was originally set up in France, the winners usually came from England, Italy, or the United States. By 1922, when the race was won by England with a flying boat designed by Mitchell and built by Supermarine, Mitchell had begun to realize that the necessary hull design of a flying boat was aerodynamically inferior and added too much weight to the airplane. He decided to sidestep the original intentions of M. Schneider by designing a sleek monoplane, basically a land-based airplane, but fitted with floats to fulfill the letter if not the spirit of the competition.

He got to work immediately but wasn't able to get a machine ready for the following year's race, which was won by a Curtis flying boat from America. The organizers decided to run the races only every other year, so that no competition was held in 1924. By the summer of 1925, Mitchell's revolutionary S.4 was in the air: a sleek monoplane, virtually a flying engine mounted on a pair of floats. At 226 miles per hour, it immediately broke the British speed record, but it crashed before the Schneider event took place.

The airplane nevertheless impressed His Majesty's government so much that they saw the future and provided funds for seven more such aircraft, three to be built by Mitchell and four assigned to a design team at Gloster Aircraft. The next Schneider race was in 1927, and by then the Supermarine design, Mitchell's S.5, was clearly the better. It dominated the race, taking both first and second places; later that year it broke the world speed record by nearly a hundred miles an hour, with a run at 319 miles per hour.

With enthusiasm high, work began immediately on an improved design for the 1929 race. This time the airplane was constructed entirely of metal (the previous winner had wooden wings) and it had a new Rolls-Royce engine. Two of them were built, and once again they took both first and second places. A week later, they set another world's speed record, raising it to 357 miles per hour.

Mitchell's group at Supermarine was ecstatic, but His Majesty's government was less so. Evidently feeling that good enough was sufficient, it withdrew all support for another seaplane. At the last moment, Lady Houston came through with a hundred thousand pounds, and the S.6 was built. The race itself was an anticlimax: Mitchell's designs were so clearly superior to anything else, both the Italians and the Americans gave up, and no one else even showed up for the 1931 competition. The S.6 cruised around the course at 340 miles per hour, winning the trophy for the third time in a row and, by the rules, retiring it permanently.

Everyone concerned with airplane development now felt that England should sponsor another such race. But Dowding realized that the emphasis on seaplanes was misplaced since the large floats they carried would always render them inferior to land-based planes. He also understood that the fantastic speeds achieved in the races meant that without the floats, Mitchell's basic design could produce a fighter plane much faster than the Luftwaffe's bombers. He argued that it was time to forget seaplanes and trophy races and instead use the technical knowledge that had developed during the years of competition to build faster fighter planes.

Reginald Mitchell felt the same, but the Air Ministry did not. In the fall of 1931 they issued Specification F.7/30, inviting firms to design a new fighter to replace the Bristol Bulldog, a traditional two-gun biplane fighter similar to those used in the Great War. Seeing his chance, Mitchell submitted a monoplane based on his Schneider winners, but in this competition it lost. Eight firms competed, and the winner was another biplane.

Vickers, the parent company of Supermarine, let Mitchell continue his work. Two years later, his newest design was labeled the Type 300 and Mitchell was diagnosed with cancer. He had an operation that, like most cancer treatments those days, was ineffective. On a trip to the Continent to recover from the operation, if not from the cancer, he visited Germany. The usual story is that he saw a demonstration of Willy Messerschmitt's new, single-winged Bf 109 fighter and realized that it totally outclassed the biplane the RAF had just ordered. The story isn't true, as the 109 wasn't built till 1935, but he did see the exuberant, warlike spirit of the Nazis. He was both impressed and terrified by it, and so he came home to ignore his rapidly growing cancer, to refuse all further treatment, and to work without rest on what would become the Spitfire.

By 1935, Dowding had managed to convince the Air Ministry that the old biplanes were an anachronism. He persuaded the ministry to issue a new specification calling for a single-winged airplane with enclosed cockpit and speed enough to catch the modern monoplane bombers. A primary objection the old guard had was that the biplanes' wings were braced together with wire, which gave them the strength to withstand the violent maneuvering of a dogfight, and obviously a single wing couldn't be braced with a second wing that doesn't exist. But new construction techniques and materials were able to provide a greatly strengthened wing, one that was more than acceptable. As an added bonus, the new single wing was actually strong enough to handle the recoil of machine guns, which could thus be placed on the wing, well outside the propeller's arc, and could therefore fire continuously. The provision was made to give the new fighter four of these guns instead of the two that the biplanes had been able to accommodate.

The head of the operational requirement's section of the Air

Ministry, a Squadron Leader named Ralph Sorley, computed that at the high speeds of both the new fighters and the bombers, a pilot would be lucky to hold the target in his sights for one or two seconds. And with such a short burst, even from four guns, the new all-metal bombers couldn't be brought down. He suggested eight guns, "causing great controversy" in the ministry, some of whose members had been fighter pilots in the Great War only twenty years previously. The standard equipment they had had, two guns firing through the propeller, continually jammed, so the breech had to be accessible to the pilot, who carried a hammer with which to bang on it. This usually worked, but if it didn't, the pilot had to take the gun apart, clear the jam, and reassemble it—all in the middle of a dogfight!

The former pilots couldn't realize how far the technology had advanced in so few years. By 1935 the RAF had the Browning .303, which was less prone to jam, while at the same time the new monoplane designs had wings strong enough to hold eight such weapons. This arrangement is what Sorley suggested, with Dowding's backing. But Sir Robert Brooke-Popham, then the Commander in Chief of Air Defense, agreed with the ongoing consensus of the establishment that "eight guns was going a bit far . . . the opinion of most people in Fighting Area is that the guns must still be placed in the cockpit." He also argued that the cockpit must not be enclosed, for when the pilots banged on the jammed guns, they'd need plenty of room to swing their hammers.

The old guard also pointed out that the weight of eight guns would be too much for a single-engine plane to handle, especially with the bomb-load it was expected to carry, since all fighters were expected to serve also as ground support for the infantry. Dowding argued that what was needed was a pure fighter; it was time to stop insisting on double duty. It was a tough fight, but Dowding won out. A new specification F.10/35 was sent out for an eight-gunned fighter, with the bombing requirement lifted.

The premier biplane fighter designer of the 1920s, a man named Sydney Camm, was working for the Hawker company. Convinced of the basic rightness of Mitchell's ideas, he came up with his own monoplane, the Hurricane, which would prove to be inferior to the Spitfire but easier to produce and maintain. Dowding recommended that the biplane winner of the 1935 competition be dropped and the Hurricane and Spitfire be built instead, and eventually he got his way. As it turned out, it was in the nick of time.

So he had, or would soon have, fighters that could reach up to the bombers' altitude, catch them, and shoot them down. He had one problem remaining: Even in the case of war, he clearly would never have enough fighters to keep a continuous patrol in the air waiting for the bombers. And even the new "Spits" and "Hurris" took more than twenty minutes to climb from the ground to the bombers' cruising altitude, whereas in half that time, the Luftwaffe would cover the thirty miles from the coast—where they would first be spotted—to London. So back to square one: "The bomber would always get through."

nine

AND BACK to the death ray, and to Winston Churchill. By the time of Rowe's memorandum and the demise of the sound location system, Churchill had been out of the government for five years. Always true to his principles rather than to party politics, he was scorned by both the Liberal Party he had left ten years before and the Conservative Party to which he now belonged. And he was no more popular among the people at large.

Twenty years ago, he had been the coming man; now he was a has-been who had never quite been. His voice roaring out the dangers of Nazi rearmament was a living example of the Zen riddle: If a tree falls in the forest and nobody hears it, does it make a sound?

Nobody wanted to hear it. The horrors of the past war were too near, the horrors of any future war too horrible, the horrors of the present were bad enough. The heroes of the Great War had come home to find the economy in ruins, and the sudden eruption of the worldwide depression had made things all the worse. Unemployment in towns around England ranged from an unacceptable 10 percent to an unbelievable 68 percent. So the people of England did not want to hear about the plight of the German Jews or about the statistics of aircraft production in the Ruhr.

Yet Churchill roared on, in Parliament and newspaper articles and political meetings, scorning the scorns—indeed, at times seeming to revel in them—stubbornly presenting the facts that the world wanted to ignore. And always searching for more. How he found his facts, everyone suspected and no one knew—and everyone suspected someone else. Some said agents in MI5, disaffected by the waffling of His Majesty's government, fed the gadfly their secrets. Others blamed Brendan Bracken, a friend so intimate that many thought he was Churchill's bastard son, whose house in North Lord Street became the headquarters for those fighting against Chamberlain's appeasement policies. Some said Churchill communicated with spirits; others said his wife was sleeping with someone in the cabinet.

The prime minister harried his security people. Perhaps it was some of these people, perhaps others, perhaps all of them. Whatever his sources, Churchill seemed to know more than anyone else about what was going on in Germany, about what the British government knew about what was going on in Germany, and about what was going on in the corridors of the British government.

And so he found out about the Rowe memo, and he faced Wimperis with it. What was being done, for instance, about the death ray? "It's all nonsense," Wimperis very properly responded, but Churchill would have none of that. He reminded Wimperis of the tank, of how that too was deemed nonsense until he, Winston, had discovered the discarded file and asked what was so nonsensical about it. When no one could tell him—when, as it turned out, there was nothing at all nonsensical or wrong with the idea except that it was new—he had roared his roars and pushed the tank through development until it became the weapon that crushed the trenches and won the Great War.

"So now," he asked again, "what are you doing about the death ray?"

Wimperis found it impossible to explain just why this weapon really was pure fantasy. It is, after all, difficult to argue with a bellicose ignorance, and that is what he was facing in Winston Churchill. A great man, certainly, but one of whom it was said, "the man's mind has astonishing gaps of total ignorance." So the Director of Scientific Research reluctantly asked his staff to investigate the possibility of a death ray, and if they couldn't come up with one, perhaps they could at least come up with a report that would convince the bombastic Churchill to sod off and leave them alone.

In the event, that is what happened. But the report led to a bit more than that.

A death ray would use electromagnetic radiation of some sort. Consequently, on January 18, 1935, Wimperis sent for Robert Watson Watt, head of the UK's Radio Research Laboratory, and asked him if he could possibly provide the military with a death ray to destroy enemy bombers. Watt was a serious Scotsman, and he did not laugh; presumably, he was just dismayed at the ignorance involved in such a question. Scientific officers should not take science fiction seriously. But Wimperis was serious, especially when he asked Watt to provide him with, if not the death ray, then specific data as to why it was impossible.

This Watt could not do on the spur of the moment. He returned to his laboratory and passed the problem on to "a junior scientific officer," as he later put it, an unassuming young man named Arnold "Skip" Wilkins, without mentioning the words *death ray* or *enemy bombers*. He liked to keep secret things secret, and Wilkins was not within his circle of trusted friends. He decided to present Wilkins with a "formalized problem," and so Wilkins returned from his lunch one day to find a used calendar leaf on his desk, turned to the blank side. He recognized this as Watt's usual method of communication. On it was scribbled a note from "S," Watt's usual notation for himself, the Superintendent. The note told Wilkins to "calculate the amount of radio-frequency power which should be radiated to raise the temperature of eight pints of water from 98°F to 105°F at a distance of 5 km and at a height of 1 km."

To bring down an enemy bomber, it wasn't necessary to kill the pilot; raising his temperature to 105° would make him delirious and incapable of keeping the plane under control. Watt—or Watson-Watt as he renamed himself after the war when he was knighted—thus framed the calculation in these terms. Wilkins, it turned out, was just as clever, and immediately realized the only possible purpose of heating eight pints of water (the amount of water in the blood of a person) to delirium temperatures five kilometers away and one kilometer up in the sky:

> It seemed clear to me that the note concerned the production of fever heat in an airman's blood by a death-ray and I supposed that Watson-Watt's opinion had been sought about the possibility of producing such a ray.
>
> My calculation showed, as expected, that a huge power would have to be generated at any radio frequency to produce a fever in the pilot of an aircraft even in the unlikely event of his body not being screened by the metal casing of the fuselage.... [As nothing remotely like the power required could be produced], it was clear that no radio death ray was possible.
>
> I said all this to Watson-Watt when handing him my calculation and he replied, "Well, then if the death ray is not possible how can we help them?" I replied to the effect that Post Office engineers had noticed disturbances to VHF reception when aircraft flew in the vicinity of their receivers and that this phenomenon might be useful for detecting enemy aircraft.

His insight went back to a day when he had been having a cup of coffee with several Post Office engineers—who in England were also responsible for radio communication—who were complaining about the problems of aircraft interference. Wilkins recognized that,

of course, metal airplanes flying between radio stations would interfere with the radio waves. In effect, they would absorb the radio
waves and reemit them in all directions, setting up interference pat-
terns. There was nothing to be done about this for the Post Office
people, since there was no way to shield the planes so that they
would pass through the airspace without causing interference. But
now he realized that such interference would be an indication of the
airplane's presence in the sky.

Wilkins explained all this to Watson-Watt, who then wrote a
memo to Wimperis stating unequivocally that a death ray was
impossible, but suggesting this use of radio interference to locate
enemy bombers before they appeared visibly in the skies. Thus was
radar invented.

But Watson-Watt was no fool. In his memo, he didn't mention
Wilkins's name, and so history records that the "Father" of radar was
Robert Watson-Watt. You will seldom find the name of Skip Wilkins
in the history books. (That's the way the game is played. As another
instance, in 1960, a Cambridge University graduate student named
Jocelyn Bell discovered the existence of pulsars. After much arguing,
she managed to convince the director of her laboratory, Anthony
Hewish, that there really are stars up there that pulse. No one understood what they could be until Tommy Gold of Cornell explained
them as the long-sought-after neutron stars, appearing to pulse
because they were rapidly spinning. The Nobel Prize went—surprise,
surprise—not to Bell or Gold, but to Hewish.) Watson-Watt, in his
memoirs, did try to resuscitate Wilkins by calling him the "Mother"
of radar for all his subsequent work in bringing it to fruition, but he
never acknowledged that the initial idea was not his own.

Well, never mind. Wimperis reported the Watson-Watt memo to
Churchill—who in his generally masterful history of the war gives
sole credit to Watson-Watt for radar—and to the first meeting of a
committee he had formed, the Committee for the Scientific Survey
of Air Defence.

I suppose there is some truth to the idea that there is nothing new under the sun, and radar is no exception. It might have been invented much earlier, for the idea was floating around out there. Radio waves had been discovered by Heinrich Hertz in 1886, and by 1900 a controversial genius and early pioneer of radio communication named Nikola Tesla suggested the idea, although of course at that time he was not thinking of airplanes: "When we raise the voice and hear an echo in reply, we know that the sound of the voice must have reached a distant wall or boundary, and must have been reflected from the same. Exactly as the sound, so an electrical wave is reflected, and the same evidence [can be used to] determine the relative position or course of a moving object such as a vessel at sea."

But nobody was interested in measuring the position of an object at sea: What was the point? And Tesla was known as a wild man who claimed to receive radio messages from Mars, so his idea disappeared, only to be resurrected a few years later when a German inventor, Christian Hulsmeyer, rediscovered the principle and proposed to use it to avoid ship collisions in foggy weather. He actually obtained funding, started his own company, gave public demonstrations, and offered the system to the German navy for a modest sum. As with the British Admiralty and its response to airplanes, the Germans were not interested. Hulsmeyer was asked by the Dutch to give a demonstration; he did, the system worked perfectly, and the Dutch then decided that they too were not interested. He offered it to the British navy, which also turned it down. One can't imagine what they there thinking—or rather, how on earth could they *not* be thinking? Ships at war were often baffled by fog or smoke; how could they not be interested in a device that could see through such obstacles?

But they weren't, and the concept disappeared again. And then again it surfaced, in 1916, when Hans Dominik and Richard Scherl invented it for a third time and offered it to the German Kriegsmarine for a second time. This time, in the midst of the Great War, the admirals were interested. They asked how soon they could have a working system installed in their ships. "Six months," Dominik and Scherl replied. "Too late," the admirals said, dismissing them. "The war will be over by then."

Oh, who is so blind as those who will not see?

The concept was used for sound waves rather than radio waves, in the systems called Asdic by the British and Sonar by the Americans, to detect submarines. A ship on the surface sent a sound wave down through the water; if a submarine was present, the sound bounced off and an echo was heard up on the surface. In 1925 King George V was given a demonstration and, revealing an intellect not often associated with royalty, pointed out that electromagnetic waves—radio waves—traveled much faster than sound waves, and so wouldn't it be better to use radio instead? The admirals coughed discreetly. "Quite impossible, sir," they murmured. "Scientific considerations, you know. Impossible to describe. No, no, quite impossible."

As indeed it was, or at least it was difficult, due to scattering and interferences in the water. King George nodded; it was only a thought, and it quickly disappeared. Not to reappear for another ten years, when Skip Wilkins made the suggestion to Watson-Watt, the ostensible father of radar, who seems to have been the only man in the past twenty-five years who *hadn't* thought of it.

ten

And so Wimperis reported to the Committee for the Scientific Survey of Air Defence that he had it on good authority that although a death ray was impossible, they might use radio waves to locate enemy bombers before they reached the English coast. With the committee's full approval, he went the next day to see Dowding to tell him the good news and to ask him to authorize, on his authority as Air Member for Research and Development, the necessary funds to begin to construct this early-warning system. The decision rested squarely on his shoulders.

Dowding said no.

Behind his stuffy exterior, his eyes must have been gleaming. This could be the third part, the missing part of the puzzle. The Spitfire and Hurricane, with their eight guns, were nearing production. If he could find the bombers with enough time for the fighters to reach them . . .

But his budget was tight and the government was adamant about not raising taxes to increase military expenditures, and he was not much impressed by calculations. He had spent the several previous years listening to requests for funds for death rays and frozen clouds, and he had seen those phantasms evaporate before the peering eyes of experiment. Was this to be just a bit more pie in the sky?

He knew about radio from his own experiences. He knew how useful it could be, and how new the technology was; he knew how bright people, those unhindered by preconceived ideas, could find new uses for it.

He had done so himself, when he had come back from Baghdad in time for the summer air exercises. When he had been put in charge of fighter defenses, he turned out to be the first ranking officer in the RAF to use radio in these exercises. Without telling anyone, he sent several trucks equipped with radio out on the roads over which the bombers would have to pass. When the airplanes did, the news was radioed back to Dowding, who then scrambled his fighters in time to intercept them—just as he would do with radar and the Luftwaffe bombers in the summer of 1940. But the umpires in the 1930s saw this as cheating. They stopped the exercises and told him to play by the rules like a gentleman, and they started over again.

Dowding saw no point in arguing with them, especially since he had another idea—an extraordinarily simple idea, which no one had ever thought of before. Airplanes did not carry radios, but, he thought, why shouldn't they? Way back in the First World War, he himself had conducted experiments in air-to-ground radio communication, and it had worked. The trials had never been followed up, since the Air Ministry in its wisdom had decided that air-to-ground communication was of no use. But Dowding thought he might as well pursue his own ideas rather than those of the Air Ministry. He installed a radio set in one of his fighters and had the airplane follow the bombers back to their base and inform him by radio when they landed. As soon as they did, Dowding sent his fighters to attack them on the ground. He caught them napping, wiped them out, and would have won the exercise if the umpires hadn't been so confused that they decided to cancel the whole business and go home.

Now, with Wimperis before him, he thought how wonderful it was that someone else was thinking about new ideas. But he had to be sure it worked. So he said no to the immediate expenditure of research funds, but not to the idea. He wanted a demonstration.

Wimperis said he didn't know how he could demonstrate the effect without funds to build the equipment. Dowding replied that there were lots of radio sets around the country; surely something could be found. Wimperis said yes, of course, he'd have a demonstration set up within two weeks.

He left Dowding's office without a clue in the world as to how this was to be done, but he knew whom to pass the buck to. He sent for Watson-Watt and asked him to set up a demonstration. Watson-Watt said certainly, and he left Wimperis's office without a clue in the world . . . but he too knew whom to pass the buck to.

He sent for Wilkins and told him to set up the proper equipment for a demonstration. Wilkins had no one to pass the buck to, so he told "W-W" the facts: "To modify a transmitter to operate suitably short pulses of high enough power to enable an aircraft echo to be displayed on a receiver was quite impossible in the time suggested."

Watson-Watt was devastated, but Wilkins was not. It was simply a question of figuring something out. There was always an answer, he thought, if one tried hard enough. And very quickly he came up with it.

The problem was to send out "suitably short pulses of high enough power." All radio wavelengths were not expected to be equally effective. Upon first working out the details for Watson-Watt, he had calculated that the equipment should use pulsed wavelengths of the same size as the wingspan of the aircraft they wanted to detect: "suitably short pulses." He now remembered that there was a rather powerful British Broadcasting Company (BBC) station that broadcast at shortwave and was located at Daventry; the station's wavelength was twice what was needed, but Wilkins thought this might be good enough, at least for a rough demonstration.

The test would be simple. They arranged for an RAF bomber to fly up and down a prearranged course south of Daventry, in the path of the BBC's broadcasts, and Wilkins would set up the equipment to find the radio echoes it sent back. Dowding arranged for Mr. Rowe to be the official RAF observer, and on the day before the scheduled test, Wilkins took an assistant in a van loaded with the equipment to find a good spot to set up.

He found an open field that gave a clear view in the right direction, and the two of them got to work. While they were setting up the aerials, an ominous black cloud began drifting in their direction. With a flash of lightning and a loud boom, it let loose just as they were finishing with the aerials but before all the connections had been made. The men dove into the van and drove off to get some dinner while they waited out the storm.

It was dark before the weather loosened up, and when they got back to the field, they realized they hadn't thought to bring any lights, having intended to finish their work in daylight. Now Wilkins worked by the intermittent light of flaring matches, which his assistant held for him, and finished just five minutes before the station went off the air at midnight. The equipment worked perfectly. Smiling a sigh of relief, he turned on the ignition—and found that the van wouldn't move: The field had turned to mud with the thunderstorm and had frozen solid around the wheels by midnight. Luckily, the men found a shovel in the van, dug themselves out, and managed a few hours' sleep in the local pub before starting out for the next day's demonstration.

Which worked perfectly. In fact, better than perfectly. The bomber flew its course, out of sight of those in the field, and they picked up the radio echoes and were able to chart its course. When they did they were puzzled: It didn't correspond to the course they had agreed on. Watson-Watt then talked to the pilot and found that he had gotten lost; the radar plot was a more accurate indication of where he had been than he himself could tell by looking out the window.

Rowe communicated all this to Wimperis, who went back to see

Dowding the next day. Dowding immediately authorized the ten thousand pounds.

The future of civilization would have come cheap at twice the price.

Now the three pieces of the puzzle were in place. With radio direction finding, or RDF as they called it, or radar as it would come to be known, the Luftwaffe's bombers could be spotted in time for the new fighters to climb into position to intercept. The fighters were fast enough to catch the bombers and, with their eight guns, would be able to bring the bombers down. All that was needed now was an army of scientists to turn the proposed warning system into reality, and a lot of effort to organize the support system that would make it all work.

eleven

You MIGHT THINK that gearing up to save the world from the horrors of Hitler would occupy a man's mind full-time, but a man's a man for a' that, and in the dark lonely hours of the night his fancy—even that of a fifty-year-old man—will perforce turn to thoughts of love. For Dowding this meant Clarice, his only love, his love for only two years; Clarice, who had died fifteen years before.

Dead.

Dead and gone? Perhaps not.

Dowding's first exposure to the other world of spirits and fairies took place in India, in 1906, when he was serving as a subaltern in the army. He wrote home from Kalabagh that it rained "every blessed day; the whole place is like one vast sponge. Tennis is impossible." He went on to mention en passant that "there is a lady here with a Planchette [Ouija board] apparatus, which writes fluently but with extreme inaccuracy; the spirit who actuates the board calls himself Nathaniel Bopp & is only ten years old; which perhaps accounts for his self-confidence and lack of veracity. The lady's husband insults 'Nat' consistently. . . ."

This casual acceptance of messages from the beyond was not at all unusual at the time. Spiritualism was in its heyday, finding interest and favor among the most educated as well as among the least. Charles Dickens, for example, was the most popular writer of his day, and such popularity has its basis in a genuine relationship to the public. He wrote not only for them but *of* them: his feelings, his outlook, his beliefs, resonated with the great mass of people. His membership in the Ghost Club, then, reflected the widespread beliefs of many in his audience.

The Ghost Club was formed in Cambridge in 1855 by Trinity College fellows who accepted the existence of ghosts and other psychic phenomena. The club harbored not only intellectuals like Dickens but also clergymen and scientists, and it continues to this day. Of course, it would be ridiculous today for a scientist to belong to such a club dedicated to communicating with the dead. But "the past is a different country; they do things differently there," and in the century of Dowding's birth, they did indeed do things differently. Science had shown that the universe was vastly more mysterious than had been believed, and even today, John Wheeler, one of our greatest physicists, has noted that "the universe is not only stranger than we suppose, but stranger than we *can* suppose."

This is not to suggest that Wheeler believes in the living dead, but to those pioneers of modern science in the nineteenth century the strangeness of the universe was even stranger than we can suppose today, and postmortem existence did not strain the faculties of the mind. Belief in a life after death and in the reality of communication across the boundary does, after all, predate all of today's religions. Its origin as a cultural phenomenon, however, can be said to have taken place just a few decades before Dowding's birth. This public fascination with the spirit world began with the explosive popularity of the Fox sisters, who, on March 31, 1848, discovered how to communicate with the spirit who inhabited their haunted house. By a series of clicks and knocks, they learned that the spirit was angry because he had been murdered five years previously. Miracle of miracles!

The story was picked up and widely circulated, and the two Fox sisters became vaudeville celebrities with their psychic demonstrations. One of the two, Margaretta, later confessed that she faked the spirit's clicks by clicking on her own double-jointed toe, but the widespread publicity the sisters received sparked a movement similar to the flying-saucer craze, which began almost precisely a hundred years later.

Spiritualism received a tremendous boost in the final decades of the nineteenth century from three widely respected figures: Arthur Conan Doyle, William Crookes, and Oliver Lodge. Conan Doyle's respect (in this respect) was unearned; he was a good writer but had no real understanding of either science or philosophy. Though the Sherlock Holmes stories he produced are topflight, the pseudoscientific utterances of Sherlock are just plain silly. Lodge and Crookes, on the other hand, were two of the most eminent scientists of the century.

In 1870 Sir William Crookes, the discoverer of thallium and the inventor of the Crookes tube—the precursor of today's television tubes—and later the president of the world's most distinguished scientific body, the British Association, embarked on a scientific investigation of this thing called spiritualism. "I consider it the duty of scientific men who have learnt exact modes of working to examine phenomena which attract the attention of the public, in order to confirm their genuineness, or to explain, if possible, the delusions of the honest and to expose the tricks of deceivers." Good try, Sir William. He concentrated on the most notable medium of the day, a delightful young lady named Florence Cook, and after a couple of years, he announced that he was satisfied that she was neither deluded nor a deceiver. She was, in fact, the genuine goods.

He maintained this stance for the next three years, defending her—and through her, all spiritualists, who loudly proclaimed William James's dictum "In order to prove that not all crows are black, you need find only one white crow." Crookes was convinced, after thorough investigation using the most stringent scientific techniques, that Miss Cook did converse with dead spirits and that she did bring them into the séances in semimaterial forms. In short, he concluded that there was life after what we call death and that communication between the two spheres of existence is open to a privileged few. Then, in 1874, he suddenly stopped all proselytizing and washed his hands of the whole business. He never reversed his findings; he just stopped writing and talking about it, and no amount of interviewing would entice him to say another word.

Which is rather peculiar. Had he lost all interest in the very nature of life and death? When we look at the whole story, at the small nuances and the large facts, it seems that the most likely explanation is that Sir William was sleeping with Miss Cook, or perhaps with the attractive young lady, Katy King, whose protoplasmic materializations at the séances were most provocative. The affair lasted several years, and when it ended, so did Sir W's interest in spiritualism.

Was Sir William a dupe or a duper? Did he really believe that Katy was pulled from the ethereal plane by Florrie to materialize for the pleasure of her customers, or was he a willing participant in her act? We have no answer to this question, but it seems to me that the answer lies in the very soul of a scientist, who attacks a problem with the tacit understanding that Mother Nature is not out to trick him. In Einstein's phrase, "the Lord is subtle, but not malicious." When scientists turn to the investigation of phenomena that may be real or may be trickery, the scientific method loses much of its power. By the very nature of science, which treats observation as the lodestone of truth, someone manipulating the observations might trick a scientist even more easily than a layperson.

Much more incredible than the idea that Sir William could have been tricked by a woman with whom he was infatuated is the idea that he would have been willing to lie about his observations. For a scientist to lie—to fabricate data—is the ultimate sin. Of course, we all sin, but I know of no episode in history in which a scientist lied about his data for love. For money, prestige, power, and government grants, yes. But not for love.

At any rate, the banner was picked up in the following decade by Sir Oliver Lodge. A physicist like Crookes, he was no less respected and no less willing to investigate phenomena that most scientists felt were beyond the pale. In 1884 (when Dowding was a child), Lodge attended several séances with an established Italian medium and reported that "there is no further room in my mind for doubt. Any person without invincible prejudice who had had the same experience would come to the same broad conclusion, viz., that things hitherto held impossible do actually occur."

Well, why not? For a scientist, this was only the beginning. In the years that followed, the law of conservation of energy seemed to be repealed by the Curies, the absolute space that formed the basis of Newton's gravity was abolished, time grew curvatures, electrons disappeared and materialized with impunity, and invisible microbes infected us all.

In 1915 Lodge's son Raymond was killed in action. In the following months, both he and his wife received many messages from Raymond, all of which they accepted as real, and his book *Raymond* was later accepted by Dowding, as it was by so many others, as whole truth and the sine qua non of spiritualism. Shortly before Sir Oliver's death, when he was asked to speak before the Modern Churchmen's Conference, he declared: "If I find myself an opportunity of communicating [after my death] I shall try to establish my identity by detailing a perfectly preposterous and absurdly childish peculiarity which I have already taken the trouble to record with some care in a sealed document deposited in the custody of the English S.P.R. I hope to remember the details of this document and relate them in no unmistakable fashion [thus proving the continuation of life after death]." Unfortunately, no such communication was ever received.

Nevertheless, the scientific researches of Oliver Lodge and William Crookes gave a cover of respectability to the claims of the spiritualists, and Hugh Dowding grew up in an atmosphere in which communication with the dead was rather routinely accepted, just as today most people (at least in the United States) believe in a God that guides our nation. This acceptance of things unseen was buttressed immeasurably by the host of scientific discoveries previously referred to, as Dowding grew up and the nineteenth century turned over into the twentieth. These discoveries had nothing to do with spiritualism per se, but raised the specter of things unseen yet absolutely real: those mysterious rays called X, the even more mysterious emanations of radioactivity, and Einstein's proclamation that space and time itself could be warped. And there was more, much more. Lord Rutherford found alpha particles bouncing in all directions from invisible atoms, while Max Planck suggested that energy was a quantized sort of thing that nobody understood at all. Anyone who cared to take the trouble, it seemed, could be attuned "to strange sights, things invisible to see." Clearly, mere communication with spirits was nothing to get upset about.

So when Watson-Watt tells him that invisible rays can detect an aircraft, does Dowding dismiss this as the ravings of a madman? Of course not. On the other hand, does he believe him? No, he does not; instead, he asks for a demonstration. Then, when Mr. A. P. Rowe tells him that he has seen it work, he does believe. So why should he not believe two of the world's top scientists, Lodge and Crookes, when they tell him they have seen people communicate with the dead?

Just as the reported demonstration of the invisible rays of radar gave him hope that England was not doomed, the reports of Lodge and Crookes gave Dowding hope that Clarice was not lost to him forever.

But it is one thing to believe, for example, the testimony of others that a man named Jesus lived, and quite another to believe you are Jesus. It would be a few more years before he would take that next step, which would lead him right around the bend.

twelve

On August 8, 1934, the *Times* published a letter headed "Science and Air Bombing":

Sir,

In the debate in the House of Commons on Monday on the proposed expansion of our Air Forces, it seemed to be taken for granted on all sides that there is, and can be, no defence against bombing aeroplanes and that we must rely entirely upon counter-attack and reprisals. That there is at present no means of preventing hostile bombers from depositing their loads of explosives, incendiary materials, gases, or bacteria upon their objectives I believe to be true; that no method can be devised to safeguard great centers of population from such a fate appears to me to be profoundly improbable.

If no protective contrivance can be found and we are reduced to a policy of reprisals, the temptation to be "quicker on the draw" will be tremendous. It seems not too much to say that bombing aeroplanes in the hands of gangster Governments might jeopardize the whole future of our Western civilization.

To adopt a defeatist attitude in the face of such a threat is inexcusable until it has definitely been shown that all the resources of science and invention have been exhausted. The problem is far too important and too urgent to be left to the casual endeavors of individuals or departments. The whole weight and influence of the Government should be thrown into the scale to endeavour to find a solution. All decent men and all honourable Governments are equally concerned to obtain security against attacks from the air and to achieve it no effort and no sacrifice is too great.

The letter was signed *F. Lindemann,* a man who would seem to be a strong advocate of Dowding's policies. The reality turned out to be quite different. Frederick Lindemann was professor of experimental philosophy, which was what physics was called at the time, at Oxford University. He was a man of great controversy. Some gave him credit for establishing Oxford as the second-best physics school in the country, others gave him credit for establishing Cambridge as the very best (by chasing away from Oxford the best students and professors). "He was an amateur among professionals, which is how Rutherford (the head of the Cambridge laboratory) always regarded him," asserted scientist-novelist C. P. Snow.

In *Fringes of Power,* John Colville (Churchill's private secretary) describes Lindemann: "To those he liked he was generous, helpful and entertaining. Against those who had displeased him he waged a vendetta.... He looked with contempt on Jews and coloured people; he was arrogant and impervious to argument when his mind was made up. Yet he was good company when in the mood, never boastful of his achievements, and a loyal friend."

Not being "boastful of his achievements" took on a rather singular form, exemplified by a legendary incident. As a recent biography puts it, "during the First World War he turned his experimental skill to warplanes, which he learned to fly to prove his theoretical method of recovering from an aircraft's spin." The story is that the "spin" was the terror of the skies, death to any pilot who slipped into one. This would happen when the airplane would stall and, if the wings were not kept absolutely level, one of them would dip and the airplane would fall over on that side. The other wing would flip over and the plane would plummet earthward, spinning faster and faster as it fell uncontrollably. Once in a spin, no one had any idea how to get out of it; the result was inevitably a fatal crash.

Lindemann worked out a theoretical description of the forces operating on the plane, and then he figured out how to counteract them. He thought that the instinctive response of pulling back on the stick (which normally points the aircraft's nose upward) was absolutely wrong; instead the pilot should first straighten out the aircraft by the use of the rudder pedals while keeping the airplane in a dive until the spin stopped and flying speed picked up. Only then should the pilot pull back on the stick.

This advice was counterintuitive to every pilot, and so to prove his theory, Lindemann decided that he should learn to fly. He did, and then he took off, climbed to fourteen thousand feet, pulled back on the stick, and held it pressed into his stomach as the nose rose and rose and the speed fell and fell, until with a shudder the plane stalled and fell out of the sky. As it did, he flipped the control stick over to one side so that the wing fell, and very quickly he was in a spin. As the earth rushed up toward him, he pushed the stick forward, straightened out the wings, and held it in a dive until the speed built up. Then he pulled back on the stick and zoomed back up into the sky.

From that day forward, his technique became the standard method of recovering from a spin, and the spin itself then became a standard method of escaping from an uneven combat, a frightening but routine maneuver taught to every fledgling pilot.

Or so the story goes. Whenever it was repeated in his presence—and, being such a lovely story, it was repeated over and over again—he never confirmed it, never boasted about it, merely smiled and went on sipping his tea. The problem is, he also didn't deny it, and the story isn't true.

In 1916 Harold Balfour, later Lord Balfour of Inchrye and Permanent Under-Secretary of the Air Staff, was a flying instructor in the RFC, and it was he who taught Lindemann to fly. In 1973, Balfour wrote: "The legend has been perpetrated that Professor Lindemann pioneered the spin and the technique of recovery. He never did anything to contradict this story, but it is just invention."

At the time he was teaching Lindemann to fly, Balfour said, the RFC pilots already knew how to come out of a spin: "Spinning was a normal and essential feature of air combat. We taught it to all our pupils." The technique had been worked out some four years previously, in 1912, by a Lt. Wilfred Parke of the Royal Navy. He had accidentally fallen into a spin, and as he said later, he knew at that point he was going to die. He tried the normal maneuver of pulling back on the stick, which didn't work. Then, resigned to death, somehow he tried the very thing that instinct told him not to do: He pushed the stick hard forward, dropping the nose even more vertically. This caused the airspeed to pick up enough for the wings to provide lift, and he was able to straighten them and recover.

Balfour concluded, "I saw Smith-Barry spin Avros while Lindemann was still wetting his instructional nappies in the front seat of an Avro in which I was trying to teach him how to fly."

Lindemann dressed formally, in a black suit and bowler hat, no matter what the occasion, and always carried an umbrella. He was an inveterate snob and at the same time a top athlete, once winning the tennis championship of Sweden. It was these two qualities that transformed him from a scientist of questionable reputation into a man of great influence on the coming war.

Many scientists are intellectual snobs, but Lindemann was a social snob. It was said of him that "he thinks his only peers are peers," and so he was happy to accept an invitation to a weekend at the Duke of Westminster's palatial Eaton Hall, where the Duchess had paired him with Churchill's wife, Clementine, who was a keen and competitive player. Winston wasn't there, but Lindemann and Clementine got along so famously that the Duke arranged a quiet evening at home for the two men to meet.

It was a match made in heaven—or perhaps in hell. Churchill admired Lindemann's brains and bravery, as exemplified by the story of the spinning airplane, a story that Lindemann didn't bother to deny. Lindemann, for his part, admired Churchill's pedigree and the sense of power that flowed through the air around him.

The combination nearly destroyed England.

In the 1930s, the position of Winston Churchill was unique. Way back before the First World War, he had been the youngest man in history to hold a post in the governing cabinet, but he had lost the position because of a military fiasco at Gallipoli. Now, as Hitler rose to power, Churchill was still a member of Parliament but had not held a cabinet post for nearly a decade. He saw the threat of Nazism early on and tried to rally England, which was disarming while Germany was rearming. He held little influence in Parliament, but as Hitler sent his armies into the Ruhr and then Austria and finally Czechoslovakia, Churchill's prestige among the public rose.

I must admit that if I had been there, not knowing the future, I would probably have taken Prime Minister Chamberlain's side against Churchill. There are several reasons for this. First, it had been only fifteen years since the Great War ended, and that had been a most horrible war. Millions of people had been slaughtered. *Millions,* and for no good reason, which would have been the second of my reasons: Nothing had been accomplished by that war. There had been no military or political aims, save victory. As Kipling, the great jingoist himself, put it after his son was killed in action: "If any ask why we died / Tell them our fathers lied." The only fruit of that war, labeled for want of any other purpose the War to End All Wars, would be if indeed there were no further wars.

Finally, nothing like Hitler had ever been seen before. He embodied a horror that was, literally, unbelievable—until it engulfed us all. To see it coming would have required second sight (which Churchill, but hardly anyone one else, had). Today we look back on the appeasers as cowards, ignorant of what was happening. But who of us would have reacted differently?

And so Churchill spoke out again and again, warning of the danger, blasting complacency, and only a few listened.

Thank God . . .

C. P. Snow, in the Godkin Lectures at Harvard University, 1960: "Nearly everyone I knew of my own age who was politically committed, that is, who had decided that fascism had at all costs to be stopped, wanted Churchill brought into the government [in the late 1930s]. . . . We wanted a government which would resist [the Nazis]. . . . But if Churchill *had* been brought back to office? . . . Lindemann would have come with him . . . different technical choices would have been made . . . and without getting radar in time we should not have stood a chance in the war that finally arrived."

As Dowding was preparing England to resist, Churchill and Lindemann would appear to have been his natural compatriots. Lindemann chaired one of the two best physics laboratories in the country, and Churchill wanted above all else to resist the coming Nazi hordes and to prepare England for the inevitable struggle. But Lindemann's personality intruded.

As already noted, he was generous, arrogant, full of contempt, good company, prejudiced, and a loyal friend. He showed these different sides to different people, and unbelievably, his appearance seemed to change as well. John Colville thought "he had a distinguished presence. His deep-set eyes looked out beneath gently arching brows and a curving, well-developed forehead. His nose was of noble Roman shape, his moustache was flat and neatly trimmed, his mouth suggested refinement.... He wore beautifully cut clothes, out of date in design... spotlessly clean, almost clinically so." But according to Snow, he was "pallid, heavy featured... [with] a faint Teutonic undertone to his English, to his inaudible, constricted mumble." Lord Birkenhead thought him "an offensive man of alien extraction... spending too much time ingratiating himself with exalted people."

In more than physical appearance, Lindemann was a man of contrasts. He presented different aspects of character, personality, and intelligence to different people. He was "a very odd and a very gifted man... he was savage, he had a suspicious malevolent sadistic turn of what he would have called humour.... If one was drawn to him at all, one wanted to alleviate it" (Snow); he "had an ear for music and [was] a skilled pianist, he was modest... and his knowledge of almost all periods of history was impressive" (Colville); he had "no interests in literature nor in any other art" (Snow); he had "a beautiful brain" (Winston Churchill); "he made himself unnecessarily objectionable to a large number of people, although... he rarely committed the sin of being rude by accident" (Ronald Clark); and, finally, "what fun it was to see him!" (Clementine Churchill).

On one point everyone agreed: He had a great talent for explaining difficult scientific problems in simple language, and this knack nearly defeated all Dowding's efforts.

England's hope of winning any coming war rested entirely on technologic change. The technologies involved were difficult for a layperson to understand, especially for an impatient man like Churchill, with a world of troubles on his mind. Churchill was famous for instructing his helpers to give him a written evaluation of any problem on one page. How could one explain the complexities of radar to a layman—especially one with "astonishing gaps of total ignorance"—on one page?

Well, Lindemann could, with his talent of explaining complex subjects in a simple manner. But this ability led to problems. The first problem was that he didn't explain the material correctly. The second problem, which probably accounts for the first, is that he—Lindemann—hadn't thought of the idea of radar himself. The third problem, which melds the first two into an insuperable obstacle, was his arrogance: If he hadn't thought of the technique, it probably wasn't worth being thought of. As a result, in his own mind, the technical problems inevitable in any new process gyrated and grew and roiled insolvably. Instead of trying to address these problems, he thought of new, different ideas. New ideas were desperately wanted, but his were totally impracticable.

Churchill's regard for him, and the manner of his influence, are illustrated by a story told by General Sir James Marshall-Cornwall about a dinner party at Chequers when Churchill had become prime minister. The news from the military men at the dinner was not good, and

the PM leant across me and addressed my neighbour on the other side: "Prof! What have you got to tell me today?" The other civilians present were wearing dinner-jackets, but Professor Lindemann was attired in a morning-coat and striped trousers. He now slowly pushed his right hand into his tail-pocket and, like a conjuror, drew forth a Mills hand-grenade. An uneasy look appeared on the faces of his fellow-guests and the PM shouted: "What's that you've got, Prof, what's that?" "This, Prime Minister, is the inefficient Mills bomb, issued to the British infantry. It is made of twelve different components which have to be machined in separate processes. Now I have designed an improved grenade which has fewer machined parts and contains a fifty per cent greater bursting charge." "Splendid, Prof, splendid! That's what I like to hear. CIGS! Have the Mills bomb scrapped at once and the Lindemann grenade introduced." The unfortunate CIGS [Commander of the Imperial General Staff] was completely taken aback; he tried to explain that contracts had been placed in England and America for millions of the Mills bombs, and that it would be impracticable to alter the design now, but the Prime Minister would not listen. . . .

It turned out, finally, that Lindemann's grenade didn't work. At the time of the dinner, he hadn't actually made one, but had just formed an idea of how it could be done. At Churchill's insistence, many man-hours were devoted to firming up the design and manufacturing several for testing, but it all came to naught. This was typical of both Lindemann and Churchill: To Lindemann (nicknamed "the Prof," by many), an idea was as good as a finished product if the idea were his, and to Churchill, whatever the Prof said was gold.

Unfortunately, it often wasn't. As mentioned earlier, Wimperis had formed a Committee for the Scientific Survey of Air Defence and had put it under the chairmanship of T. H. Tizard, a universally respected scientist who had learned to fly with Lindemann and who had been his friend and colleague. More recently, however, Tizard had joined the list of the Prof's enemies for no other reason than Tizard's increasing reputation in government circles, envy being another of Lindemann's characteristics.

When Churchill heard about the committee, he insisted on Lindemann's inclusion. Although Churchill had no official authority to do so, such was the force of his personality that Tizard reluctantly agreed. The result was instant chaos.

We turn again to C. P. Snow, who as both scientist and politician knew well how things worked in England in those days (and perhaps still do today). There would have been "a great deal of that apparently casual to-ing and fro-ing by which high English business gets done. As soon as the Tizard committee thought there was something in radar, one can take it that Tizard would lunch with [Sir Maurice] Hankey at the Athenaeum; Hankey, the secretary of the Cabinet, would find it convenient to have a cup of tea with (Lord) Swinton (Secretary of State for Air) and [Prime Minister] Baldwin. If the Establishment had not trusted Tizard as one of their own, there might have been a waste of months or years. In fact, everything went through with the smoothness, the lack of friction, and the effortless speed which can only happen in England when the Establishment is behind one."

At the committee's first meeting, Wimperis had presented them with Watson-Watt's (actually, Wilkins's) idea, and they had agreed that Wimperis should take it to Dowding. At subsequent meetings, Wimperis reported that Dowding had asked for a demonstration, and, later, that the demonstration had been a success and that Dowding had initiated funding. The committee was unanimous in backing the development of radar as a most propitious—and indeed the only—hope of protecting their homes from enemy bombers. From that moment on, "everything went through with the smoothness, the lack of friction, and the effortless speed which can only happen in England when the Establishment is behind one."

And then Lindemann dropped in. One is reminded of a couple of couplets referring to Newton and Einstein. The first one was written by Alexander Pope:

> *All was clothed in darkness and night.*
> *God said, "Let Newton be!" and all was light.*

And then in the twentieth century, Anonymous wrote this one:

> *The devil, howling "Ho!*
> *Let Einstein be!" restored the status quo.*

Replace *Newton* with *the committee,* and *Einstein* with *Lindemann,* and there you have the situation. The Prof burst into the committee and scattered their unanimity like so much chaff. He immediately saw everything that might go wrong with radar, presented all these problems as insoluble, and then swept on to present his own proposals.

Some measure of the value of his ideas may be gained by an anecdote told by Sholto Douglas, who would later replace Dowding as Commander in Chief of Fighter Command. During the First World War, one of the pilots in Douglas's squadron got the bright idea of tying a hand grenade to a long wire and trying to fly just above an enemy plane, lowering the wire so that it would tangle in the enemy's propeller and explode the grenade. The scheme never worked. "It was an idea that smacked all too strongly of the flavour that I came to know later of some of the schemes put forward in all seriousness during the second war by Professor Lindemann with the backing of Winston Churchill."

The first of these schemes was one Lindemann had filched from R. V. Jones, a graduate student in his laboratory. He quickly managed to convince himself that he had thought of it himself, in much the same way that Watson-Watt had appropriated Wilkins's idea. Instead of building transmitters to produce radiation and then receivers to detect the echoes, why not detect the natural infrared radiation produced by the aircraft engines, thus cutting the problems in half?

It was an interesting proposal, and it eventually worked—some thirty years later, in Vietnam. Lindemann was right that with infrared they wouldn't have the problems involved in transmitting, but they would have the additional problems associated with differentiating the aircraft's infrared from all the other natural infrared radiation in the world. For radar, they could use a single frequency, one that commercial radio stations did not use, but every warm object in the world produces a spectrum of infrared radiation.

Lindemann brushed aside any such problems, but the rest of the committee felt strongly that radar would be much more likely to work. After much argument and wasted time, Lindemann finally announced that he was willing to compromise: Both radar and infrared should be pursued. But splitting the scarce research funds between the two projects would have meant that neither would have been ready in time.

Tizard told him: "I think the way you put the facts is extremely misleading, and may lead to entirely wrong decisions being reached, with a consequent disastrous effect on the war. I think, too, that you have got your facts wrong." Lindemann shrugged that off and blithely came up with other ideas. He appropriated the World War I idea that British airplanes could fly in front of and above the incoming bombers and drop strands of wire with grenades attached. But he made it even better: They could drop bombs onto the enemy formations! Even as the committee members began bringing up the obvious objections that you couldn't expect the enemy to fly straight and level, and that it would be easy for them to evade such weapons, he came up with other ideas. Antiaircraft shells could be fit with fuses that would magnetically detect when they came close to an airplane and would then explode. This would mean that the shells didn't have to actually hit an airplane to destroy it.

Colville recorded some of these conversations in his diary that summer: "I talked to the Prof about his secret weapons . . . he thinks these may be really effective next year and if they are, there is a distinct possibility that aircraft will be ruled out as a weapon of war." In fact, the proximity fuse for antiaircraft shells did become effective late in the war, but wasn't even close to being ready that summer, when it was needed, or even the next year, as Lindemann had predicted. And of course it didn't mean that aircraft were ruled out as a weapon of war.

Lindemann's other projects were eventually tried, when Churchill became prime minister and brought Lindemann along with him into the cabinet, but they never worked. All they succeeded in doing was wasting time and money and turning the committee meetings into roiling controversy instead of amiable cooperation. Finally, the problem was solved by dissolving the committee, and the next day reforming it.

Without Lindemann.

Although he could no longer bully the committee, Lindemann still had the ear of Churchill, who, responding to his insistence, repeatedly fought against all the available research funds going to radar. This was the beginning of a strong love-hate relationship between Churchill and Dowding, who strongly supported radar. Well, perhaps the love part had begun several years before, when Churchill, as Colonial Secretary, had been impressed with Dowding's work in keeping peace in Iraq with a few bombers. Now, when they should have been working together on their overall purpose of preparing England for war, they were instead warring over the details, arguing about spending scarce research funds on entangling wires or air-to-air bombs or, most importantly, on infrared versus radar.

Churchill's method was to bluster and rant, avoiding details, conjuring all-powerful images, and then daring his opponent to bring up a single argument against him. His command of the English language was masterful (in contrast to his command of science), and he would use it to sweep all objections aside and to carry his opponent away on a flood of words and eloquent phrases. Dowding's method was to sit quietly and listen rather than attempting to stem that inexorable flow of rodomontade, and then not to try to counter arguments that were so far-flung as to be indefensible, but instead to simply say no.

No, he would not reassign his little supply of research moneys. No, his committee told him that radar was not inferior to infrared. No, he would not accept Churchill's statistics (which had been supplied by Lindemann, whose love of statistics was so great that he was well-known to frequently make up his own). No, no, and again no. Dowding was adamant, indefatigable, unmovable. He would put his trust in God, and pray for radar.

thirteen

In 1936 the Royal Air Force underwent a total rearrangement into four main commands: Training Command, Coastal Command, Bomber Command, and Fighter Command, the last organized out of the former Air Defence Great Britain. Boom Trenchard had retired, and Dowding, as the most senior officer in the RAF after Chief of the Air Staff (CAS) Edward Ellington, was appointed the first Commander in Chief of Fighter Command. Ellington told him that upon his (Ellington's) retirement the next year, Dowding would take his place as CAS, the top RAF position.

The appointment to Fighter Command was a natural one in view of his activities as Air Member for Research and Development the past several years. Now he was in a position to put the fruits of his labors to work, integrating the new eight-gun fighters that were slated soon to come off the production lines with a radar system that was slated soon to work.

This appointment suited Dowding perfectly. He believed in radar and the Spitfire, and this was what he wanted: a chance to put it all together and defend his homeland against the bombers. But he was still very much alone in the belief that it could be done. The plum appointment, given to a slightly younger contemporary named Arthur Harris, was thought to be that of Bomber Command.

It was clear by now that Hitler was a growing menace. What was not clear was how to defend against him. The Prime Minister, Neville Chamberlain, thought Hitler could be reasoned with. Chamberlain's opponents in Parliament, headed by Winston Churchill, applied the term *appeasement* rather than reason. In the Air Ministry, the thinking was in favor of strength through a bomber force that would deter any attack, and so the majority of available funds were funneled to Bomber Harris. Dowding stood alone, yet resolute, in his belief that a strong fighter force would be a better deterrent.

"The best defence of the country is the fear of the fighter," he argued, and halfway measures would be disastrous. Given a sufficient force, no one would dare attack. Given a halfway decent force, he could stop an attack eventually, but only after severe damage was done. Given an insufficient force, enemy bombers would "destroy the productive capacity of the country," and then what use was Bomber Command?

By 1936, the hillside property of Bentley Priory had passed into the hands of His Majesty's government and was newly established as the headquarters of Fighter Command. At nine o'clock in the morning of July 14, Air Chief Marshal Hugh Caswall Tremenheere Dowding presented himself at the front gate of the priory for the first time. His uniform was correct to the smallest detail, his hat sat firmly and perfectly horizontal on his head. Contrary to military custom worldwide, he did not take over his new command with brass bands blaring and flags flying and ceremonial speeches flowing. He arrived alone and unannounced; the guard at the gate didn't know who he was and inspected his pass carefully before allowing him entrance. No one knew he was coming. The officer in charge of the priory wasn't even there, and so an embarrassed sergeant took him over the grounds.

This suited Stuffy perfectly. He took as his office—which is kept today just as he left it—a large room with floor-to-ceiling French windows overlooking a rose garden. He had his desk placed with the windows to his left and back to take advantage of the sunlight and so that he might easily swivel around to look out of them over Harrow Hill to London sprawling in the distance. He took off his hat and, without any fuss, got down to work. He had also taken a large white house called Montrose, in Stanmore, the adjacent village, down the hill from the priory, and had brought his sister Hilda to keep house for him. Leaving the domestic details to her, he began setting up his command immediately.

In the still of the night, he would lie in bed in that old house, thinking those thoughts that are best left unthought, of death and desire and loneliness, of the empty void and dark despair, of his lost love, Clarice, wandering alone and frightened through the void. Was she trying to reach him, as he was trying to reach her? To think of her gone forever was terrible; to think of her reaching out helplessly while he lay here blind and deaf was even worse.

But for now these were thoughts that slid into his mind only in the dark and lonely moments of the night. With the dawn he awoke, pulled himself out of bed, and was driven up the hill. His waking hours were filled, every minute of them, with the task of putting together England's defense. In this he was bound on one hand by the strict budgetary restrictions of a government still reeling from the worldwide depression, and on the other hand by the stubborn resistance to new ideas that permeated the Air Ministry and his colleagues on the Air Staff. Finally, he had to face the normal recalcitrance of people asked to do something they had never heard of before—and to do it in a hurry.

He needed, for example, modern airports that wouldn't sink in a sea of mud when it rained. The two main fighter airfields, Biggin Hill and Kenley, like nearly all of those scattered around England, were made of grass over a clay base. When it rained, the grass would sink and the clay would rise and it all became a nonoperational quagmire. Dowding wanted concrete runways.

According to Lord Balfour, "senior officers who long ago had surrendered the pilot's seat for the office chair resisted this innovation which they considered unnecessary, dangerous, and expensive.... Dowding pleaded for hard runways, telling the Air Staff 'During the winter of 1936/37 there were three consecutive weeks during which not a single aircraft could take off or land at Kenley.' But as late as 1938 the Air Staff declared there was no need to plan for hard runways." The idea of training on anything except a grass field was blasphemy to those who had been brought up on pure, natural, organic grass. They argued that training accidents would increase in number and severity, since on a grass field, you could wander around as you pleased when you landed, but with concrete runways, the slightest deviation would lead to the plane's swerving off the runway onto ... the grass?

The argument didn't make sense, but perhaps for that very reason, it was made heatedly. (If you can't generate light, settle for heat.) Dowding also needed a brand new operational system to pass the information from the incoming radar plots to his fighter pilots. This began with telephone lines that wouldn't be easily disrupted by bombs. He went to the Air Staff for funds to put in place a web of underground lines connecting all the eastern and southeastern coast. The staff argued that it would be a ridiculous waste of funds to provide such a costly scheme, which would be useful only if the proposed radar system actually turned out to work. Dowding replied that it had to work.

"Yes, well, let's just wait and see," was the reply.

"We can't afford to wait," he said, looking over his shoulder at the Luftwaffe growing like a cancer in Germany.

"Hard runways, underground telephone lines," they grumbled. "The man's mad."

Which is what they had said about the man who first proposed the tank. But also what has been said about every man who thinks he's Napoleon or Jesus. And so day after day he argued, they objected, he came back with answers to their objections, they objected to his answers ...

Watson-Watt and Wilkins proposed a system of radio transmitters, to be named the Chain Home, or CH, towers, lining the southeastern coasts, sending their beams out over the waters, linked to receivers that would pick up the echoes of any plane venturing into their airspace. Dowding embraced the scheme enthusiastically and took it to the Air Ministry. Grudgingly, he was given permission to begin constructing them, but only with the solemn provision that no towers were to be built anywhere they might interfere with the grouse shooting. Dowding didn't react to that restriction with horror, with a growl, or even a grumble. He nodded, and got on with it.

And so, inch by inch, month by month, argument by argument, Dowding began building the aerial defense of England, turning the country once more back into an island.

For each improvement, he had to fight for funding and production priority with Harris, who thought that anyone who couldn't see the prime importance of bombers was a lunatic. He and Dowding went back a long way, and all along the way, they had been adversaries. When Dowding had been in Research, Harris had been in Plans, and their research and their plans had collided headlong. "I had so many differences of opinion with Stuffy. . . . I had a major fight [about] instruments for navigation and blind flying [for my bombers]—and I couldn't afford to be polite when he started laying his ears back and being stubborn. Stubborn as a mule, but a nice old boy really. He was just out of touch with flying."

To Harris, anyone who couldn't understand that the future lay with bombers rather than fighters was "just out of touch." He insisted that all aircraft production should be concentrated on bombers, but Dowding managed to convince the Air Staff that he would need fifty-two squadrons of fighters to mount a suitable defense over England. As of 1938, he had twenty-nine, with no Spitfires and fewer than a hundred Hurricanes, none of which could climb above fifteen thousand feet, while the Luftwaffe bombers could reach twenty-five thousand.

We tend to get the impression that people involved in Great Things do not have the same petty irritations that clutter our own lives, but they are human too. Despite being told by Ellington in 1936 that he (Dowding) would replace Ellington as CAS upon the senior man's retirement in the next year, Dowding was told in 1937 that this was not to be the case. "The S. of S. [Secretary of State for Air Viscount Swinton] has asked me to let you know," Ellington wrote, ". . . that he has decided that Newall will succeed me as C.A.S."

This was the same Cyril Newall whom Dowding had bested in a field exercise in their subaltern days in India by rousing his own men at four A.M. and attacking Newall's group while they were eating breakfast. Though they were near contemporaries, Dowding was senior to Newall by a few months and had hoped "to reach the top of the tree," as he put it. So, "naturally it came as somewhat of a blow. But when I look back on this incident in the light of later events, I see how fortunate this decision really was."

It was more than "somewhat" of a blow. He and Newall were the two most senior men in the RAF, and their careers had grown side by side with the normal competition between two keen officers. Before the higher-ups' change of heart, when Dowding had heard that he himself would be the next CAS, Dowding had been pleased but not surprised. As slightly the senior of the two, he would expect to be the natural choice unless there was a serious problem with him. And now he was told that indeed he was not the choice; the clear inference was that there certainly was a serious problem with him.

As in fact there was. He saw the future of war in the air more clearly than anyone else, but the result was not the immediate admiration of his peers but rather their contempt, sprinkled liberally with irritation. Harris's opinion that he was out of touch with flying was the consensus among those who advocated the bomber offense over the fighter defense, and they were in the majority. Thus the contempt and the irritation grew steadily as Dowding, without regard for the feelings and needs of others, with characteristic obstinacy and without taking the time or making the effort to schmooze his compatriots, relentlessly fought for what he saw as his God-given light.

He wanted concrete runways and telephone lines and steel towers—even if they might interfere with the grouse hunting. He wanted armor plating and bulletproof glass to protect his pilots: "I can't understand why Chicago gangsters can have bulletproof glass in their cars and I can't get it in my Spitfires," he complained. Above all, he wanted a radar system that worked.

The concept that Wilkins had put forward was clear in principle, but foggy in details. It was something totally new, and all the parameters had to be worked out one by one in difficult experiments. The proper wavelength for maximum efficiency had to be determined, and transmitters and receivers built to that specification. Spurious echoes from other sources had to be disentangled, and the bugs in new designs had to be eliminated. Everything had to be tested, and it seemed that every test would fail: There were echoes where there were no planes, and planes where there were no echoes. Back again to the drawing board, and back again and again.

The Air Ministry parted with twenty-five thousand pounds to buy Bawdsey Hall, the isolated ancestral home of Sir Cuthbert Quilter overlooking the North Sea, and here a band of electronics engineers and physicists were gathered from universities and research laboratories all over England. An eccentric Scotsman named John Logie Baird had just invented a workable television system, but before he could put it into commercial operation, his business was shut down and all his technicians taken to work on this most secret project, leaving him fuming and cursing.

It was a maelstrom of activity, at the center of which sat old Stuffy Dowding, rejected by the powers that be, no longer in line to be the next chief of the RAF, but still relentlessly doing his thing: cutting red tape, riding roughshod over hurdles, hurting sensitive feelings, and making enemies at each step of the way—and getting things done. But things went slowly, so slowly—an inch at a time, and often two inches back—that it drove him to desperation. He wrote to the Secretary of State for Air: "I can say without fear of contradiction that since I have held my present post I have dealt with or am in the process of dealing with a number of vital matters which generations of Air Staff have neglected for the last 15 years. . . . This work has had to be carried out against the inertia of the Air Staff—a statement which I can abundantly prove if necessary. Further I have continually had to complain that the Air Staff take decisions vitally affecting my command without the slightest consultation with me or my Staff."

Then suddenly, at the beginning of September 1939, Hitler invaded Poland.

part two

Springtime for Hitler

fourteen

ONE YEAR PREVIOUSLY, in September 1938, Europe had come to the brink of war over Czechoslovakia. Hitler had insisted that part of that country, the Sudetenland, was demographically and culturally German and should be returned to Germany. It was a reasonable point of view, difficult to argue against.

Czechoslovakia had been carved out of Germany and Austria-Hungary by the League of Nations—basically by France and England—after the First World War, to serve as one of a series of buffer states hemming in Germany so that it couldn't cause any more trouble. The Sudetenland was, as Hitler claimed, in reality German, and he would invade, if necessary, to rescue the German population there from "oppressive" Czech rule. The basic contention of the League was that national preferences should be determined by plebiscite, by the will of the people actually living there, and if this had been done in the Sudetenland there is no question but that the people would vote to belong to Germany rather than to Czechoslovakia.

There were two problems. One was that the Sudetenland contained a mountain range that presented a natural border between it and Germany. Removing the Sudetenland from Czechoslovakia meant removing the mountains, which meant leaving the Czech state without a defensible border. The other problem was Hitler. Although he loudly proclaimed to have "no other territorial demands in Europe," how could anyone believe him?

On September 15 Prime Minister Neville Chamberlain flew to Berchtesgaden to, in his words, reason with the leader of a great country, or, in Churchill's words, to appease the madman. It was the first time in history that a head of state had taken the bold step of flying to another country, serving to underscore the need for quick action to prevent war.

Acting virtually unilaterally, he ceded to Hitler the Sudetenland and returned to convince both his Parliament and the French—and, after much argument, the Czechs—that reneging on promises and ceding territory was better than war. But when he brought this agreement back to Hitler the following week, the German dictator told him flatly that it was not enough! Further negotiations followed, until at Munich on September 29 a four-power conference of Germany, England, France, and Italy—but not Czechoslovakia—agreed to all of Hitler's demands. The Czech republic was left without allies, and they capitulated.

In return, on the following day, Chamberlain obtained Hitler's signature on a paper he had drafted overnight, promising to settle all future territorial demands by "consultation." He flew back to England, triumphantly waving the piece of paper with Hitler's signature, proclaiming "peace in our time."

Churchill rose in Parliament, thunderously proclaiming that piece of paper a stain on the honor of His Majesty's government. Britain had guaranteed the existence of the state of Czechoslovakia, and with the Munich Agreement, Chamberlain had ripped it asunder without even giving the Czech government a word in the negotiations. Six months later, without provocation and despite his claim of "no further territorial demands," Hitler sent his troops across the now-indefensible border and occupied all of Czechoslovakia.

Thus ended appeasement, and reason, and peace in our time.

The verdict of history has been harsh, and in agreement with Churchill's oratory at the time. *Appeasement* has become a dirty word, negotiation a sign of weakness. But in truth Chamberlain was right; Churchill was wrong. If Churchill had had his way, England would have gone to war, would have retained its honor, and would have been crushed by Hitler. Chamberlain had groveled before Hitler, had sold England's honor, but had given his nation the opportunity to regain it. In reality, he had no choice.

His actions were dictated by an overwhelming desire for peace, which was seen as cowardice, but also by the knowledge that England was simply not yet ready for war. Earlier that year, Dowding had written a concise statement setting forth the condition of Fighter Command. He stated with confidence that he could defend the island against the German Luftwaffe with fifty-two squadrons of Spitfires and Hurricanes.

At the time of the Munich crisis, he had twenty-nine squadrons, which included not a single Spitfire and fewer than a hundred Hurricanes—and the Hurricanes were useless against bombers, being limited to a ceiling of fifteen thousand feet, more than a mile below the Luftwaffe bombers' cruising altitude. Worst of all, radar was not yet working. The CH chain of transmitters was still being built (the grouse hunting was suffering terribly), and even those that were completed were not working properly. On a good day, they were able to "see" incoming bombers and measure their position with reasonable accuracy, but they couldn't get the height correctly—and that made the system just about useless, for the air is a three-dimensional space. To understand how serious this was, imagine the analogous problem in two dimensions. If you want to go from Miami to New York and you're told the distance is thirteen hundred miles but you don't know the direction, you're never going to get there. (On a bad day—and there were many of them—the radar system couldn't even get the position right.) And this was for the areas where the CH transmitters were built and operating; many areas of the coast had no radar at all.

Chamberlain knew if he didn't give in to Hitler's demands, England would quickly lie burning, devastated, in ruins. He put a good face on it, hoping against hope that Hitler might live up to his promises, that indeed there might be peace in his time, but whatever the outcome, Chamberlain knew that he had no choice but to buy time at the expense, sadly but unavoidably, of Czechoslovakia.

He almost succeeded.

It was now clear that Hitler would not stop until he was stopped, and war preparations began in earnest. The Hurricanes were modified to increase their altitude, and the first few Spitfires began to come off the production line. Compared to 1936, when he took over Fighter Command, Dowding was stronger. Then, he had had eleven squadrons of obsolete twin-gunned biplanes. By 1938, his strength was more than doubled, but he also had new responsibilities. He was now expected to provide air cover to protect shipping through the Channel and along the southern coast. Since attacks might hit such targets before radar could provide warning, this would mean standing patrols, which in turn meant a terrible waste of time, fuel, and pilots' energy. He was given four more squadrons, which looked good on paper, but these new squadrons were fitted with twin-engine Blenheims—bombers converted to fighters by the addition of machine guns. Calling them fighters didn't actually make them fighters; in the event, they proved useless for the task.

Dowding was also asked to provide air cover for the navy's home base at Scapa Flow in the Orkney Islands, north of Scotland. He was given two more squadrons for this, but these new squadrons were even less effective than the Blenheims—they had no planes at all, and no pilots to fly the no-planes; they existed only on paper. Finally, he was given another paper squadron and told that with this group, he was expected to protect Belfast.

He realized that although the squadrons were imaginary, the tasks were not. If Scapa Flow, Belfast, or the convoys were attacked, he would surely be ordered to protect them, which would mean reducing the already meager forces he was gathering for the protection of the island kingdom itself. Even worse was the arrangement he had inherited, that four squadrons of fighters would be sent with the British Expeditionary Force to France, if and when that force actually embarked. Far from convincing the Air Staff that this was impossible, he found himself instead fighting a rearguard action against constant threats of increasing the allotment. In March 1939, he was ordered to have an additional six squadrons ready to go at a moment's notice.

In July he wrote to the Air Ministry: "If this policy is implemented and ten regular squadrons are withdrawn from the country, the air defence of Great Britain will be gravely imperiled. The Air Staff estimate that fifty squadrons are necessary for its defence. I calculate that by January 1940 I shall have twenty-five equipped with modern types, plus fourteen Auxiliary squadrons . . . but only six of these will be even nearly as efficient as the Regulars. If ten regular squadrons were withdrawn, the remaining resources would be altogether inadequate for the defence of this country."

What was needed was increased production of fighter aircraft and increased numbers of well-trained pilots assigned to Fighter Command. But Bomber Harris was arguing as strongly for more bombers and pilots, and the Air Ministry was still convinced that a large bomber force might yet deter Hitler. Day after day, Dowding and Harris fought each other for the slowly swelling trickle of planes and men.

Just as bad was the state of radar. The CH chain of transmitters was nearing completion, but the apparatus was beset with gremlins. Yesterday it worked, today it didn't, tomorrow...?

The days hurried by, and before preparations were anywhere near complete, Hitler invaded Poland. England and France ordered him to leave, and when he refused they declared war. It was September 3, 1939, and the world would never again be quite the same.

fifteen

IMMEDIATELY AFTER the outbreak of war, Churchill was brought back into the government in his old role as First Lord of the Admiralty, and Britain's army, the British Expeditionary Force (BEF), moved to France. With it went the four Hurricane squadrons that had been promised. Dowding knew this had long been the plan, but the plan had also included an increase in Fighter Command to fifty squadrons. He had assumed that the former would not be taken from him until the latter had been achieved, but in this he was mistaken. The leader of the BEF insisted on his four squadrons, and off they went.

Dowding was furious. He stormed off to his old compatriot, Cyril Newall, the Chief of the Air Staff, and was fobbed off onto his deputy, who listened quietly, sadly commiserating and shaking his head at the perversities of fortune, but said his hands were tied. Whereupon Dowding roared off to the Secretary of State for Air, in whose office the sad shaking of the head was repeated. Infuriated, he retired to the priory and dashed off an angry letter to the Air Council. Were the Council members aware, he asked, of what was happening? Had they not agreed that fifty squadrons were the minimum necessary for the defense of the homeland? Did they understand that not only were the fifty not in place, but four had been subtracted and plans were in place for more diversions?

Yes, yes, he understood that arrangements had been made for the four squadrons to leave him to accompany the BEF to France, but he had always been assured "that these squadrons would never be dispatched until the safety of the Home Bases [England] had been assured." Yet off they had been sent with no regard for the safety of England.

Well, they were lost, he knew that. He knew enough of military life to understand the nine-tenths rule; he would never get them back. But what of the further six squadrons earmarked for France "if necessity arose"? It would certainly arise, and what would be done then? He knew that the Council had assured him that these squadrons would not be withdrawn from his command until the island's defenses were in place, but, he wrote bitterly, "I know now how much reliance to place on these assurances."

And yes, he knew how much the BEF needed air support, and how pressure from the army must have been exerted on the Air Council to provide the four squadrons, but "similar pressure is likely to be applied to dispatch the further six squadrons," and then another four and then another six, and so on . . . He saw a future that contained a continual drain from his command to the exigencies of a continental war. He saw the day-to-day necessities overwhelming any long-range plans for the defense of the kingdom against aerial onslaught. He complained strongly that the defenses were inadequate, that with only the thirty-five squadrons he now had, he could not guarantee the safety of the population against bombing, and that any further reduction in his forces would be disastrous. He needed more fighters, not fewer.

He was right, of course. The Air Council realized this. But they wanted him to understand their position vis-à-vis the BEF and the contradictory demands of the several armed forces. There simply weren't enough fighters to go around. What were they to do? To

Dowding's mind, the answer was simple: They were to stand up like men and fight for Fighter Command, for if the defenses were inadequate when the bombers came, the war would certainly be lost. But they didn't see the future as clearly as he did. Their answer was that their subordinate commanders—men like Dowding—should see the bigger picture, the political situation, and should do the best they could with what they had and should above all shut up.

This Dowding would not do. He wrote letter after letter, he besieged them with advice and demands, he would not be satisfied until England was safe. He was, they all agreed, a bloody damned nuisance. He was piling up enemies, but he made some meager headway. He convinced Newall, who thereupon insisted that eighteen more fighter squadrons must be formed immediately. The problem was, of course, that although it was easy to list on paper these squadrons, they had no aircraft. And although this sounds silly, it did have some effect. As slowly more and more Spitfires came out of the factory, they would be assigned to these new squadrons, and slowly they took shape. By the time the Battle of Britain began in the following summer, Dowding had his fifty squadrons, although not all of them were outfitted with proper airplanes.

In the meantime, nothing much was happening. England had gone to war on behalf of Poland, but there was no way it could help that eastern country. Poland fell in a few weeks, and then everyone looked around and wondered what to do next. The BEF was basically an adjunct to the French army, waiting on French initiative. But the French had no initiative. They had learned their lesson in the First World War. Then, their motto had been "*Élan, élan, toujours élan!*" and the result had been the slaughter of an entire generation of young men. Now their strategy was defensive. They were dug in behind their impregnable Maginot Line, waiting for the Royal Navy to blockade Germany and starve it into submission.

And Christmas came and went, and the horrors of war did not appear. No bombers appeared in the sky, no artillery fire boomed across the trenches. The satirists came out and named this affair the Bore War, a screamingly funny pun on the Boer War, and everyone had a chuckle and went back to sleep.

In April 1940, there was a slight awakening when the Germans invaded Denmark and Norway. This gave Churchill his chance, and he unleashed the navy to cut the Germans' overwater supply lines and drive them out. The result was an unmitigated British defeat.

It was a bad plan, properly executed. In the First World War, Churchill had sent the navy through the Bosporus into Turkey, a good plan that was badly executed. Though the fault then had been with the commander in the field, Churchill had been blamed and was drummed out of the government. Now, because of Churchill's poor plan in Norway, Chamberlain was blamed and drummed out of the government. The next day, May 10, 1940, Churchill was installed as Prime Minister. He was greeted, not with brass bands, but with the news that on this same day, the German army was smashing through and around the Maginot Line into France.

The Germans, you see, had also learned a lesson from the First World War, when the British tanks broke over their trenches, overwhelmed their machine-gun nests, and broke their back. This time, the Germans built their army around the tank corps, the Panzers, but with a new wrinkle.

Britain had accepted the Douhet principle that the next war would be fought by fleets of bombers attacking cities in what has been called strategic bombing. Germany instead saw the bombers as long-range artillery, attacking tactical targets with pinpoint accuracy. They ignored development of long-range heavy bombers and built instead a fleet of dive-bombers, *Sturzkampfflugzeugen,* which means "vertical battle airplanes," called Stukas for short, to accompany the Panzer Korps, and with these they swept through Poland in a Blitzkrieg, or lightning war.

The French thought they were safe from the Panzers behind their Maginot Line, but that line had two problems, one economic and one political, and both stupid. The line stretched across the border between France and Germany. To save a few francs when building it, France ignored the stretch of border that was lined with the Ardennes forest because that ground was obviously impenetrable to heavy artillery. Moreover, the Maginot Line ended at the western end of France's border with Germany, where Belgium sat stuck between the two. Belgium had refused to allow the line to continue along its border with Germany because it didn't want to provoke the Nazis; instead the small country relied on a diplomatic agreement of nonaggression.

So everyone was surprised on May 10, 1940, when the Panzers broke out of the Ardennes onto French soil, leaving their heavy artillery behind but supported instead by waves of Stukas blasting everything in sight. To the west, more Panzers swept into Belgium and kept right on going into France.

The French army collapsed. The French air force was destroyed in the air and on the ground as waves of Stukas and Messerschmitt fighters swept over their aerodromes and caught them unawares, for they had no radar. Élan gave way to despair.

Churchill, too, was caught unawares. He had monitored the growth of Nazi military might, but he hadn't realized how completely the French were depending on their Maginot Line and how weak they were behind it. British strategy relied on a great French army, merely reinforced by the BEF. Now, day by day, the French retreated, surrendered, threw down their arms, and ran from the German tanks. Inexorably the Panzers raced over the countryside, wildly the Stukas screamed out of the clouds, and daily the telegrams poured into 10 Downing Street pleading for help.

What help could the British give? The BEF comprised all the British army that was prepared for war; there wasn't any more. Except for the Royal Air Force.

But without radar, the RAF planes that were sent to France were overwhelmed. Within the first three days, half the bomber force was lost. Lord Gort, commanding the BEF, and Air Marshal Barratt, in charge of air support, demanded reinforcements. Dowding was ordered to send two more squadrons of Hurricanes.

The next day, a group of tactical bombers, Fairey Battles, was put under French orders. On May 13, thirty-one of them were dispatched to attack pontoon bridges the Germans were building across the Meuse River. The orders sending the Battles into action were incredibly stupid, for there was nothing to be gained by destroying such easily reparable structures. The Battles were slow and poorly armed, they were meat on the table for the Messerschmitts, but they pushed their attack to the limit and destroyed the bridges. And the Messerschmitts destroyed the Battles. Twenty-four bombers—77 percent!—were lost, and within a few hours, the Germans had rebuilt the bridges, monuments to brass hat stupidity.

The Messerschmitts were dominating the air. Prime Minister Reynaud, acting on demands from the French general staff, made a personal appeal to Churchill for ten more fighter squadrons. Lord Gort seconded this request: "Our main defence in the air is fighters. . . . I earnestly hope the War Cabinet will decide to give additional air assistance for Allied success in the coming battle." Churchill brought these appeals to his War Cabinet, which agreed that ten more squadrons should be prepared to fly to France.

Dowding was appalled. "I was responsible for the Air Defence of Great Britain, and I saw my resources slipping away like sand in an hourglass. The pressure for more and more assistance to France was relentless and inexorable." He gave up on the Air Ministry, on playing the game and either following orders or going through the proper channels. Instead he appealed directly to Churchill, telling him that the requested squadrons would have little effect on the war since they would be operating without radar and so would be helpless against the overwhelming numbers of German fighters. They would be a sacrificial lamb, accomplishing no military purpose.

Churchill responded that there was more than mere military purposes on the line here. There were political promises to be kept and emotions to be dealt with. Above all else, French morale had to be rebuilt; they must be assured that Britain would stand by them or they might give up and leave England to face Hitler alone.

Dowding said, point blank, that taking more squadrons from him would do nothing for France and would leave him unable to defend England. Churchill was adamant. Dowding then asked him for permission to take his case to the War Cabinet personally. "I had to do it because I believed that the Air Ministry would not support me firmly enough against the Prime Minister in his strong wish to send more fighter squadrons to France in response to the frantic appeals coming from across the Channel. . . . It was confounded impertinence on my part, but I could not be sure that the Air Ministry were fighting tooth and nail [against sending the fighters]."

Thirty years later, Dowding was asked, "In your whole life, what was the most important decision you ever had to take?" His answer: "The decision to ask for an interview with the War Cabinet to prevent our fighters being handed over to the French."

Churchill was shaken by his sincerity, and agreed. The next day, May 15, Dowding was driven to the underground bunker known as the War Rooms on Prince George Street, one block from No. 10 Downing Street, to argue his case before the War Cabinet.

He argued briskly, efficiently, and, as always, alone. Although the Air Ministry was well represented at the meeting, they remained silent. "I should have been able to count on them for support in what I was saying, but I got none. Newall [Chief of Air Staff] had been rebuffed a little earlier by Churchill over something inconsequential, and he was silent. Sinclair [Secretary of State for Air] was sitting forward with his arms on the table eagerly trying to guess what Churchill was going to say next."

Churchill, though affected by Dowding's words, repeated his own argument: The French were collapsing, and without French resistance, Hitler would become master of Europe, and England would have to face the Nazi hordes alone. The French needed bolstering, and they needed it today. The BEF was doing all it could, but if the French army collapsed, the British army would be lost along with it. The only help England could provide was airplanes, fighter airplanes. Churchill asked that the cabinet authorize the immediate departure of ten more fighter squadrons to France.

The room was quiet. Dowding waited for Newall or Sinclair to speak up, but they remained silent. "The Air Ministry representatives took no part in this discussion, despite [their later protestations]. I felt that everybody was too frightened of Winston Churchill," Dowding remembered. Finally, Dowding rose to his feet. He took up a graph he had prepared showing the daily losses of his Hurricane fighters in France. "I walked around to the seat occupied by the Prime Minister. I leant forward and laid the graph on the table in front of him, and I said: 'If the present rate of wastage continues for another fortnight we shall not have a single Hurricane left in France or in this country.' I laid a particular emphasis on *or in this country.*"

Then he sat down again. No one said a word. The air circulation system went on whirring. Wing Commander William Elliott (later Air Chief Marshal Sir William) was in the room that day: "The atmosphere was the most highly charged emotionally that [I] had ever known. . . . Dowding was white in the face with strain . . . but when [he] came to make his statement it was put so ably and sincerely, and with such feeling, that there was no room left for any further discussion."

Everyone waited for Churchill to speak. He did not. What could he say? Quietly, the cabinet agreed unanimously that no more fighters should be sent to France, but added the cautionary phrase "for the present." That last phrase was bothersome, but Dowding decided not to argue it but rather to take his victory and remain vigilant. He left the meeting and wrote that afternoon to Keith Park, his chief assistant: "We had a notable victory on the Home Front this morning and the orders to send more Hurricanes were cancelled. Appeals for help will doubtless be renewed, however, with increasing insistency and I do not know how this morning's work will stand the test of time, but I will never relax my efforts to prevent the dissipation of the Home fighter forces."

He didn't know that "this morning's work" had already failed the test of time, for after he left, Churchill began to have second thoughts, and he unilaterally decided to send four more squadrons to France. When he was in that mood, the cabinet never stood up to him. And so, without further debate, the morning's "decision was reversed," according to General Sir Ian Jacob, one of those present. "I believe it was the only occasion in the whole war on which, a firm decision having been reached, the Prime Minister changed his mind." Churchill then flew off to France to deliver the glad tidings to Reynaud, but instead, Reynaud's despair infected him. Churchill began to think the unthinkable: that France might totally collapse and surrender. That must not be allowed to happen. He telegraphed his cabinet, telling them to send six more squadrons immediately, adding that he expected a reply by midnight.

In his diary, Churchill's private secretary, John Colville, described the dilemma the cabinet now faced: "The Cabinet met at 11.00 pm to discuss a terrifying telegram Winston has sent from Paris. Winston wants us to mass all our air strength to stop the [German] advance in order to save the collapsing French morale. . . . The Cabinet's decision was to send the ten fighter squadrons for which the French asked. That means denuding this country of a quarter of its first line fighter defence."

In *Their Finest Hour,* Churchill describes it all: "In the morning, before I started [for France], the Cabinet had given me authority to move four more squadrons to France. On our return to the Embassy and after talking it over . . . I decided to ask sanction for the despatch of six more. This would leave us with only the twenty-five fighter squadrons at home, and that was the final limit."

And that is it, the whole story according to Churchill. It is historical emendations such as these that prompted Sir John Slessor, a later Air Chief Marshal of the RAF, to remark, "The enormous interest and value of Sir Winston's memoirs sometimes suffers from his occasional genius for self-deception."

Not only does Churchill ignore the entire cabinet meeting at which Dowding fought against the departure of any more fighters from England—and at which the cabinet agreed with him—but he says that twenty-five fighter squadrons at home was what was required to defend England. In truth, Dowding and the Air Staff had always agreed that a bare minimum of fifty squadrons would be necessary—they argued over whether it should be fifty, fifty-one, or fifty-two—and the RAF was already down to thirty-seven. Nor was even this "the final limit," for the French collapse continued, and the BEF was now in danger of being surrounded and cut off from the Channel ports. Churchill now had to face not only the loss of his only ally, France, but the loss of his own army as well.

Colville, again writing in his diary for Saturday, May 18, described the potentially dire consequences of either decision the cabinet had to make: "The Cabinet have now got to take a fundamental decision. They can either send most of the fighters from this country in the hope of turning the scale of the western front, in which case the war might be appreciably shortened; or they can maintain them here for defensive purposes. . . . If we send the fighters and lose them, then this country will be left at the mercy of concentrated German air attack and we can hardly avoid destruction. It would be a terrifying gamble, but I am afraid it is one we ought to take."

It was a gamble that they probably would have taken, if not for Dowding. Not knowing about the reversal of the decision he had pushed through at the meeting, or of the subsequent order to dispatch even more fighters to France, he was nevertheless distrustful of the cabinet, and particularly of Churchill. As soon as he returned to the priory, he sat down and wrote a letter to the Chief of the Air Staff, hoping that the CAS would show it to Churchill.

Sir,

I have the honour to refer to the very serious calls which have recently been made upon the Home Defence Fighter Units in an attempt to stem the German invasion on the continent.

I hope and believe that our Armies may yet be victorious in France and Belgium, but we have to face the possibility that they may be defeated.

In this case I presume that there is no one who will deny that England should fight on, even though the remainder of the Continent of Europe is dominated by the Germans.

For this purpose it is necessary to retain some minimum fighter strength in this country and I must . . . remind the Air Council that the last estimate . . . as to the force necessary to defend this country was 52 squadrons, and my strength has now been reduced to the equivalent of 36 squadrons.

Once a decision has been reached as to the limit on which the Air Council and the Cabinet are prepared to stake the existence of the country, it should be made clear to the Allied Commanders on the Continent that not a single aeroplane from Fighter Command beyond the limit will be sent across the Channel, no matter how desperate the situation may become. . . .

I believe that, if an adequate fighter force is kept in this country, if the fleet remains in being, and if Home Forces are suitably organized to resist invasion, we should be able to carry on the war single handed for some time, if not indefinitely. But, if the Home Defence Force is drained away in desperate attempts to remedy the situation in France, defeat in France will involve the final, complete and irremediable defeat of this country.

Finally, this letter took effect. Newall presented the letter to his cohorts, the army and navy Chiefs of Staff, and he strongly urged that no more fighters be sent. The chiefs reluctantly agreed, and at last Churchill surrendered to the inevitable. He wrote to General Sir Hastings "Pug" Ismay (his Chief of Staff): "No more squadrons of fighters will leave the country whatever the need of France...."

On this same day, May 19, they received the news that the French army south of the BEF had melted away. The British retreated to the Channel port of Dunkerque and dug in. The victorious Wehrmacht pursued them, paused to gather its forces, and prepared to destroy them—and Hitler called time out.

Göring had persuaded him. Reichsmarschall Hermann Göring, an ace pilot who had led Baron Manfred von Richthofen's squadron after the Rittmeister had been killed, had risen to command the Luftwaffe. But he had morphed from a fighter pilot into a gluttonous sycophant, a strutting, fat peacock far removed from the realities of the air war. Infatuated to the point of drunkenness over the Luftwaffe's victories in Poland and France, he now saw his greatest opportunity. He convinced Hitler that he could destroy the BEF from the air.

Hitler liked the idea. Like Churchill, he thought he was a better general than his generals. Unlike Churchill, he always sought to play them off against each other, to undermine them, to humiliate them. Göring was his boy, firmly in his pocket, and now Hitler saw the chance to use his court jester to show the army generals he could do without them. He halted the Panzers and sent in the Stukas.

And, across the Channel, Dowding sent in the Spitfires.

When the army reached Dunkerque, Britain set to work. Three centuries of naval heritage came to life; not only the Royal Navy but every sailboat, motorboat, yacht, and spinnaker came floating, sailing, putt-putting down the rivers and coastlines of England, headed across the waters to France. Every weekend sailor, every farmer who vacationed on the sea, every man in England in whom the blood of Drake and Nelson coursed brought his four-man or seven-man skiff and set off across the Channel to bring the army home.

The navy sent every ship it had, freighters to load the soldiers by the hundreds and destroyers to guard the sailboats while they picked two, three, four men out of the surging surf. Above them the Hurricanes patrolled, and with them came the Spitfires, finally committed to action by Dowding, together with every other plane that could fly and carry a gun.

And sometimes the Stukas broke through and slaughtered the boys waiting on the beach and those struggling through the water to reach the ships. And sometimes the bombers hit the ships and men died, while, hidden above the clouds, the Hurris and Spits flashed into greater hordes of German bombers and shot them down and drove them away.

The British soldiers died blown to bits, machine-gunned, strafed, drowned; they died by the hundreds, but they were saved by the thousands. Two hundred thousand of them came home. Although it was impossible to keep every German bomber away, the great masses of them that Göring had promised would destroy the BEF were beaten off, and that raggedy flotilla of professional and amateur sailors brought the army home, brought their lads back to Blighty.

A few days later, France surrendered. Of 250 Hurricanes sent there, only 66 returned; the loss amounted to half the total number of Hurricanes in the RAF.

The Battle of France is over. I expect that the Battle of Britain is about to begin. . . . Hitler knows that he will have to break us in this island or lose the war. If we can stand up to him, all Europe may be free and the life of the world may move forward into broad, sunlit uplands. But if we fail, then the whole world, including the United States . . . will sink into the abyss of a new Dark Age, made more sinister . . . by the lights of perverted science. Let us therefore brace ourselves to our duties, and so bear ourselves that, if the British Empire and its Commonwealth last for a thousand years, men will still say, *"This* was their finest hour."

part three

The Long Hot Summer

WELL! The man certainly had a way with words. And he kept it up. After France surrendered but before the Battle of Britain began, Lord Halifax led a coterie of Englishmen seeking to negotiate a peace with Hitler. When Hitler replied that he had no demands on England, that England could keep its empire and he would keep the Continent he had conquered, Churchill bellowed, No! Not bloody likely! "All the conquered people of Europe shall share the gains— aye, and freedom shall be restored to *all*. We abate nothing of our just demands; not one jot or tittle do we recede. . . . Czechs, Poles, Norwegians, Dutch, Belgians, have joined their causes to our own. *All these shall be restored!"*

The man was magnificent. As Hitler, furious at this rebuff, geared up to invade England, Churchill warned him and warmed the hearts of every free person: "We shall defend our island whatever the cost may be," he roared. "We shall fight on the beaches, we shall fight on the landing grounds, we shall fight in the fields and in the streets, we shall fight in the hills; we shall *never* surrender!"

Of course, he had nothing to fight with. The army had come home from Dunkirk, but they had left all their weapons behind. They brought back no tanks or artillery, no machine guns or bullets. They had no hope of defeating the powerful Wehrmacht, which was flushed with victory and armed with the best tanks in the world and what appeared to be the most powerful air force.

The British had only one thing going for them: the courage that sprung like a lion out of Churchill's heart and reverberated with his gruff voice throughout the land.

And, oh yes, they had the defensive system of radar, Spitfires, and Hurricanes that Dowding had put in place.

Dowding's relationship with Churchill is one of the unsolved mysteries of history. Dowding himself said, "After the meeting of 15 May there was no chance of our ever becoming friendly. I had opposed him, and he had had to change his very stubborn mind in front of a large gathering of senior officers and officials over a very important issue." This feeling was shared by Dowding's friend, Field Marshal Archibald Wavell, who upon hearing of the May 15 meeting, warned him to beware of Churchill's enmity. Indeed, after the Battle of Britain was over, Dowding was summarily fired, and the feeling among the fighter pilots was that they would never forgive Churchill for that. But earlier this summer, when others, irritated by Dowding's long intransigence, tried to fire him, Churchill angrily vetoed them.

Churchill was a complex man. As Neville Chamberlain put it, "What a brilliant creature he is! I like him. I like his humour and vitality. I like his courage. . . . But not for all the joys of Paradise would I be a member of his staff!" He would come storming into a meeting and bark out his thoughts as if they were commands, then fix everyone with his glowering eyes and silently dare them to answer. According to Lord Esher, "he handles great subjects in rhythmical language and becomes quickly enslaved by his own phrases. He deceives himself into the belief that he takes broad views, when his mind is fixed upon one comparatively small aspect of the question." Others said, "It is like arguing with a brass band."

So, more often than not, they didn't even try, and then he would win the war with his tanks or nearly lose it in the Dardanelles. Sometimes they would try to answer him with the beginnings of a long-winded argument, but he would cut them off rudely; he didn't have time for such meanderings, for long explanations.

But many of these arguments were by their nature subtle and complex; they needed long explanations. No matter, he would not listen. His own statements were, if colorful and brilliant, always clear and concise, and if you couldn't answer them in the same way, it was because your mind was muddied and your thinking muddled, and to cheery blazes with you!

This was why he valued Lindemann so much. The Prof could always give a short explanation of what he was proposing, and if in doing so, he skipped over a few vital details—details that often meant that his conclusion was totally wrong—well, he didn't care and neither did Churchill. Meanwhile, those more knowledgeable at the meeting would break a tooth or two as they silently gritted them and as their blood pressure rose.

Dowding was lucky; he didn't have to shave the truth to simplify it. His message was by its nature simple and direct: "If the present rate of wastage continues for another fortnight we shall not have a single Hurricane left in France *or in this country.*" It was a message Churchill could understand. He didn't like it, he didn't like having it shoved down his throat, but he could understand it and appreciate it. And when France did fall and the Luftwaffe came sailing over the horizon, he was damned glad and appreciative of the Hurricanes and Spitfires Dowding had saved from Churchill's misplaced love of France. Out of the embarrassment and ire arising at the May 15 cabinet meeting, there grew, like a phoenix, admiration for a man Churchill knew he could trust not to kowtow, not to be overawed by rhetoric. Above all else, Dowding knew what he was doing and could say so in plain words.

Not everyone felt the same way about Dowding. His forthrightness was seen by some as stubbornness (Lord Halifax regretted "the proneness of Dowding to give expression to purely personal views even if they clash or seriously detract from official views"); by some as pure nastiness (when Robert Watson-Watt offered him some hundreds of airborne radar sets, Stuffy said with some asperity, "Just give me ten that work!"); and by others, such as Bomber Harris, as downright stupidity ("out of touch with flying"). His 1936 appointment to put Fighter Command together had been a natural one in view of his seniority and his championing of radar and the new fighters when he was head of Research. But once in charge there, he was even more peremptory and dismissive of everyone's opinions than he had ever been.

Some thought it was because of the broken promise that he would become chief of Air Staff in 1937, when instead, Cyril Newall was appointed the new CAS. (Dowding was also told then that he would stay in the RAF in his present or an equivalent position until 1942, another promise to be broken.) Others thought it was just the natural tendency of one's nature to become intensified as one became older; in Dowding's case, his natural perversity was becoming unbearable. Whatever the reason, they wanted him gone.

And so, although in 1937 Secretary of State for Air Ellington informed him that "an officer of your rank will be employed... up to the age of 60 [i.e., 1942]," in August 1938 the Air Ministry informed him that he would be asked to retire and relinquish Fighter Command to Air Vice-Marshal C. L. Courtney the following June (1938). Then, three days before the proposed takeover, Courtney was injured in an air crash and the decision was revoked. So too was the promise that he would remain "in an equivalent position" until 1942. He was told that he should stay on with Fighter Command for another year, but that was all: "We will be unable to offer you employment in the RAF after June 1939." Then in February 1939— six months early—without prior notice to him, the *Evening Standard* publicly announced his retirement.

Next, Sir Archibald Sinclair (now Secretary of State for Air and head of the Air Ministry) telephoned to tell him that the retirement would be deferred until the end of the year. Dowding replied that he "was not willing to extend service unless I had the confidence and support of the Air Council hitherto denied me." He received Sinclair's verbal assurance and was asked to continue to serve till the end of March 1940.

One day before his scheduled March retirement, Newall asked him to stay on until July 14. On July 11, just three days before this new retirement date, Churchill wrote a private and confidential letter to Sinclair: "I was very much taken aback the other night, when you told me that you had been considering removing Sir Hugh Dowding at the expiration of his present appointment . . . he is one of the very best men you have got." He went on to say that talk of enforced retirement should be discontinued and Dowding should be kept in office as long as the war lasted. He even suggested that Dowding was the proper man to be made chief of the Air Staff.

Sinclair immediately rescinded the July retirement, writing to Dowding and asking him to stay on throughout the summer in his present position, ignoring Churchill's suggestions that he be promoted to CAS and kept on until the end of the war. Dowding replied that despite the "discourtesy and lack of consideration" that the Air Ministry had shown him in retiring and unretiring him five times, he would be happy to stay on. He himself added the words "without any date for my retirement being fixed," because everyone else seemed to be intent on reducing the strength of Fighter Command "below the extreme danger point . . . and no one else will fight as I do" against these proposals. In reply, Sinclair wrote him a nice letter that said nothing except to thank him for agreeing to stay on, and that the summer would be quite long enough, thank you very much. October 31 would be his new retirement date.

Churchill made no further comment.

And so the long, hot summer began, with Churchill a lion bearded in his den, roaring his fury at the enemy pacing outside, and with Dowding glowering at his political masters, but inwardly glowing and exultant.

Exultant? Yes, for he had begun to see beyond the evils of this world into a higher realm. Sir Maurice Dean, Permanent Under-Secretary of State for Air at the time, remembered that Dowding strode into Whitehall on the day France surrendered, mounted the stairs to the Air Staff offices where Dean worked, and announced, "Now we cannot lose."

"His face was shining. His words and demeanour would have become a major prophet. Marshal of the RAF or not, for practical purposes that was what he was at that moment."

Of course, Dowding was immensely relieved that, with France gone, no more fighters would be sent across the Channel. And with his forces intact, he was confident that he could withstand the Luftwaffe and that therefore England could withstand Germany.

Or . . .

Had he just gotten the word from God?

Lord Halifax, writing in his diary about the fall of France, quoted Dowding as saying, "I went on my knees and thanked God." Now a belief in God is reasonably normal, especially in wartime, when everyone believes that God is on his side, but Dowding went a bit further—not quite around the bend yet, but well on his way. He was beginning to have visions. Although he didn't yet announce these to the public during the summer, he did ask close friends whether he shouldn't publish his experiences to reassure the British people that they had nothing to fear in this war.

What did he mean by his "experiences"? An experience is more than a belief, as indeed it was for Dowding. He meant he was actually speaking to spirits from "the other side"—spirits that told him clearly that God was working on behalf of the British people. Convinced of this, he explained to friends—and later published—his conviction that "God will not allow our nation to be obliterated in this war, and He has already intervened in our behalf." The first part of that statement is, again, the sort of thing that many people cling to in times of duress, but the second part? What did he mean?

He meant the "miracle" of Dunkirk. He told his friends now, and later published, that God had "stilled the waters of the Channel into an unnatural calm for days on end" so that the fleet of small boats might bring the army back safely to England. Of course, you might reason that if God could do that, and were inclined to do it, then He could just as easily have prevented the military defeat that rendered the "miracle" of Dunkirk necessary in the first place. God might also have prevented the Luftwaffe bombers from killing all those soldiers on the Dunkirk beaches, and later in the war from razing London—not to mention what the Almighty might have done about Buchenwald and Auschwitz.

But Dowding had no doubt that he was literally marching arm in arm with the Lord of Hosts. How could he doubt it? The spirits told him so. Later that summer, his own wife, Clarice, would appear to him, confirming all this. And yet, while his mind was wandering amid the faeries and cacodaemons, his feet remained planted firmly on the solid ground—on the ground where the radar towers were anchored, from which the radio beams soared up into the air to detect whatever waves of bombers might appear over the horizon.

Somehow the spirit voices cleared his mind rather than clouding it, somehow he remained rooted both in the ethereal realm and in our own, somehow he remained in control, directing Fighter Command against the onslaught that now began.

seventeen

A T T H E T I M E of the Munich Agreement in 1938, Dowding had about half the fighter squadrons needed to defend England, and all were fitted with outmoded biplane fighters. He had neither radar, Spitfires, nor Hurricanes. One year later, when the war began, he had the beginnings of a comprehensive radar system set up, but as discussed earlier, it wasn't yet operating properly. He had a few squadrons of Hurricanes, and the Spitfires were beginning to be pro-duced. In the spring of 1940, Chamberlain, in nearly his last speech as Prime Minister, goaded Hitler for having "missed the bus," for not having attacked when England was still unprepared. A few days later Hitler did attack, sweeping over France.

In the Battle of France, Dowding lost half his Hurricanes, and more were lost over Dunkirk, together with some of his hoarded Spitfires, which were first committed to action there. Then came another respite, shorter this time, during which more Hurris and Spits came off the production lines, more pilots were trained, and the worst of the radar glitches were fixed. When the Battle of Britain began, in that summer that was both too long and too short, too bright and too terrible, Dowding and his chicks were still not quite ready, but they were slowly getting there.

Just barely in the nick of time.

The summer was too long in that it seemed to take forever for autumn to come, and with it the autumnal gales that would sweep in from the Atlantic to roil the Channel and make it impossible for any invasion force to cross. The function of Fighter Command was not to defeat the Luftwaffe but to prevent its own defeat, to stay in existence and prevent the Luftwaffe from gaining air superiority until those saving winds should blow.

The summer was too short in that there wasn't enough time to prepare, to manufacture enough Spitfires and Hurricanes, to cure the glitches in the radar system, to train the masses of operators who would have to run the observers' sightings and the radar plots into a controlled system of fighter deployment, to produce more fighter pilots to replace those killed. Every day seemed a race against time, while every month seemed to stretch out endlessly.

The summer was too bright; it never seemed to rain. Every morning, the pilots would roll out of bed and look up at the clear bright sky and ask each other, What's happened to the typical English summer? Where the fuck are the clouds, the fog, the rain that would give us a day's respite from the Luftwaffe?

The summer was too terrible, as planes and pilots tumbled burning out of the sky.

The battle that began that summer was different from the one everyone had prepared for. When Dowding had argued that he needed fifty squadrons of fighters to defend England, he and everyone else had been thinking of German bombers coming from Germany, from so far away that German fighters could not make the trip. Now the German bombers would be coming from much closer bases in occupied France, and they would be accompanied by escorting fighters. The British Spitfires would have to fight their way through a cloud of Messerschmitts to reach the bombers, and fifty squadrons was no longer sufficient. But that was all they had.

This unanticipated problem was somewhat countered by Hitler's having built his air force as a tactical weapon of light bombers to support the army, and not, as Giulio Douhet had envisaged, a strategic force of heavy bombers to destroy cities. Hitler intended to win the war not by terror bombing but by invasion, and to do this, he had to destroy Fighter Command rather than England's cities.

Lindemann, incidentally, misunderstood this problem. "I assume that day bombers are not the problem," he wrote, "as our fighters can deal with them." He was worried about night bombing, which did in fact present a problem later, but in the summer of 1940 the day bombers were the menace. Night bombers could not be found in the dark skies, let alone shot down, but their effect was minimal since the same darkness that shielded them also shielded their targets. Churchill, while still as fond as ever of the Prof, had learned by this time that the defense of the realm was to be left to Dowding. Lindemann's schemes against night bombers, including searchlights mounted on night fighters and aerial mines dropped by parachute onto the bombers, were given their trial, and failed, and that was that. The real fight took place in the light of day.

During June, the Luftwaffe probed England's air defenses with single bombers by day and night, doing little damage. Dowding responded with flights of three fighters at a time. A few bombers were shot down in the daylight hours, a few fighters were lost—mostly by accidents and mostly during abortive attempts to send off the Spits and Hurris by night. Radar had not yet advanced far enough to be made small enough to be fit into an airplane, and these high-spirited thoroughbred planes were difficult enough to fly by day, let alone by night. No night fighter ever caught sight of a German bomber, let alone got into position to attack one, let alone shoot one down.

On July 4, the Luftwaffe attacked for the first time in force. At 8:41 that morning, thirty-three Stukas suddenly dropped out of the clouds to hit the Portsmouth naval base. Although radar had picked them up, it had not done so soon enough. What's more, because the aerodrome Dowding had fought for in this sector wasn't yet completed, the Hurricanes were still miles away when the bombs began dropping. In four minutes a merchant tanker and an antiaircraft ship were left burning and sinking, and the Stukas had disappeared. One of them was shot down by antiaircraft fire, but the British fighters arrived on the scene too late.

At two o'clock that afternoon, a convoy sailing through the Straits of Dover was hit by a formation of twin-engine Dorniers. This time eight Hurricanes intercepted them, but were beaten away by thirty escorting Messerschmitts.

At six-thirty that evening, radar reported an incoming raid, and nine Hurris were scrambled. This time there were no bombers approaching; there was nothing but an overwhelming force of Messerschmitts. Two British fighters were shot down, one Me was lost.

Such was the opening phase of the Battle of Britain. Göring's strategy was obvious and clever, and there wasn't much Dowding could do about it. Although with the fall of France and the availability of the French coastal aerodromes, England was within the range of the German fighters, it was just barely within their range. The further inland they had to fly, the less gas they would have to enable them to fight. Therefore Göring ordered attacks on coastal targets, ships, and naval bases, which the RAF would have to defend. When the British fighters come up, he ordered, shoot them down.

Dowding's strategy was more subtle, and poor Göring never did catch on. When the July 4 fighting was over, the morning Stukas returned to base and reported that they had encountered no fighter defense. The afternoon Dorniers came home and reported only an ineffective fighter defense. The thirty-six evening Messerschmitts came home and reported they had been opposed by only nine Hurricanes.

What was Göring to conclude from all this? The prime strategy of any general from time immemorial, since before the time of

Alexander the Great, was to attempt to meet enemy forces with superior numbers. When the Stukas were unopposed, perhaps the RAF had been caught by surprise, but when the Dorniers and the Messerschmitts were met by only a few fighters, and when Dowding sent eight Hurricanes up against thirty Messerschmitts in the afternoon and nine up against thirty-six in the evening, it was clear to Göring that Dowding had only a very few fighters at his disposal.

It was the obvious conclusion, and it was wrong. As the battle commenced that summer, the Luftwaffe enjoyed only a slight advantage in numbers of fighters. (The Germans, however, did have hundreds of bombers, which the RAF had to attack. Moreover, Göring could pick the targets and therefore concentrate his fighters, while Fighter Command had to spread its force over the entire prospective battlefield, namely, the length and breadth of England.) Dowding's strategy was based on his understanding that he didn't have to win the battle; he only had to avoid losing it. He had to keep Fighter Command viable throughout the summer; he had to keep it ready to oppose the invasion. He had to keep his planes flying until the autumn winds came blasting in.

Göring's orders were different. He had to destroy Dowding. He never understood that Dowding didn't have to destroy him, but had only to survive. So throughout the month of July, Göring sent his bombers against the British convoys and their naval bases and coastal defenses, and time after time, a few British fighters—"penny-packets," Dowding called them—would rise up to defend as best they could. Göring was happy to report to Hitler that his failure to wipe out the BEF at Dunkirk wasn't really a failure after all: The aerial fighting over France and particularly over Dunkirk had practically wiped out the British fighters; there were only a few left.

In that first week of July, Hitler issued his Directive No. 15, ordering his army, navy, and air staffs to begin coordinated planning for the invasion of England.

Lord Dowding

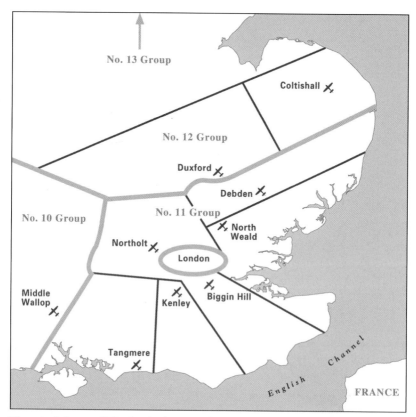

No. 13 Group

Coltishall

No. 12 Group

Duxford

Debden

No. 11 Group

No. 10 Group

North Weald

Northolt

London

Middle Wallop

Kenley

Biggin Hill

Tangmere

English Channel

FRANCE

The air defense of England, showing the responsibilities of Fighter Command Groups, with each Group divided into Sectors. Also shown are the main airfields in each sector.

Lord Trenchard

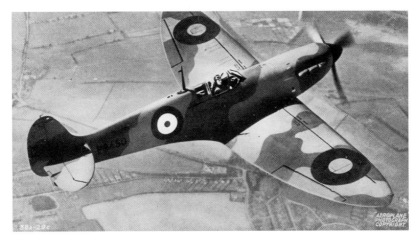

The Spitfire

The Hurricane

Radar Towers

Bentley Priory, outside Dowding's office

Professor Lindemann

Douglas Bader, lifting his leg to clamber into his Spitfire

Keith Park

W. L. FISKE

Billy Fiske, on a British cigarette
card from the 1930s

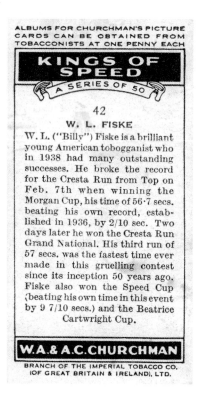

KINGS OF
SPEED

A SERIES OF 50

42

W. L. FISKE

W. L. ("Billy") Fiske is a brilliant
young American tobogganist who
in 1938 had many outstanding
successes. He broke the record
for the Cresta Run from Top on
Feb. 7th when winning the
Morgan Cup, his time of 56·7 secs.
beating his own record, established in 1936, by 2/10 sec. Two
days later he won the Cresta Run
Grand National. His third run of
57 secs. was the fastest time ever
made in this gruelling contest
since its inception 50 years ago.
Fiske also won the Speed Cup
(beating his own time in this event
by 9 7/10 secs.) and the Beatrice
Cartwright Cup.

The Bristol Beaufighter

Dowding's office at Bentley Priory. The unclut-
tered desk is just as he kept it day by day.

The plotting table at Fighter Command headquarters, showing
the incoming plots as they were on September 15, 1940. On the
wall is the listing of fighter squadrons in No. 11 Group, indicating whether they are at readiness, in the air, or available.

Dowding's statue in front of the Church of
St. Clement Dane in the Strand, the "official"
RAF church.

eighteen

Dowding was staking the entire outcome of the war on two diaphanous hopes. One was a fatherly God who had let His people down rather continuously throughout history, and the second was a complex, untried system of control revolving around a brand new technologic development: the detection of airplanes by radio waves.

To realize how vulnerable was his trust in God, one has only to study the history of the Jewish people for the past three thousand years. To realize how nearly impossible it was to organize a military system around a new technology, consider the time when the tank was first proposed ("The man's mad!"). Or consider that by the time of the Japanese attack on Pearl Harbor in December 1941—a full year and a half after radar had proved decisive in the Battle of Britain—American generals still had not integrated radar into the U.S. defense. (An experimental set actually detected the approaching Japanese forces, but the warning was ignored. Had it been acted on, the disaster would have been prevented.)

Nevertheless, this is what Dowding proposed to do. And, in fact, what he did.

He divided Fighter Command into Groups, the two most important of which were Nos. 11 and 12. No. 12 Group was assigned the northeast coast, which was the closest to the German airfields and so was expected to bear the brunt of any attack from that quarter. To establish command of this most important Group, in 1937 he chose Air Vice-Marshal Trafford Leigh-Mallory, to Dowding's everlasting regret.

Leigh-Mallory was an imposing man, especially once he reached high rank. He was large, big-boned, and husky but not fat, with an impressive moustache. In the First World War, he had been a pilot with the RFC, but in Army Cooperation rather than fighters. Some people with that background, being given command of a Fighter Group, would have been rather reserved, unwilling to push their opinions. Leigh-Mallory belonged to the other group, those who would compensate for a lack of experience by being overly aggressive. This characteristic may have been even more exaggerated by his family circumstance. Though an intelligent man with an honors degree in history from Cambridge and an excellent athlete, he was always overshadowed by his brother George Mallory, the most famous mountain climber in England's history, who had recently died on the crest of Mount Everest. On Mount Snowdon, there is a celebrated climb known as Mallory's Pipe, the official description of which concludes: "This climb is totally impossible. It has been performed once, in failing light, by Mr. G. H. L. Mallory."

Put it all together, and you have an intelligent, strong, aggressive and ambitious Air Vice-Marshal, not prone to tolerate the opinions of others. He was perhaps a good man to be in command, but not such a good man to be second in command.

For No. 11 Group, Dowding chose Keith Park, a small, wiry, tough New Zealander who had become a fighter ace in the First World War after being wounded and hospitalized in some of the worst infantry battles of that war. He had left New Zealand as a common mud soldier, but after the Somme, he had had enough. He might be crazy, but he wasn't stupid. He tried to join the RFC, to fight in the nice, clean air high above the sopping trenches, but the RFC wasn't accepting anyone with wounds as severe as his. So through a compassionate medical officer, his medical records were "lost," and as a healthy soldier with combat experience, he was taken in by the RFC, eventually becoming New Zealand's top ace.

In April 1940, Dowding gave him command of No. 11 Group, which guarded the southeastern corner of England, facing France across the Channel. The original intention had been to expect German bombers coming across the North Sea from Germany into No. 12 Group's territory, with 11 Group serving as backup. But then in May, France had fallen and the Luftwaffe had occupied the French airfields, bringing the southeastern coast into the spotlight as the expected hot spot.

Leigh-Mallory, as Dowding's most senior subordinate commander, expected to lead the defenses wherever the Germans might attack. He immediately asked for transfer to command 11 Group, but Dowding had confidence in Park and kept the two men where they were.

His confidence in Park was justified by later events. Moving Leigh-Mallory to 11 Group would have been disastrous. As it was, Leigh-Mallory nearly brought the whole system crashing down around its ears.

Leigh-Mallory and Park couldn't stand each other. As Lord Balfour, the Under-Secretary for Air, put it, "These two very different characters had individual views on air fighting strategy and tactics. They disliked each other to the point of strong personal antipathy and took no trouble to hide this fact from their staffs."

It all began with Park's suddenly becoming the hot-shot commander of the prime fighting force in Fighter Command. It was as if Leigh-Mallory took as a personal affront the surrender of France and the shifting focus of the Luftwaffe's assault on Britain. Well, what he really took as an affront was Dowding's refusal to switch his and

Park's commands when the defensive shift took place. Added to this was their personal opposites: They were as different emotionally as they were physically—the big, strong, overpowering presence of Leigh-Mallory as compared to the small, wiry, springlike tension of Park. They were bound to dislike each other.

Finally, and most importantly, they held different views on how to fight the Luftwaffe. Park was in total agreement with Dowding's strategy of sending up small flights of fighters to attack overwhelming forces, in order to sustain a fighting force capable of resisting invasion. This was nonsense to Leigh-Mallory. Attack in force—this was his motto. Bring in the strongest concentrations of aircraft you have, and wipe the skies clean of the Luftwaffe.

This is, of course, the normal strategy in warfare. But it didn't work, for two reasons. One was that the RAF didn't have to defeat the Luftwaffe; they just had to avoid being defeated. Leigh-Mallory's strategy would have resulted in gigantic, pitched air battles between the two forces, which was just what Göring wanted and just what Dowding wanted to deprive him of.

The second reason is the time it took to bring large formations of fighters together. The Big Wing, as Leigh-Mallory's tactic became known, consisted of several squadrons of fighters sailing in to attack en masse. But the airfields weren't large enough to enable an entire squadron—let alone several squadrons—to take off all at once. Individual flights of three planes would take off, and then the first ones would have to circle and form up with the later ones. This took time, and radar wasn't yet good enough to provide enough time for such aerial organizing. So to get several squadrons into the air at one place and time, and to organize them into a fighting unit, took time that the RAF did not have. The German bombers would have reached their targets and unloaded their bombs before the Big Wing caught them.

Nonsense, said Leigh-Mallory, all it takes is a bit of practice. And even if this were true, he continued, so what? We'll hit them so hard that they won't come back again.

In the event, it often did prove true that the Big Wing was too late to intercept the bombers before they did their bombing, so what was left of his strategy was the second part: Hit them so hard that they won't come back again.

If they were fighting the war they had expected to fight—a Douhet campaign of bombers against cities—then the Big Wing tactic might have been a reasonable approach. But that was *not* the war they were fighting. Dowding's strategy was to hit the bombers as quickly as possible, albeit with small penny-packets of fighters. Disrupt the bombers if you can, but mainly keep alive to fight another day and thereby frustrate Hitler's plan to invade.

If Dowding and Leigh-Mallory had been equally in command, a vigorous discussion of the two strategies would have been in order. But Dowding was solely in command. Leigh-Mallory was his subordinate and should have followed his orders—which were to stand by and act as backup to Park's No. 11 Group. When the bombers came over, Park would be in command, sending up his fighters in accordance with Dowding's strategy to foil as much of the bombing as he could. When his forces were overwhelmed by the large numbers of attackers, as would often be the case, Park was to bring in Leigh-Mallory's Group.

When given these orders, Leigh-Mallory's mouth went taut and smoke began pouring out of his ears. Sit back and wait to take orders from that kiwi Park? His frustration erupting like Krakatoa, he disobeyed the orders.

Dowding's biggest mistake—his only mistake, really—in the battle was not to crack down on Leigh-Mallory. Long after the battle was over, Dowding reflected, "Looking back on things now, I believe that I ought to have been very much firmer, in fact stricter, with Leigh-Mallory." Balfour suggested that, regarding Dowding's comment, "for Leigh-Mallory, read both [Leigh-Mallory and Park]." But that is nonsense. Park was obeying Dowding's commands; Leigh-Mallory was not. We may as well get this straight from the outset.

The heroes here are Dowding and Park; the villain of the piece is Leigh-Mallory.

This assessment is not universally accepted. One can make a case for either side; there is good and bad in every man. There are also pros and cons to every decision, as there are two sides to every story. And of course, the verdicts of history are often shuffled and reshuffled according to the changing fashions of the times. Nevertheless, Leigh-Mallory is my villain.

You may come to disagree, but first listen to the tale as I believe it should be told.

nineteen

THE BASIC CONCEPT of Dowding's scheme was that the four Groups were the core, but they were to flow into and out of each other as needed, as directed by Dowding or as the exigencies of battle demanded. Nos. 11 and 12 Groups would do most of the fighting, while 10 Group, in the far west out of Luftwaffe range, would be used for training and replacement purposes, backing up Park's 11 Group with reinforcements. No. 13, in the far north, would defend Scapa Flow, train pilots, and be ready to back up Leigh-Mallory's 12 Group if necessary.

If the Luftwaffe attacked one Group's area of responsibility, for example, fighters in the adjoining Groups were to be held in readiness and released into the fight immediately when—but only when—called on by the primary Group Commander.

Leigh-Mallory did not like this concept, which limited his powers. His idea was total autonomy for the Group AOCs (Air Officers Commanding), particularly before the fall of France, when he expected that the attacks would come into his sector. He issued a memo emphasizing control of his immediate area without regard for what might be going on elsewhere. At that time, Fighter Command had forty-one squadrons of fighters; he asked for twenty-nine of these to be placed under his immediate control. Dowding replied that this memo showed "a misconception of the basic ideas of fighter defence." He might have considered replacing Leigh-Mallory at this time, but his attitude was to pick the people he thought best for the job and then leave them alone. His assumption that they would follow orders turned out to be unrealistic.

In a fighter defense exercise early in 1939, the radar hadn't managed to pick up a group of "enemy" bombers that suddenly appeared over one of Leigh-Mallory's aerodromes. He reacted by instituting standing patrols, so as not to be caught flat-footed again. Dowding pointed out that the purpose of the exercise was to find weaknesses and fix them, not to change strategy. In the coming war, the RAF would not have sufficient planes to mount standing patrols; they would have to rely on radar. He informed Leigh-Mallory that he was not to institute such strategic changes on his own. Dowding might as well have stood outside his office at Bentley Priory and shouted into the wind. Leigh-Mallory came storming out of the meeting, swearing that "he would move heaven and earth to get Dowding sacked from his job." In the end, that is what he did.

When the war began, Dowding reminded his Group Commanders not to issue special Group orders in addition to those of Fighter Command. This was necessary because squadrons might be freely moved into and out of particular Groups as the constantly changing flow of the situation demanded, and it would be confusing if pilots found themselves in a Group where orders that they did not know about were standard operating procedure.

Two days after the war began, Leigh-Mallory introduced a new set of special orders to his own Group. Dowding immediately ordered him to cancel them and not to issue any others. Leigh-Mallory continued, however, to do so, as when he transferred several squadrons that Dowding had assigned to particular airfields to other bases, including some that were overcrowded. This was a serious breach, since Dowding would assign a squadron to one base with primary responsibility for local defense, but also with an eye to where it might be needed elsewhere. Leigh-Mallory was concerned only with his own local defense, a narrow view that could not be tolerated.

Dowding wrote what he considered to be a severe note: "I have delegated tactical control almost completely to Groups and Sectors, but I have not delegated strategical control, and the threat to the line must be regarded as a whole and not parochially." He also pointed out that three squadrons were the maximum that any aerodrome could hold if central organization was to be in control, and Leigh-Mallory now had as many as seven squadrons at some aerodromes. "I would only ask you to remember that Fighter Command has to operate as a whole," Dowding concluded.

With this message, Leigh-Mallory subsided, and as the winter months marched through the Bore War and on into the beginning phases of the summer's battle, he gave Fighter Command little more grief. Dowding turned his attention to the other myriad details needed to turn Fighter Command into an efficient, strong organization, as summer arrived.

On July 16, Hitler issued Directive No. 16:

PREPARATION FOR A LANDING OPERATION AGAINST ENGLAND:
    As England, despite her hopeless military situation, still shows no sign of willingness to come to terms, I have decided to prepare, and if necessary to carry out, an invasion against her.

He went on to state that the British army, having lost all its equipment at Dunkirk, would not be able to mount any effective opposition. But he demanded, as a prerequisite to the invasion, that the Luftwaffe must first annihilate Fighter Command.

On July 21, Göring met with the German naval staff, who complained that the British navy still seemed to own the English Channel. It was imperative, he was told, that the Channel be denied them. No responsibility could be assumed for transporting the Wehrmacht across the waters in the presence of the Royal Navy. Göring promised to destroy the English Channel ports and any ship that dared set sail. He told his Luftwaffe commanders that these tactics would surely bring up the last few British fighters. They were to be destroyed.

Nearly all the Chain Home radar stations were now complete and linked by secured telephone lines to the central command system. They kept a constant watch over the French coastline. The worst of the technical problems had been worked out. Chief among these were the backward echoes and the difficulty of distinguishing friendly aircraft from enemy. The backward-echo problem was solved by the shielding of transmissions so that only the forward half got out, and the friend-versus-enemy problem was solved by the installation of a small transmitter in the British fighters so that they sent out an identifiable signal. This IFF (Identification-Friend-or-Foe) apparatus by now had been installed in virtually all aircraft of Fighter Command, although many bombers and Coastal Command flying boats had not yet been fitted and were occasionally the objects of an interception.

The height problem was actually two problems, and progress was being made on both. The original CH transmitters fired their transmissions up into the sky, allowing low-flying bombers to slip under undetected. It wasn't simply a matter of aiming the transmitters lower; the problem was ground interference, which bounced the waves around in a manner to make their interpretation impossible. The solution, to find a wavelength that the ground didn't seem to reflect, had now been found. The first Chain Home Low station was operating by July. Seven others had been built, but weren't yet bug-free and in operation.

Height determination was still a problem and would remain so throughout the battle. Because an error of a few thousand feet was all too frequent, pilots were understandably reluctant to commit themselves to battle, only to find the enemy unexpectedly above them. The World War I slogan "Beware of the Hun in the sun" was still operable. Since gravity had not yet been repealed, height meant life and death to a fighter pilot.

The fighter pilots were the glamorous heroes of the fight, but just as a quarterback needs his linemen, the pilots needed their work-horses on the ground. To make the system work, the RAF had to train radar operators by the thousands, and here Dowding had a rev-olutionary idea: women. When he suggested training them for this work, the consensus around him was that it wasn't reasonable, for the radar operators would be working beside the transmitting towers in wooden shacks, which would be obvious targets for Luftwaffe bombers. The women would panic, leaving the radar screens untended, and catastrophe would ensue.

Dowding didn't think so. He pushed his idea through, and the women worked out perfectly, proving to be just as tough as the men when under attack.

The other ground workhorse that needed to be fit into the system was the Controller, who would take the radar information and direct the fighters to the attack. The problem, which Dowding anticipated correctly, was that once in the cockpit and off into the wild blue, a fighter pilot is a law unto himself, readily willing to ignore radioed instructions from silly groundlings. The solution Dowding applied was to take the fighter pilots themselves and train them as Con-trollers. Hearing instructions from one of their own, they were more easily controlled and directed onto the incoming bombers (although many of them did like to put a few thousand extra feet onto their altitude).

Throughout the Bore War winter, the RAF practiced intercepting every English airplane that flew. Many a student pilot concentrating on keeping his altitude constant and his nose on the horizon through a figure eight would be thrown into a sudden panic as a flight of Spitfires came diving out of the clouds, zooming under him close enough to kiss and disappearing again in a wild zoom that left the trainer shuddering in their prop-wash.

And now as the July days followed one another, Dowding and his chicks were ready.

The first German attacks on convoys and port towns were small skirmishes, but by the end of the month, the Luftwaffe, urged on by Göring, was mounting increasingly heavy attacks and Fighter Command was beginning to suffer. The sky over the Channel waters now seemed to be raining burning Spitfires and Hurricanes, blazing Messerschmitts and disintegrating Heinkels; the green fields of the coast were being carpeted with burned-out hulks carrying black crosses and bright RAF roundels—and bullet-holed, shattered, bloody, and burnt bodies.

twenty

THE CHAIN OF radar stations consisted of individual stations operating independently, but with their data analyzed as a whole. Unfortunately, each station was subject to its own distortions of data. One of the problems was that the performance of each station depended largely on its position. Height determination, the primary source of error, was made when a given echo reached the tower by two different routes: one coming in straight from the target airplane and the other hitting the ground in front of the tower and bouncing up to be detected a minimicrofraction of a second later. It was an ingenious and complex system, it was the best they had, and it suffered because the ground in front of each tower was different, with its own individual characteristics. Some towers had obstructions, trees or hills, in front of them; some had flat land; some looked from a height out over the sea; some had hills to the left and forests to the right; others had hills to the right and forests to the left. Each of these towers, looking at the same target, would give different altitudes.

And, of course, each station was manned (or womanned) by different people with different natural abilities and different training, most of them by necessity trained as quickly as possible, which meant not as well as possible. The saving grace of the system was that these problems didn't come on them out of the blue, as it were, but had been foreseen from the beginning, and so efforts had been incorporated to minimize the resultant errors. The RAF would fly a bomber back and forth in front of each tower as it was completed, and the radar would plot the position and altitude. These would then be compared with the real position and altitude, and a correction factor for each altitude and an azimuth indication for each station would be obtained.

Every station had its own "fruit machine," a newly contrived apparatus that resembled a slot machine but was really a sophisticated calculator. When a target was sighted, the radar operator would plug its apparent range and direction into the fruit machine, which would then automatically apply the already tabulated corrections and transfer these by simple trigonometry into map coordinates. The operator would then repeat the process to determine the altitude of the incoming aircraft. The areas covered by the individual CH stations overlapped, so a raid usually would be detected by at least two separate towers. The data from each one would be sent to the filter room at Fighter Command headquarters, Bentley Priory. Here the two sets of data would be combined and analyzed, and with luck, a fairly precise location and altitude could be obtained and sent down to the underground plotting room. There, filtering officers on the balcony looked down and added a further correction: Sometimes towers A and B would report an incoming raid, and so would B and C. Because of the errors alluded to, the two sets of data would not exactly correlate and two markers would be placed on the table. The filter officers had to decide if this was one raid they both alluded to, or two separate raids coming in close to each other.

Another group of officers, watching as the markers were moved across the map by the WAAFs, would extrapolate their speed and direction to guess at the bombers' targets and thus to direct particular radar stations to follow them, at the same time alerting the pertinent Fighter Command Groups. Once the raiders came over the coast, the Observer Corps would phone their sightings in to their local Group, each of which had its own operations room, where the filtered radar data were now combined with the Observer data, and decisions made for a precise reaction to each threat. From there the information went to sector operations rooms, which would translate Group's orders into individual fighter squadron scrambles.

It was too complicated, with possibilities of error all along the line. If the radar data had been perfect, if the Observer Corps never made a mistake, it still would have been impossible. The raiders came over at hundreds of miles an hour, which meant that the plots changed by roughly four miles every minute. And the Luftwaffe bombers didn't come in straight lines, like arrows toward their target. No, they feinted, they had formations break off and head in different directions, they did all they could to throw the defenders off.

Now add in the fact that the radar data were never perfect, the Observer Corps did make mistakes, and the sky was filled with hundreds of attacking planes heading for different targets. It was impossible to decide which planes were heading where and at what altitude, how many of them there were, and which defenders should be sent off to intercept them.

It was impossible, but it was done, and more often than not, they got it right.

During July, the fighting was concentrated in the Channel and along the southeastern coast, areas assigned to Keith Park's No. 11 Group. The squadrons were based on large, permanent aerodromes near London, such as Kenley and Biggin Hill, but every morning at dawn, Dowding sent a three-plane flight to a small forward aerodrome near the coast. When an incoming raid was picked up by radar, the flight would be in position to make an early intercept to disrupt the raid. More flights would then move up to the forward aerodrome, or even go right in to the attack if the raid was large enough.

There were two problems with this strategy. Obviously, that first flight would meet overwhelming numbers, but this was unavoidable; the Luftwaffe were able to choose when and where to attack, and Dowding didn't have enough fighters to cover the whole area with full squadrons. The second danger was that the airfields were left unattended while their planes were attacking the forward raids. The Germans so far didn't realize this opportunity, attacking instead convoys and naval ports, but if they should ever catch on, and if the airfields were destroyed, the British fighters would have been neutralized, so No. 12 Group was ordered to stand in readiness to intercept any follow-up raids that might be aimed at 11 Group's airfields. The system would work since, although the 12 Group fighters would have to fly from their own aerodromes to those further south that would be under attack, the radar system would give them enough time to get there—if 12 Group's fighters were scrambled efficiently and followed the Sector Controller's orders.

This meant that in these early days of the battle, it was 11 Group that did all the fighting while 12 Group sat home and waited. In later days, in Vietnam, Korea, and Iraq, you didn't find many reserve troops upset because they were being kept out of the fighting. But this was a different war and these were different warriors. The Few, as they came to be known, have often described themselves with words like "the gayest band of warriors that ever flew into battle," and this war is often spoken of as "the last good war." It wasn't good, of course, and no one is gay when he faces death daily, but these warriors were fighting for their homes, for survival against an enemy that was truly evil.

And they were young—oh, so young—and the young are immortal. Before he wrote *Charlie and the Chocolate Factory,* Roald Dahl was a fighter pilot in the RAF. He describes his war experience: "It was wonderful. I loved doing it because it was exciting, because the waiting on the aerodrome was nothing more than the waiting before a football game or before going in to bat." After a while, after combat day after day, it began to change: "But then always going back and always getting away with it . . . each time now it gets worse . . . it whispers to you that you are almost certain to buy it sooner or later, and that when you do . . . you will just be a charred corpse . . . black . . . twisted and brittle."

The pilots of 12 Group hadn't yet reached that second stage. They wanted to go into battle; they yearned for it. Instead they sat around their aerodromes safely in the north and listened to the fighting on their radios; they fretted, complained, and battered their superiors with requests, with demands.

But they were kept where they were. Aside from the necessity of protecting 11 Group's airfields if the Luftwaffe should ever wake up to the realization that they were easy prey, No. 12 Group was needed to protect the north. Dowding realized that though the French airfields were closest to England, the original German airfields were still within range, and if ever Göring thought that there were no fighters left in the north, he would come there with devastating raids. Unopposed attacks in that quarter could finally break the British spirit.

So 12 Group was told to obey orders, to sit back and wait. They saw themselves as backups to 11 Group, as substitutes, as second-raters, and they didn't like that one little bit. Led by their chief, Leigh-Mallory, they couldn't understand why the fighting in the south pitted small numbers of Brits against large numbers of Huns, while they sat on their arses, as they put it. The pilots waited on their deck chairs in the grass beside their planes and played cards and grumbled. Leigh-Mallory sat in his office and fumed.

Of all the 12 Group pilots, Squadron Leader Douglas Bader was the most charismatic. That was understandable, for he had something going for him that no one else in the RAF did: He had no legs. He had lost both before the war, when, during an exhibition of aerobatics, he crashed a fighter by flying it upside down a few inches above the grass. At the end, it flew a few inches *below* the grass, the prop dug into the ground, the plane flipped over and crashed, and Bader was pulled out. That is, most of Bader was pulled out; his legs—one above the knee, one just below—remained in the burning wreck.

He awoke in hospital to hear a nurse outside his door shushing a crowd passing by: "Please be quiet, can't you? There's a boy dying in there." But Bader was the most stubborn of men, and he refused to die. He was invalided out of the RAF, and he refused to stop flying. He learned to walk on his artificial legs without help—well, he learned to hobble on them, at any rate—and he got back into airplanes and learned to fly them again. He badgered the RAF to let him back in, he bombarded them with requests and doctor's certificates, he flew with his old RAF friends, who all backed him up until, finally, when the war began and the RAF desperately needed pilots, they took him back in.

They even gave him a Spitfire. The story goes that as evening fell one day in March 1940, "Pingo" Lester, the station commander of Duxford aerodrome, was watching the last Spitfire come in from the day's practice. Instead of sailing in at landing speed, it came speeding toward the aerodrome out of a power dive, leveling off at the last moment to come skimming across the grass, and then, before Pingo's unbelieving eyes, it rolled over.

Inches above the grass, engine roaring at full power, it turned upside down and skimmed along the entire length of the runway, rolled back upright, zoomed up into the sky, looped over, and came sailing back down to make a perfect landing. It taxied up to Pingo, and the cockpit hood was swung back. The pilot heaved himself upright and then leaned down. With his hands, he lifted his legs one at a time out of the cockpit, clumped them down on the wing, stood precariously on them, and slid down to the ground. As he limped over toward the station commander, Pingo sighed resignedly,

"Douglas, I do wish you wouldn't do that. You had *such* a nasty accident last time."

From all over the British Empire and Commonwealth they came to defend the home country: from New Zealand and Australia, from India and South Africa, and from Canada. No. 242 Squadron, composed entirely of Canadians, had been sent to France with their Hurricanes and had been savaged there. Now back in England, they had lost their squadron commander, most of their pilots, and all their planes. They were a bedraggled, dispirited lot, assigned to No. 12 Group to keep them out of the fight while they reorganized.

They didn't want to reorganize. They thought of themselves as wild colonial boys, and they had seen the mess their superiors had made of the battle in France and they wanted no more of it. They wanted to go home. Instead, they got a batch of new Hurricanes and they got Douglas Bader as their new commander.

You can imagine their reaction when he showed up without his legs. They were going to be led by a cripple. That was the best that Fighter Command could do for them. It showed just where they stood in the estimation of the hierarchy: somewhere just above the latrine cleaners and just below the janitors.

Bader called them all together for a squadron meeting. He told them what he expected of them, that they were going to be one of the finest fighting squadrons in the RAF. There was silence for a moment. Then from the back of the room came the clear comment, "Bollocks!" Then, a moment later, the voice added, "Sir."

Bader later said it was the "Sir" that amused him and let him think he had a chance with them. Without another word he limped out of the room and across the field to his Hurricane. Using his arms, he pulled himself up on the wing, balanced himself by leaning against the fuselage, and, lifting his right leg with both hands, he pushed it over the side into the cockpit. He braced himself against the canopy and lifted his other leg in his hands and pulled it in, half-falling into the cockpit with it as he always did.

He took off but instead of safely reaching for height before retracting the wheels, he pulled them up as soon as they left the ground, keeping his nose inches off the ground while the airspeed wound up. Then he pulled the Hurri steeply up, rolled off the top, and came screaming down again straight at the group gathered to watch. He knocked their hats off with his slipstream and zoomed back up into the sky.

They had never seen anything like what they saw that day; they didn't think it was possible to do what Bader was doing. He swung low over the grass, pulled up into a loop, went over the top and straight down into another loop—which is something absolutely prohibited by the book. If the first had not been precisely perfect, if he had lost any altitude in it, he would have crashed on the second. He didn't crash. And he didn't stop. He went right on into another consecutive loop, a third, and then a fourth.

They looked at each other. Not one of them would have dared try that.

He came roaring back down to grass-top height and rolled upside down: his old specialty. He held it there right across the aerodrome in front of their wide-open eyes. Then he flipped over upright again and took it straight up in a tight, looping climb. At the top of the loop, he flicked into a roll, dropped off into a spin, and came right out of that into another loop. He used to do that at the prewar air shows, but they were too young; they had never seen it done before.

When he came down a half hour later, dropping the Hurricane softly into a perfect landing as if it were a feathery bird instead of a ton of metal and canvas, they were still standing there in perfect attention. He pulled himself heavily out of the seat and dropped off the wing onto the ground, a cripple once again. He hobbled across the grass past them, glancing at their faces, and disappeared into his quarters.

As he closed the door behind him, he smiled. Bollocks, indeed!

An ambitious commander of No. 12 Group, jealous of the commander of No. 11 Group.

A daring, charismatic squadron leader, eager for battle.

A group of the gayest young men ever to fly into battle, impatient for battle, denied that battle.

And a sober, patient commander in chief.

A situation waiting to explode.

twenty-one

Im Westen Nichts Neues was the title of the best novel to come out of the First World War. It was translated as *All Quiet on the Western Front.* A more accurate translation would be *Nothing New on the Western Front,* and that would be a good description of the fighting as July turned into August. Sporadic attacks on convoys continued, but as the English cut down on their shipping, the attacks became less frequent. To the fighter pilots, it seemed that the fighting might peter out, but Winston Churchill knew better because of the work being done in an old Victorian mansion built in 1882 by Sir Herbert Leon.

In 1938 His Majesty's government acquired the site, Bletchley Park, for its Code and Cypher School. The stables were converted into garages, the tack and feed house and the apple and plum store into work cottages. A radio station was set up under the rooftop water tower. The pigeon loft was left alone.

On July 25, 1939, two of the Bletchley Park inmates met with a small group of Poles in the Pyry forest. The British were given a set of sheets documenting the use of the German cryptography machine, which consisted of two typewriters, one of which would convert a message into code and the other would then receive the message and retype it back into ordinary language. Using several wheels to vary the codes, the system was unbreakable, but with the Polish information, the British had a chance. Working together with three Polish mathematicians, Rozecki, Zygalski, and Rejewski, who had escaped to Paris, Alan Turing put together the forerunner of today's computers, and by 1940, the group at Bletchley had broken the Luftwaffe's code.

The code was named Enigma, the intercepted messages Ultra. Throughout the rest of the war, an expanded group of mathematicians, cryptologists, linguists, chess players, and engineers worked constantly to decipher the intercepted German radio messages. The system was so important that only a handful of people besides Churchill had access to Ultra. Dowding was not put on the list until very near the end of the battle.

On August 1, 1940, an Ultra copy of Hitler's Directive No. 17 was sent to Churchill:

> FOR THE CONDUCT OF THE AIR AND SEA WAR AGAINST ENGLAND.
> I intend to intensify air and sea warfare against the English in their homeland. I therefore order the Luftwaffe to overpower the Royal Air Force with all the forces at its command, in the shortest possible time. After achieving air superiority the Luftwaffe is to be ready to participate in full force in Fall Seelöwe.

The code name *Fall Seelöwe,* Operation Sea Lion, had already been identified by the code breakers at Bletchley. It was the plan for the invasion of England.

A couple of false starts ensued. Göring, with his customary panache, named the coming Luftwaffe offensive *Adlerangriff,* Attack of the Eagles, and many histories list it as beginning on August 8. That day's fighting did not signal the beginning of anything new but rather the last of the old. Because of the slackening off of attacks during the previous few days, the Admiralty decided to try sending another convoy down from the north and through the Dover straits. When it was sighted, the Luftwaffe—still operating under its old orders of striking at all shipping—sprung at it in force.

Radar picked up the incoming raid and a pitched battle ensued, with mixed results. The convoy was destroyed, with seven of the twenty ships sunk and six so damaged they had to head for the nearest port; only four made their destination without damage. But the victory came at a high cost: The Luftwaffe lost twenty-four aircraft, with another dozen heavily damaged; fifteen British fighters were shot down.

The next day began with scattered attacks against ports, with other bombers searching for convoys that did not set sail because of the previous day's losses. The actual date set for *Adlerangriff* was August 10, but bad weather blew across France and the day's activity was canceled and reset for August 13.

REICHSMARSCHALL GÖRING TO ALL UNITS:
   Adlerangriff! You will proceed to smash the British Air Force out of the sky. *Heil Hitler!*

Enough already with the convoys and the seaports. The mission of the Luftwaffe now was to destroy Fighter Command, to sweep the skies clear so the navy and the army could proceed with the invasion of England. They would attack the British fighters in the air and on the ground, overwhelming them with hordes of Messerschmitts in the air and, if they didn't rise to fight, destroying them on the ground by attacking their airfields. The Luftwaffe would even destroy the aircraft before they were built, by bombing the Hawker and Supermarine factories where the Hurricanes and Spitfires were constructed.

But the German reconnaissance planes sent to find the aerodromes and factories did not do a good job. They found the Upavon aerodrome, which their analysts gave a highest priority, but it was an outmoded field no longer used by Fighter Command. They also found one of Fighter Command's most important fields, Tangmere, but all the Spits and Hurris had been scrambled before the Luftwaffe arrived, so their photographs showed nothing but the night-fighter squadron of twin-engine Blenheims on the grass. When the Germans misidentified these as bombers, they dismissed Tangmere as a target. The Woolston factory had unfortunately been built in an exposed position right on the south coast, but the Luftwaffe never found out that it was an outsource of Supermarine and was building Spitfires, so they never targeted it. They got it all wrong.

And as for the radar towers . . .

Every nation spies on every other nation, even if it is not planning to go to war, but especially if it *is* planning war. In 1938, several groups of "tourists" returned from England to Germany with reports of strange Eiffel-like towers being constructed on the south and east coasts. It did not take any stroke of genius to understand that they were military in nature. But what were they? Radar seemed a reasonable choice.

Radar is viewed as an English invention, but scientific discoveries are often simultaneously made in more than one place. Science is funny that way. Well, perhaps it's not so funny. Events have a way of coming together at a particular time so that simultaneous discoveries are perhaps inevitable. In the late 1930s, the interference of airplanes with radio waves would have been observed in many countries, many of which were either preparing for war or worrying about those that were. The airplane was the coming weapon of mass destruction, and so means of detecting their onslaught would be on the minds of people all over the world.

The difference was that England had Dowding, a man who both appreciated the possibilities and had the power to do something about it. No other country had such a man, and so although work did progress on radar systems in Germany, Japan, Russia, and the United States, only England had a working system that was integral to its defense when the war began.

In Germany the man who had the power to bring radar along was Göring, but he had not the intelligence. The man there who had the intelligence was the Luftwaffe's Director General of Radio Signals, General Wolfgang Martini (a man unique in that each of his names reflects a singular glory of Western civilization). After long argument, he persuaded Göring to let him fit a zeppelin with radio detection instruments and fly along the coast of England to find out what those towers were emitting.

On May 9, 1939, he cruised off what he thought was the east coast of England. In reality, he was lost in fog and drifted over Yorkshire. His course was plotted by the British radar, and the officer in charge of the radar reported, "We were sorely tempted to radio a position correction to the airship, but this would have revealed we were seeing her on radar, so we kept silent." Martini's equipment wasn't working that night, and all he got was static.

He had time for one last try before war began, on August 2, after checking and double-checking his equipment. But on this night, it was England's radar system that failed. None of the operators saw him on their screens, and he received no signal from them. He returned to Germany and reported to Göring that the towers seemed to be inactive.

By the summer of 1940, the Germans had their own radar system, but Martini hadn't been able to integrate it into the military machine. German thoroughness and technical superiority are well-known, particularly to the Germans, and since Göring didn't think of his own radar as important he couldn't believe that the British system was. Yes, he admitted to Martini, those towers were probably a sort of radar system, but it couldn't be very good. Not worth wasting bombs on.

But Martini kept at him. He showed Göring pictures the

reconnaissance aircraft had brought back: flimsy towers and wooden shacks. Such an easy target!

Göring laughed, shaking his head in amusement. These technical types! All right, he said. All right, we'll bomb your little wooden shacks.

Tomorrow, August 11.

Though Dowding wasn't yet on the Ultra list, Churchill did let him know—without revealing the source—that *Adlerangriff* was scheduled for August 13. Otherwise, Dowding might have thought it started on Sunday, August 11. But no, this was just a warm-up. Batting practice.

Large bands of Messerschmitts came streaming over the coast shortly after dawn, escorting a few bombers, which hit Dover but caused no damage. The damage was done by the Messerschmitts, which swarmed over the defending fighters. A few hours later, more than a hundred bombers attacked the Portland naval base, and four squadrons were sent up against them and their escorts. Eighteen German planes fell flaming this day, but so did sixteen Hurricanes and one Spitfire.

The next day, Monday, August 12, again began with a sweep by Me 109 fighters, but this was just a prelude to attacks on the radar stations. Just after 8:30 in the morning, sixteen twin-engine Messerschmitt 110 fighter-bombers took off from Calais. They crossed the Channel south of Dover and flew along the coast.

In the wooden shack next to the radar transmitters at Dover, the WAAF operator was watching the blip they produced on her screen as they headed west. The Controller at Sector headquarters was studying the map table, following the marker that signaled their progress and trying to guess at their target. Then suddenly they broke into four sections and swerved directly north.

The blip on the radar screen in the shack at Dover reflected that change of course, and the WAAF operator called it to the attention of the duty officer, who called in the news to Sector Control. He murmured to the WAAF, "Looks like they're coming right at us."

She nodded assent, reached up to the hook over her head, put on her tin hat, and continued to read off the coordinates as the bombers dove in to the attack. The bombs hit a few moments later.

The bombers had broken into four sections. They hit the radar stations at Dover, Rye, Pevensey, and Dunkirk (in Kent). The wooden huts burst apart; the tin hats were no protection for the WAAFs. The electronics, the power supplies, the men and women were shattered. Pieces of arms and legs, tubes and cables, blood and electric sparks mingled in the wind, and the stations went off the air. Other raids swept in unseen by the blinded radar and hit airfields at Hawkinge and Lympne.

The wooden shacks were destroyed but the towers still stood. Fragile and skinny, they appeared highly vulnerable, but the shock waves of the bombs passed right through their open structure. And the shacks that fell apart with the first bombs were just as easily rebuilt. The electronics damage was more difficult to repair, the pieces of the people blown apart were harder to gather, but by late afternoon, the WAAF operators who survived had had their cups of tea and the stations were back on the air.

In the afternoon, the Luftwaffe came back, this time heading for the fighter aerodromes and expecting to sweep in unseen past the blasted radars, but again they were met by Spitfires and Hurricanes in precisely the right place at the right time.

Göring was convinced by this that he had been right all along. Martini was a fool. It was the same with all specialists, he said. They exaggerated the importance of whatever they were working on. They didn't see the whole picture. "There doesn't appear to be any point in continuing attacks on radar sites," he wrote to his commanders, "since not one of those attacked has been put out of action."

But, he continued, it didn't matter. The bombers had demolished the RAF main airfield at Manston and destroyed all the Spitfires there, he said. In truth, they had hit Manston hard, but the bombs had scattered around the grounds; not one Spit had been hit. They had destroyed forty fighters the previous day, according to the reports brought back by the Luftwaffe pilots, and another thirty-five today; the actual losses were seventeen the previous day and the same number today. The Luftwaffe reconnaissance photographs showed empty fighter bases, but in reality most of the photos showed abandoned bases or those used by training or bomber squadrons, so the absence of fighters on them was meaningless.

Göring believed the photos and the reports of his pilots. The RAF was down to its last few Spitfires, he assured them. One or two more days of dedicated action would finish the fighters off. The Attack of the Eagles would end the history of England; the nation of shopkeepers would drown in its own blood.

twenty-two

August 13.
Adlerangriff!
It rained.

Dark clouds, heavy rain blanketed the French airfields. The Luft-waffe commanders got out of bed, looked out the window, and went back to bed. All of them did, except for two Group leaders.

Oberst Johannes Fink, commanding seventy-four Dornier bombers, wasn't going to let the weather interfere with his mission for *der Führer.* Just before dawn he led his planes off the ground and through the muck, and was happy to find that the commander of his fighter escort also had not been deterred by the rain. They ren-dezvoused off the French coast and headed for England.

But they were alone. Nobody else took off, and as dawn failed to lighten the dark sky, Göring decided to postpone the Attack of the Eagles. Meanwhile, as Fink steered around a large cloud formation over the Channel he found that the fighters, which had gone around the other side of the cloud, had abruptly disappeared. He didn't know they had received a radio signal canceling their mission. Radio communications were haphazard in those days, and Fink never heard the signal. He wondered about the fighters' disappearance, he worried about continuing alone, and then he flew on.

His bad luck at missing the recall message turned around. Although his bombers were picked up by radar, the Observer Corps gave faulty directions as they passed overland. Sector Control sent five squadrons, but four of them went off to the wrong place. One British fighter squadron found them, but there were too many bombers to stop, and Fink's planes bombed the Eastchurch fighter base.

That is, they bombed Eastchurch, which they thought was a fighter base but which was no longer in regular use. A squadron of Spitfires did happen to be using it temporarily, and on the Germans' return, Oberst Fink reported the squadron destroyed. In fact, although the airfield was badly damaged, only one Spit was destroyed.

Dowding, following events as they unfolded, was worried. The Luftwaffe had been attacking shipping and naval ports, and his chicks had been fighting them evenly in the air but had still been unable to stop the massacre of the convoys. Now, if the Germans started attacking his airfields, why wouldn't they have the same success they had with the convoys? If they did, Fighter Command was doomed.

He hoped that this morning's attack on Eastchurch was an isolated event; perhaps the Dorniers had gotten lost in the bad weather and had simply attacked the first thing they saw. Please, he thought, dear God.

During the raids all summer long he would sit in the Operations Room at Bentley Priory and listen to the radio chatter as plots showed up on the radar screens and as fighters were sent off to meet them. It had been bad enough in the first war, when he had to send his boys off to be killed. Waiting on the tarmac for the sound of their engines returning, counting them as they came limping home. Six planes taking off and three or four coming back, four planes taking off and one or two coming back, smoking, shot up, on a wing and a prayer, as they said.

It was worse in this war because they had radios, and he could hear them, from the first "Tally-ho, buggers at six o'clock!" to the final, heartrending screams:

"Get this bastard off my tail!"

"Break! Break right!"

"I'm hit! Shit, I'm hit! Oh God—"

And then the screams, rattling in Dowding's ears, and the visions scorching his brain behind his eyes: the Spitfires, the Hurricanes, his chicks clawing the canopy as fire clawed at their clothes, at their skin, at their eyes, and the long, slow spin downward from twenty thousand feet, and then finally the burst of flame as they hit the ground.

Sometimes they managed to bail out. It wasn't easy, in a hail of bullets, in a diving, spinning plane flipping over and over at three hundred miles an hour. Too often they didn't, too often the screams reverberated over and over and . . .

Late in the afternoon, the clouds parted, the rain stopped, and the Attack of the Eagles began in earnest. In Bentley Priory, Dowding watched the markers on the map table being placed one after the other, heading not for the Channel ports but for his airfields. There was no longer any hope that the morning's raid had been an anomaly; no, it was the beginning of a shift in German tactics. He watched in dismay as the raids came in one after the other, sailing right past the coastal targets and heading straight for his airfields.

He kept his face inscrutable, for a commander must not show fear, but he was afraid. When he had fought Churchill, had railed against sending his boys to France, he hadn't been afraid of their facing the Luftwaffe in the air there, but he was afraid that without radar they would be destroyed on the ground. Here in England, they had radar warning, but they couldn't stay in the air continuously. If the Luftwaffe were able to send in continuous fleets of bombers, the second fleet would catch his fighters refueling on the ground after fighting off the first fleet.

Even if the bombers came over while the fighters were in the air and found only empty airfields, they could destroy the hangars, runways, and supporting equipment; without these, his chicks could not fly, his fighters could not fight. The battle would be lost.

All afternoon the bombers came, roaming over the countryside, searching out Dowding's airfields. But the German reconnaissance proved faulty; the intelligence they had reaped from prewar spies proved out-of-date. The bombers hit the Eastchurch and Worthy Down aerodromes, but these hadn't been used by Fighter Command for years. They bombed Lee-on-Solent, which housed only naval bombers. They bombed the city of Southampton but missed the Spitfire factory there.

Even when they had the right targets, they missed. Middle Wallop was a vital airfield, but the bombers hit an empty field close by at Andover instead. They did catch Detling and practically destroyed it along with twenty-two parked airplanes—but Detling was not one of Dowding's airfields, and none of the planes destroyed were fighters.

At the end of the day Göring was triumphant. The returning Messerschmitt pilots claimed they had destroyed eighty-four British fighters in the air, while the bomber crews chimed in with an additional fifty-plus destroyed on the ground. The Attack of the Eagles had been a success, he wired Hitler; in a few more days, there would be no British fighters in the sky. Plans for the invasion could proceed.

The true numbers were different. Dowding had lost thirteen of his chicks in the air, not eighty-four. The bomber crews were more realistic in their estimate, for nearly fifty planes had been destroyed on the ground. But only one of them was a fighter. The Luftwaffe lost sixty-four.

Only thirteen of his lads had died in the air. Only thirteen young, healthy boys with their whole lives ahead of them had had those lives gauged out, had died in the most horrible way imaginable, alone in the sky four miles above the earth, falling, burning, screaming for their mothers. Radio silence was supposed to be practiced; they weren't supposed to use their radios for anything other than to warn of incoming bandits. But when the flames leaped up between the seats, when their throats were belching blood, when the canopy was jammed and they couldn't get out, couldn't escape the flames and the bullets and the cannon, they did tend to forget standing orders. They did tend to scream.

In the evening, when the day's battle was over, Dowding would have his chauffeur drive him to one or two of the neighboring airfields to talk to his boys, not so much to encourage them as to learn from their lips what was happening up in the fighting skies. Then back he would go to his office in the priory to finish off the day's paperwork. Finally, late at night, exhausted yet needing to be up in a few hours at dawn to be ready for the next day's onslaught, he would be driven back down the hill to his home, Montrose. The car would leave him at the front of that large white house, where two short steps led up to the door that was locked in the old-fashioned way, to be opened by his large brass key. It usually took him a few moments to fit the key in, for there was no light in the blackout. The driver would wait until he found the lock and opened the door, and then would drive away.

These days were terrible, yet the nights were worse. During the day he would concentrate on the battle, would worry about what was happening, would wonder if they could hold out until the autumn. That was bad enough, but at night, inside his quiet house, he would struggle to put away these thoughts of despair, and it was then that the voices of his chicks came back to him. It was then that their faces shone bright and eager—only to be torn away by the horrible flames.

The house would be dark. His wife was dead and his son was a fighter pilot, flying a Spitfire with No. 74 Squadron at Hornchurch, in the heart of the battle. Dowding's sister, Hilda, kept house for him. She would not have left any lights on, so that when he opened the door, there would be no telltale streak of light into the blacked-out night. But one night as he closed the door behind him and for a moment leaned against it, worn out, feeling old, vulnerable, and guilty for being alive when so many were dead, the dark was broken by a soft, diffuse light coming from the parlor.

Walking to it, he saw a small fire burning in the fireplace. Though the days were hot, the summer evenings were often chilly and Hilda must have lit the fire and forgotten about it when she went to bed. He smiled. This would be something to tease her about in the morning. He sat down in front of it, staring hypnotized into the flickering flames, thinking of his fighter pilots, his boys, his chicks. The gayest band of brothers that ever flew into battle.

But that was only because they were so young. At that age of immortality they hadn't the imagination to visualize the hungry flames waiting for them. But *he* knew. He knew they were not immortal; he could see the flames tearing at their scarred and twisted bodies. Oh God, if only they didn't have to die! If only—

What right had he to send these young, healthy boys off to die, to speed those eager heroes up the line to death? Well, he knew the answer to that. It wasn't his right, but his duty. It was an onerous burden that he was too weak to bear; it was breaking him. But he *couldn't* break. His duty was clear. He had to remain strong, he had to send them off to die, he had to save his country. It was God's will. God had saved them at Dunkirk. He had stilled the waters, He had brought the army home, and He would give him the strength to carry his burden. But if only...

He sighed. He wanted to rest the boys, give them some time off, but he hadn't enough Spitfires or pilots to fly them; he needed every one, every day. They were magnificent, sailing in to attack again and again, fighting desperate odds, but how long could they prevail? He stared into the flames and began to float away into a peaceful...

There was a movement in the room, and as he turned, he saw in the dark corner a pilot get awkwardly to attention, obviously flustered. "I must have dozed off, sir. I'm terribly sorry."

"Quite all right," Dowding said. He waited, but the boy seemed bewildered, as if he didn't know where he was. He was still in his flying boots, a white scarf around his neck, so he must have been flying that day and would be off again tomorrow. And yet he could fall asleep on a strange sofa in his commanding officer's house. Dowding thought he would have given a good deal for one night's untroubled deep sleep, for the sleep of the young.

"Is there something I can do for you?" he asked.

"I . . . ," the boy stopped. "I'm afraid I'm confused," he said. "I don't really know why I'm here."

It was probably a mild case of shell shock, Dowding thought sadly. He would take the boy off operations for a few days, if he could. If he could spare him. Oh, dear Lord. How could he spare any of them?

"I mean," the boy began again, and this time his voice began to rise in agitation, "I don't know where I am!"

Dowding leaned forward into the firelight. "Do you know who I am?" he asked gently. He was just a bit surprised that he wasn't surprised at all by the boy's puzzlement, nor by the incipient panic in his voice; he just wanted to calm him down, to help him.

The boy squinted through the dark. "Why, you're Stuffy," he said. "Excuse me, sir. Air Marshal Dowding, sir."

"It's quite all right then, isn't it?"

"But what am I doing here? Did you bring me here, sir?"

"Not to worry," Dowding assured him. "You've fallen asleep, you're exhausted. Just relax and it'll all come back. What's the last thing you remember?"

"We were scrambled this afternoon, just after tea. Paddy was leading, I was flying number three on his wing." He broke off, beginning to shake. "What's going on?"

"What do you mean?"

He sat there, his voice trembling. "Fire," he said. "Someone yelled to break, and there was fire everywhere—how did I get out?" He stared at his hands, holding them up shakily in front of his face. "My hands were on fire. Oh God, my face—"

"It's all right, you don't have to worry," a soft, familiar voice said, and Dowding turned to see a woman in Red Cross uniform coming across the room. He couldn't see her face in the shadows, but he knew that he knew her, and that she would take care of the lad. "We lost you for a moment, but here you are safe and sound," she said. She took the boy's hand, but he pulled it away from her.

"It's burning," he said.

"But you can see it isn't," she replied.

"It *was!*"

"But it isn't now, is it? Everything's quite all right now."

The boy was shaking violently, beginning to call out spasmodically, uncontrollably. The Red Cross nurse turned to Dowding for help, and as she did the fire lit her face and he saw that it was his wife, Clarice. He stood up and went to the boy and put his hand on his shoulder and said, "This is my wife. You can go with her, you can trust her. She'll take care of you."

The boy snapped back to attention. "Yes sir!"

Dowding smiled at him. The boy hesitated for just one second, then he smiled back, and Dowding could see how he must have looked a few years ago when he was in school, a few weeks ago with his mother, a few hours ago with his mates, before he took off in his Hurricane and was shot down in flames.

"Thank you," Clarice said. "He'll be all right now." And she took him by the hand and led him away into the darkness.

Dowding stared after them for some time. Then he put out the fire and, tottering from exhaustion, climbed the narrow wooden stairs to his bed.

twenty-three

THAT WAS the first time he saw Clarice after she died. Soon she became a regular visitor as he helped her guide his dead pilots to their afterlife. In his book, *Lychgate*, Dowding described the next time they met. He had for some time been participating in séances, and this time, he said, "I had been told that I might ask any questions; and so I asked about my own people, whether they were well and happy. After my mother had come and told me of my father, L. L. [his séance 'guide'] said: 'Here is a lady, very quiet, peaceful and dignified.' I said, 'Well, that's not my wife anyway; she was always full of laughter and fun and gaiety.' Shouts of laughter from Clarice who always enjoyed dressing up and acting. She puts on her natural appearance. Astonishment on the part of L. L. 'Why, she has been in my circle for a long time now. I had no idea who she was, or that she had anything to do with you.' To Clarice: 'What have you been doing in my circle all this time?' Clarice: 'Oh, I just came to see if you were a proper person for Hugh to associate with.'"

He went on to explain to his readers that "Clarice is my wife who is a very active member of our group. She died in 1920 . . . but nothing prevents her from manifesting as opportunity arises."

Clarice helped calm him, helped him get through the dark nights of that summer. She brought him assurance that his dead chicks weren't really dead; they had merely passed on to another level of existence. She also assured him that despite the awful bombings, despite the terrible threat of Hitler's planned invasion and all its awful consequences, he had nothing to fear. He would write, "It is only by personal experience that complete conviction [of life after death and of God's love] is possible. I had this personal experience in the Battle of Britain."

He had taken that final step; he had gone round the bend. It was perfectly possible for a man of Dowding's generation to believe in life after death and still be completely sane, for he had the testimony of well-respected scientists in that regard. But it is one thing to believe in the possibility of ghosts, and quite another to actually see them and talk with them.

With all the goodwill in the world for his accomplishments, one has to accept that Dowding was quite mad.

And the war went on.

That night, while Dowding was conversing with Clarice, the Luft-waffe sent bombers to more than a dozen cities in Britain, ranging from Scotland to Wales and Ireland. They did little damage, for they were hard-pressed to even find the cities they were looking for in the blacked-out night, let alone to hit specific targets. They were not a present danger, but their invisibility in the night was a harbinger of horrors to come.

Adlerangriff had been postponed until August 15, but on August 14 the attack was continued against Fighter Command's airfields. The sheer force of numbers overwhelmed the defenders, and although no permanent damage was done, several airfields were ren-dered inactive while dozens of bomb craters were filled in. But only three Hurricanes and one Spitfire were lost, against twenty-one Luftwaffe aircraft.

Preparing for the onslaught to come, Dowding rotated several of the squadrons that had been hardest hit, taking them out of the line to refresh and retrain, and bringing in new squadrons to the forward aerodromes.

For the official start of *Adlerangriff,* Göring prepared a total knockout blow aimed at breaking the back of Fighter Command in one glorious battle. Till now all the fighting had been in the southeastern corner of England, and Göring was convinced—by the small numbers of fighters sent up to combat the raids—that these were all Dowding had left. He was sure that Dowding, like any sensible commander, would by now have called in all his reserves, would have brought in every fighter from all over the island.

This conclusion was reinforced by the results of the reconnaissance flights the Reichsmarschall had sent out on the fourteenth: The amazing thing was not the photos they brought back, but that the planes themselves had come back. Every one of them had come back. This was the first time all summer that none of them had been attacked and shot down by the RAF. Clearly, he assured his flight commanders in a top-level meeting at Karinhall, there were only a few Spitfires left.

He was wrong. His planes had come home because six of the Chain Home radar stations—nearly half the defensive network in that southeast corner of England—had been knocked out by the last few days' raids. They hadn't picked up the reconnaissance planes, and so no interceptions had been made. But to Göring, the safe return of the planes served to confirm his own idea that Fighter Command was down to its last few fighters. If they could be hit again, hard, today, before they had time to rest and repair their damaged Spitfires, it would all be over.

Therefore, Göring smiled, he would attack in the north as well as the south. His bombers based in Scandinavia would fly over the North Sea to strike at the heart of the industrial north. They would have to fly without escorts of Me 109s because of the distance, but no fighters would be needed, since they would encounter no defense. The helplessness of the Royal Air Force would be plain for everyone in England to see. And if that wasn't enough to convince the British to surrender, he would overwhelm their last fighters in the south.

The morning dawned cloudy, with occasional fog. There were no enemy attacks at dawn, or for the next few hours. The Operations Room at Bentley Priory was quiet, the WAAFs and the control officers stood around with nothing to do. Morning tea was brought and sipped quietly. The black markers for enemy aircraft and the red ones for British were not touched. On the airfields the pilots lounged in their garden chairs, sleeping or just snoozing, playing poker or draughts, looking up at the empty sky.

The only planes flying were German weather aircraft, sniffing around to poke at the clouds and the winds. As they came back to the French airfields their data were analyzed and sent in to headquarters, reporting that the weather was bad—but that it was clearing.

The air crews had been briefed for the day's assault, and then had been held at readiness. On bases in France, Belgium, and Holland, the bombers and their fighter escorts were waiting. In Norway and Denmark there were no fighters, but the bombers were ready to go. In a wide semicircle around England they waited for the weather to clear, releasing them to show England that there was to be no respite, there was no hope, there was nothing in the future but complete and utter destruction.

At eleven o'clock in the morning the fog lifted, the clouds parted, the weather cleared.

Minutes later, the first radar blips appeared, showing a massive buildup of enemy formations over the French coast. Standing orders for the Sector Controllers were to wait until they knew exactly where the raids were going and then to scramble as few fighters as possible. But today the formations were growing so large, and with every minute another one appeared, that it was impossible to count them or to determine where they were going. The entire air seemed to be filled with so many Stukas and Messerschmitts, Junkers and Dorniers and Heinkels, that the Controllers lost control. They began to order every available fighter into the air with orders to attack whatever they saw. And what they saw were hordes of bombers attacking their aerodromes, surrounded by clouds of Messerschmitts. The fighter pilots stared at them, like African natives staring in horror at an incoming cloud of locusts. For one long moment they were transfixed, and then they dove in to the attack. Six Spits attacking thirty-six Me's, seven Hurris plunging through to a hundred bombers.

Meanwhile, lumbering over the North Sea, the bombers from Norway and Denmark plowed on. Göring had managed to give them a phony escort of Me 110s. These were twin-engine fighters that had been withdrawn from the south because they had turned out to be helpless against the Spitfires and Hurricanes. They were here today to provide emotional support, to give the appearance of an escort. Nothing more would be needed, Göring was sure.

This would be the first day of action in the north of England, and the last. The "undefended" north, to Göring's complete surprise, was bristling with fighters.

On the bombers flew, across the North Sea waters and into the waiting arms of Fighter Command.

In Newcastle, the 13 Group Controller couldn't believe his eyes when the blips appeared on the radar screens. Dowding had kept the Group intact, had not sent them down south to join the fighting, waiting for just this to happen. The Group Controller almost laughed out loud. Old Stuffy knew what he was doing. The Controller gave the orders, scrambling No. 72 Squadron from Acklington, with No. 79 Squadron placed on readiness in reserve. He scrambled 605 Squadron from Drem. Then No. 49 Squadron roared into the air from Catterick, and as the blips grew in number, No. 79 Squadron was sent after them.

No. 72 Squadron caught them first. Eleven Spitfires came around a cloud and ran head-on into more than one hundred bombers and Me 110s. A few minutes later, five Hurricanes from 605 Squadron found them, and then Nos. 41 and 79 Squadrons joined in. The Messerschmitt 110s were no match for the Spits and Hurris; the bombers they were supposed to protect began to fall flaming from the skies, while not a single British fighter was lost. The Scandinavian bomber squadrons were wiped out; aside from small sorties, they would never again attack.

Churchill sent Dowding a telegram of congratulations, acknowledging that those critics were wrong—and they were many, in the Air Staff and Ministry, who had railed against the fighters' being kept in the north while the fighting was concentrated in the south. In his later writings, the Prime Minister was effusive in his praise of Dowding: "We must regard the generalship here shown as an example of genius in the face of war."

To the Scandinavian Luftwaffe bomber groups, August 15 became known not as *Adlerangriff,* but as Black Thursday.

But in the south, where the Messerschmitt 109s were shepherding the bombers, things were not quite as easy. The morning raids were beaten back with heavy losses to both sides and with great destruction rained on Fighter Command's airfields. A quiet spell followed as the bombers went home, and then, just after two o'clock, the Kent and Essex radars reported new buildups along a wide front. With the fighters still rearming and refueling, the Controllers waited, thinking they'd still have time to scramble before the slow bombers could attack. But then suddenly a fast, low-flying squadron of 110s burst over Martlesham. They were no good as fighters, but these were carrying bombs. Three Hurricanes got off the ground, but the 110s escaped without loss after destroying the airfield.

Upward of two hundred bombers and fighters came in headed for Deal, and radar picked up another group coming in over Kent. Forty fighters were scrambled from Biggin Hill and split up, headed for the two groups. The radar couldn't differentiate between bombers and fighters, and the second group turned out to consist only of fighters, more than sixty of them. They drew half the defenders, and the bombers got through. Eastchurch and Rochester were wiped out.

Another raid of more than a hundred bombers hit the fighter airfields at Middle Wallop, Worthy Down, and Andover. Portland was bombed by another hundred-plus raid, and two final raids headed for the heart of the defense: the Sector Control airfields at Kenley and Biggin Hill. In both cases, the sheer number of the attackers swamped the defense and the bombers lumbered in and dropped their bombs—luckily (or, as Dowding thought, by the intervention of God) on the wrong targets. The Kenley bombers hit the smaller airfield at Croydon, and the Biggin Hill bombers hit the unused field at West Malling.

Finally the sun began to set, the day drew to an end. Göring had mounted the largest aerial attack in history, with more than two thousand German sorties blackening the skies. They had been hard hit, they had met more resistance than he had expected, but he reported to Hitler that they had done their job, they had finished off the RAF. The twelve most important airfields of Fighter Command had been destroyed, together with ninety-nine fighters in the air and uncounted numbers on the ground.

In London the mood was just as ecstatic. The newspaper headlines showed a gigantic victory for England. Hitler had done his worst, and the result was that 182 German planes had been knocked down.

At Bentley Priory, Dowding knew better. He was well aware, as Göring should have been, that with the skies full of airplanes the counting was not likely to be accurate. Fighter pilots were an ebullient bunch, prone to believe that anything they shot at was doomed. And with all those planes shooting at each other there were bound to be cases in which two or even three shot at the same target without seeing their comrades, so that one downed plane would be claimed by all of them. Dowding had more sense than Göring, more patience, and one important advantage: The planes all fell on English soil, so he would get an accurate assessment when the wrecks were counted.

The Home Guard spread out over the land and found 75 German wrecks, not 182, and 34 British fighters, not 99. It was an impressive victory for Dowding in the air, but the damage to his airfields was worrying. So too were the losses of his pilots. The factories were replacing his fighters as quickly as they were shot down, but it took time to train a pilot, and more time to give him the experience to fight. He prayed that God would grant him the time.

twenty-four

AUGUST 15 may have been Black Thursday to the German bomber groups based in Scandinavia, but it was Bewildering Thursday in Nottingham, where Leigh-Mallory's No. 12 Group sat out the action. He and his staff sat there in their control room listening to the radio chatter as plane after plane from both 11 Group to the south of them and 13 Group to the north were scrambled. They saw the markers placed on the map table; they saw the table growing black with the markers, with so many markers signaling so many raids that it seemed the table must collapse under their weight just as England must collapse under the weight of the bombs being dropped—and still they were not called.

For the past month and more, Leigh-Mallory had grumbled and cursed as 11 Group's fighters were scrambled and his were held in reserve, but now to his amazement even 13 Group was brought into the fighting! Bombers to the right of him, bombers to the left of him, and here he sat twiddling his thumbs, biting his lips, cursing Park and Dowding. His Spitfires waited silently on the grass, the only sound the occasional roar as the erks kept the engines warmed, waiting for the call that never came.

At Coltishall aerodrome Douglas Bader waited with 242 Squadron. He had built them up again into a military weapon; he had brought them from a group of despondent whiners into a fighting unit, and now they wanted to fight. Bader stood looking out the window of the readiness hut, seeing nothing but a hot sun in an empty sky. Where were the Germans?

They were hitting the southern aerodromes, and Bader's planes and all those of No. 12 Group were being held in readiness, waiting to see if 11 Group needed help. And they were being cleared out of the sky to the north by 13 Group. One raid of more than forty Ju 88s flew from Denmark toward 12 Group's territory, but their path as plotted by radar led to two possible targets: the industrial north or a convoy off the eastern coast. No. 12 Group was ordered to scramble one squadron to guard the convoy, but the bombers swerved north, bringing them closer to 13 Group, which intercepted and wiped them out.

The convoy was not attacked, and that was the closest 12 Group came to action that day.

In a more perfect world, things would be, well, more perfect. No. 13 Group had beaten off the attacks by the Scandinavian bombers, had decimated them, but hadn't shot *all* of them down. They should have brought in more fighters to complete the massacre by calling on 12 Group. But this was 13 Group's first action, the radar system wasn't perfect, and the Controllers hadn't analyzed the data perfectly. Following their standing orders, they scrambled 13 Group's fighters and held 12 Group in reserve, in case more raids followed. By the time the first fighters made contact and radioed back how many there were, it was too late to call in 12 Group.

To the south the story was the same, but different. The 11 Group Controllers there had lots of experience dealing with incoming raids, but today they were swamped by the thousands of enemy sorties. In effect, they lost control. Afterward, analyzing the day's actions, they realized they should have scrambled some of the 12 Group squadrons to guard 11 Group's aerodromes that had been left undefended, but there were so many planes in the air that the Controllers simply couldn't keep track of them all, and they failed to do so.

If there is one criticism that can be made of Dowding's handling of the battle, it would be this: He should have realized the frustration of an ambitious commander and fresh, eager troops surrounded on both sides by combat, ignored as the battle raged on. But his style of command was to pick the best people he could, and then trust them to behave as they should. The style worked perfectly for Park in 11 Group, Saul in 13 Group, and Brand in 10 Group. It did not work for Leigh-Mallory and 12 Group. Trouble was brewing.

The trouble took two directions. The first was the irritation of Leigh-Mallory and his pilots about being left out of the action. This was partly due to Dowding's strategy of not committing all his forces, so that Göring should never know what strength Fighter Command had. This was a brilliant strategy, requiring almost superhuman restraint, but it had one flaw: 12 Group was to be held in readiness unless called in by 11 Group, but the 11 Group Controllers either faced small raids, in which case they didn't need backup, or faced large raids, in which case they usually became overwhelmed and were too busy trying to take charge of their own Group to bring in anyone else. Either way, 12 Group was left out of the action.

The second direction the trouble led to followed from the first. Frustrated by Dowding's policy and the dilatoriness of 11 Group, it was probably natural for Leigh-Mallory's pilots to begin to question the overall strategy. Douglas Bader, in particular, disagreed strongly with Dowding's decision to face large raids with small numbers of fighters. It was clear to him that this was no way to fight a war, indicating nothing but a pusillanimous commander in chief. The way to win the war, he argued loudly both to his pilots and to Leigh-Mallory, was to attack the bastards in force. This not only would have the advantage of hitting them with superior numbers, but would also mean that 12 Group would be involved in the fighting right from the start instead of waiting till 11 Group needed them.

His message was received loud and clear by his pilots, who were straining at the leash. This was understandable, even laudable, for you want your troops to want to get into the fight. But as commander of the Group, superior in chain of command to Bader and inferior to Dowding, Leigh-Mallory should have restrained Bader while commending him for his fighting spirit. Instead, he set him loose, and this was unforgivable. He told him that whenever he was asked for help by 11 Group he should respond in any way he wished.

The opportunity came on August 10, when a fleet of bombers attacked the Boulton Paul factory in Norwich. Since the closest aerodrome was Coltishall, where Bader was based, he was called on to defend the factory. Instead of quickly dispatching a three-plane flight to break up the attack, he had his airplanes circle the airfield to form up in a full squadron. Unfortunately, the radar didn't work perfectly, possibly due to several scattered thunderstorms that reflected the radar beams, and several false directions were given. By the time Bader's squadron arrived over the factory, they found it cratered and burning and the bombers long gone.

Ignoring the slow takeoff and formation time of the squadron, Bader reported to Leigh-Mallory that all the Group needed was quicker and better radar information. Give him that, and he would destroy the enemy. He had the man-of-action's lofty disdain for mere technical details and didn't bother to consider that the state of the radar art was what it was, not what he would like it to be. He also had the man-of-action's imperial disdain for obfuscating qualifications: To his mind, simple problems demanded simple solutions. He had a squadron of highly trained fighter pilots, and if he could hit the enemy with his entire squadron at one go, he could destroy them.

But the problem was not simple, and there were no simple solutions. The problem was complex, involving not so much destroying the enemy as keeping the enemy from destroying them. And even if you ignored that part of the problem, the simple premise of hitting the enemy with an entire squadron depended on much better radar warning, which was just not possible.

But it fit in well with Leigh-Mallory's anger at how he was being subordinated to Park. The simplicity of Bader's plan seemed all too plain to Leigh-Mallory's eyes. He loved it. He told Bader to ignore any orders emanating from 11 Group or even from Fighter Command headquarters. Just damn the torpedoes and full speed ahead!

Dowding should have intervened. He should have come down hard on Leigh-Mallory and insisted he in turn come down hard on Bader. He should have taken a firm hand, as he had after the air defense exercises in 1939. When Leigh-Mallory had tried to insist on his right to override Command orders, Dowding had told him, in front of other senior officers: "The trouble with you, Leigh-Mallory, is that sometimes you cannot see further than the end of your little nose."

But he didn't realize the extent of the problem. How could he? The man was only human. He was spending all day, every day, in Bentley Priory monitoring the battle, and every evening he went to visit the pilots who were bearing the brunt of the fighting. This did not include 12 Group's pilots, but he didn't have time for everyone; he wanted to talk to those most involved, the 11 Group men at Kenley, Biggin Hill, Tangmere. He would return to Montrose in the dead of night, often after midnight, and be up at dawn. He had only those few hours between to think, and what he thought about was the danger for England and the deaths awaiting those who fought in the skies, and what God had in store.

Churchill often invited his top commanders to dine with him at Chequers, to review the day's actions and to talk of the future. John Colville reported that "one night at Chequers [Dowding] told us that the battle was going well. The only things that worried him were his dreams. The previous night he had dreamed there was only one man in England capable of operating a Bofors gun and his name was William Shakespeare. We supposed we were intended to laugh, but I looked at Dowding's face and was sure he was speaking in deadly earnest."

He took his dreams as real warnings from the beyond and wasn't sure what they meant. With all this, he had no time for Leigh-Mallory's little fussings.

twenty-five

THE ATTACKS continued without letup. Although the Luftwaffe had lost nearly a hundred planes on the first day of *Adlerangriff,* they had plenty more. The first raid on August 16 came in just before eleven o'clock, hitting the West Malling aerodrome while workers were still clearing the rubble and filling in craters from yesterday's raid. The last raid of the day came just after five o'clock, aiming for Biggin Hill. This one was beaten off, but in between, hundreds of bombers roared all over 11 Group's area. The Hornchurch aerodrome was well defended, but Tangmere was demolished. The Ventnor radar station was put out of action, despite Göring's decision that the radar stations weren't worth the effort of destroying them; with so many bombers, the Luftwaffe was able to spare enough to hit low-priority targets.

It was on this day, the second day of *Adlerangriff,* the sixteenth day of August, that Billy Fiske attacked a *Staffel* of Stukas.

Billy was the son of a Chicago banker, an American golden boy who led the charmed life of young Americans born into the aristocracy of wealth in the early twentieth century. He grew up as much at home in the pleasure palaces of Europe as in America; he was bright, clever, witty, handsome, and athletic, and everyone loved him. In 1928, at the age of sixteen, he was already the champion bobsledder at Saint Moritz and was chosen to lead the American team in the Winter Olympics at Lake Placid in 1932. When the team won the gold, he became the youngest gold-medal winner ever in that sport.

He began college at Cambridge University that same year and was immediately and for the next ten years one of the leaders of the set known as the Bright Young Things, playing golf, partying and dancing, driving the convertible Bentley his father had bought him, learning to fly, and finally marrying the former Countess of Warwick. He also put in a spot of work in the London office of a New York banking firm. Then, in the spring of 1939, life became serious: His firm gave him the choice of continuing his party life or coming back to New York and getting serious about banking. With a sigh, he decided that it was time to give up childish things, and he sailed home.

A few months later Hitler invaded Poland, Britain declared war, and Billy Fiske decided that banking was too dull after all.

The Royal Air Force was then made up of three distinct groups: the regular air force, composed of—as it was said—pilots who wished to be gentlemen; the part-time Auxiliary, composed of gentlemen who wished to be pilots; and the working-class Reserve, composed of those who were neither and wished to be both. In 1924 Lord Edward Grosvenor had gathered those members of his club, White's of St James's, who had learned to fly and formed the 601 (County of London) Auxiliary Air Force Squadron, henceforth known affectionately (or enviously) as the Millionaires Squadron. A number of Billy's friends had joined, and now he sailed back to England on the *Aquitania* to join them.

Despite being an American citizen, he was accepted into the RAF. After passing the Elementary Flying Training School, he moved on to the advanced Flying Training School at Brize Norton, and on July 12 he was granted his wish and assigned to 601 Squadron, which was part of 11 Group, based at Tangmere.

His welcome there was not as enthusiastic as he had hoped. The members of the squadron were by now experienced Hurricane pilots, and despite his training, Billy wasn't ready to fly combat. But the fighting hadn't yet heated up, and they were able to keep him out of it for the next two weeks while he trained hard. By the end of the month, he began to fly operational patrols, although he was told to stick to his leader and keep his head down, and in another couple of weeks, he felt himself an old hand. Today, August 16, when the Klaxon sounded at Tangmere, he was ready.

"Buzzard scramble! Buzzard scramble!"

Forty-three seconds of confusion, chaos, and pandemonium erupted on the aerodrome. Cards went flying through the air, tables were overturned, and Billy ran with the other pilots out of the dispersal hut. Grass and dirt and chalk were kicked into the air as the erks hit the starter buttons and the propellers spun into life, black fumes spread through the air as the exhaust pipes coughed and sputtered, and on the forty-fourth second eight Hurricanes of Buzzard Squadron were taxiing into position and racing down the grass, lifting into the air, folding their wheels into their wings, and slipping off away from the aerodrome. As the second hand ticked around the clock to begin the second minute, the sounds of chaos died away and the black specks disappeared into the bright blue sky.

"Buzzard Leader."

"Buzzard Control. Vector 190," the radio responded. "Twelve bandits angels twelve just a few miles in front of you. Do you see them?"

"Hello, Buzzard Control. Sighting negative. Listening out."

Billy listened on the radiotelephone, but said nothing; it wasn't his place to talk. Instead he searched the skies ahead of them, and watched his squadron leader lead them up to fifteen thousand feet. They should have seen the enemy formation by now, but there was nothing in sight. The sun was high in the sky, on his eleven o'clock, and he wondered about the possibility of a passel of Messerschmitts hiding up there, ready to pounce.

"Buzzard Leader, this is Buzzard Control, are you reading?"

"Buzzard Leader, roger."

"Vector 050. We have you behind them now."

The leader's wings dipped and turned, and the others followed him around in a wide curve to port. "There's fuck all up here, laddie," he called in.

"You should be right behind them now," Control called in.

"I should be back in me bed, right enough," the leader answered.

And then there was silence, silence, as the Hurricanes cut through the thin air and young eyes scanned the skies—

"Tally-ho! Bandits at two o'clock low!"

There they were, coming out of the haze three thousand feet below them, a formation of Stukas cruising along without a care in the world. The squadron leader didn't like this: Stukas never came alone. There should be Messerschmitts about. He looked up, squinting into the sun. Up there, hidden in the glare . . .

But the Stukas were headed for Tangmere, for his aerodrome, and he couldn't hesitate any longer. "Keep an eye open, laddies," he warned, and his exhaust belched a purple puff as he shoved the throttle into the wall, and every one of his mates followed suit, diving down onto their prey.

Billy picked out one for himself and followed it down as he peeled off, aiming his sight at the rear gunner, centering right on the flash of the gun spitting at him—

"Break! Break! Messerschmitts—"

There was a flash of black wings and a rainfall of red tracer bullets simultaneous with the warning, and as Billy broke left, his plane shuddered and his canopy shattered, and the control panel in front of his face splintered into fragments. Instinctively he pushed his nose down and spun out of there.

Luckily no one followed him, and even more luckily, when he moved the controls, they responded. As he pulled out over the trees he was alone. The controls were sloppy but they worked. His face felt warm and sticky, and his right hand was covered in blood, but nothing hurt, he felt nothing. He steered back toward the aerodrome.

It was only a few minutes away, but by the time he reached it he was feeling a whole lot worse. He had to fight to keep his eyes open. He could see the Stukas flashing overhead, he could see bomb splashes and black smoke on the aerodrome, but he had no choice. He had to go in.

He came in high and fast, then sideslipped at the last minute to lose height and speed. With his windscreen covered in oil, he had to lean out to see where he was going. As he did, a bomb erupted on the grass right in front of him. He swerved away, thought for a moment of going around again—that would be doing it by the book, but the guy who wrote the book wasn't bleeding to death. He lowered his wheels and dropped down between the jagged craters, trying to steer around them but as his tail wheel touched the ground, his nose came up and he couldn't see where he was going.

He didn't care. He was down, safe on the ground, that was all he knew as his eyes closed and his head fell forward and all the noise faded away.

The ground crews watching from their slit trenches saw his Hurricane roll to a stop, and then it sat there. They looked at each other. They could see the pilot in the cockpit, but he wasn't moving and the bombs were still falling. They saw four black-crossed Messerschmitts swoop over the Hurricane, saw the splatter of their bullets as they rocked it, saw the pilot disappear into a sudden roaring cascade of flames.

They jumped up from their trenches, ran through the bullets and bombs, climbed onto the burning wings, and reached with their bare hands into the flaming oil that filled the cockpit and was scorching the face of Billy Fiske. They lifted him burning and smoking out of hell and down onto the grass, they flung themselves on him to put out the flames, they lifted him onto their shoulders and half-ran, half-stumbled back across the dangerous open grass through the shrapnel and bombs and the splattering of bullets, and fell back with him into their slit trench.

When the raid was over, an ambulance rushed him to hospital, where he died the next day, never regaining consciousness. He was the golden boy, the *beau vivant,* the Olympic champion, the envy and idol of all who knew him, the epitome of the times.

He was the first American to die in combat in World War II.

The Luftwaffe lost more than fifty airplanes that day; the RAF nearly forty. But contrary to what Göring thought, the loss of airplanes was not serious for Dowding, since the factories were putting out more every day than were lost. The real problems were the damage to the aerodromes and the supporting structures, the radar stations, and the pilots. Without radar, Dowding would be lost. Without the aerodromes in operating conditions, his planes couldn't fly. And without pilots . . . well, of course, he did have his angels.

Not really. This is one of the fallacies that have grown up around Dowding. In his book *Angels,* Billy Graham writes that when he wanted to preach a sermon on angels, he found that almost nothing had been written on the subject in this century. Then he discovered the book *Tell No Man,* by Adela Rogers St. John. As Billy Graham describes the scene recounted there: "A celebration [was] held some months after the war, honoring Air Chief Marshal Lord Hugh Dowding. The King, the Prime Minister and scores of dignitaries were there . . . the Air Chief Marshal recounted the story of his legendary conflict where his pitifully small complement of men rarely slept, and their planes never stopped flying. He told about airmen on a mission who, having been hit, were either incapacitated or dead. Yet their planes kept flying and fighting... [with] a figure still operating the controls. What was the explanation? The Air Chief Marshal said he believed angels had actually flown some of the planes whose pilots sat dead in their cockpits."

What Graham doesn't say, or perhaps didn't realize, was that the book he quotes is a novel. It's fiction. It's made up. What Rogers St. John actually has her made-up character say is this: "Some months after the war, I was at a banquet honoring Air Chief Marshal Lord Hugh Dowding... as the cheers kept rocketing, he held up his hand, they lifted him up onto the table and you never heard such quiet.... [This was] the man who planned every move of the strategy of that flying show that saved England when she stood alone to save a free world.... He told us that night that angels had flown the planes for pilots already dead. When they came down the crew told him their pilot had been hit by the first burst, but the plane kept on flying and fighting, and sometimes they saw a figure at the controls."

If either Rogers St. John or Billy Graham had understood anything about the battle they would have realized that the British fighters were single-seaters: There wasn't any crew, there wasn't anyone except the pilot, there wasn't anyone who could have seen the pilot dead and another figure at the controls. The whole story was just made up by the novelist, but now millions of people have Billy Graham's word that the world was saved by angels. He ended his sermon by quoting again from Rogers St. John's novel: "There just wasn't any other way to explain how the RAF, outnumbered by planes so much better and outgunned 100 to 1, how they won the Battle of Britain—even now, with hindsight and information, nobody can figure that one."

Well, we can figure it. The German planes weren't better; there was nothing better than the Spitfire. And although the Brits were outnumbered, it was nothing like 100 to 1; it was more like 3 to 2. Finally, above all, the British won because they had radar and the proper organization to back it up. *That* was Dowding's contribution, not his angels.

He didn't need angels; he needed pilots. A Spitfire that rolled out of the factory was immediately as good as, or even better than, the lost one it replaced, but a new pilot was little better than fodder for the Messerschmitts' cannon until he learned to fly the Spit as if he were part of it, and this was not easy to do. A modern fighter was a high-spirited airplane, and a dogfight was a contest of twisting, gut-wrenching aerobatics. Learning to throw these beasts around in the air, taking them to the extreme that their structures could bear without going an inch past it, took long training. America's first ace in the war, Buzz Wagner, and our top-scoring ace, Dick Bong, both lost their lives in training accidents after their fighting was done, learning to fly new fighters.

Dowding was back in the nightmare of his past. In the First World War, he had railed against his chief's orders to send his fledgling pilots up to fight, arguing passionately that they needed more experience, that they would just go up to be killed. Now it was the same, only more so; now he was the chief, and he had no choice but to send them up.

Because every day the Luftwaffe came back. Every day the radar would report massive formations building up over France, heading out over the Channel, coming in to bomb Dowding's airports and his radar stations. On Saturday and Sunday, August 17 and 18, the bombers returned. Inexorably they blackened the skies, and the radar shacks exploded and the aerodromes were ruined with craters and the hangars were burned down, and the wrecks of Spitfires and Hurricanes littered the runways and the countryside.

Every day more Spitfires came out of the factories, and new pilots, trained barely enough to take off and land, came out of Training Command to fly them. Every day they clambered into the air to defend the land, following the directions of the remaining radar stations, small penny-packets of fighters diving out of the sun to attack the intruders. Somehow those "last few Spitfires" kept clawing at the Messerschmitts and dropping the Dorniers from the bright, sunlit sky.

At noon on the eighteenth, twelve Spits were scrambled to attack three hundred enemy aircraft over Kent. At one o'clock, Biggin Hill was attacked, and at the same time fifty bombers hit Kenley high up. Meanwhile, another German squadron zoomed in low, strewing bombs across the aerodrome, cutting all communications, leaving this important sector station in such ruins that ambulances blocked every access road. It was useless for the next three days.

At two o'clock a massive raid came in to the east. Fighter Command responded by protecting its airfields there, but the bombers went for the Poling radar station and knocked it out of action for a week. An hour later, a formation of Me 109s swept in over Manston and destroyed more aircraft on the ground before they had a chance to take off. In the early evening, five more raids hit Kent, dropping their bombs throughout a wide area.

At the end of the day, the Luftwaffe had lost nearly a hundred planes, but the British had lost fifty. More importantly, the RAF had lost more than twenty irreplaceable pilots dead or in hospital, lost one of their prime radar stations, and suffered severe damage to several aerodromes. The straws were piling high, and the camel's back was breaking.

On Monday, August 19, it rained.

The aerodromes were quiet. The pilots slept. Exhausted, worn out, finally they had a day of rest. The WAAFs deep underground in the Operations Rooms couldn't hear the rain, but they could hear the quiet in their earphones, the lovely, calming quiet.

The mechanics had time to tune their engines. The craters that maimed the airfields were filled in. The bullet holes were repaired. Dowding had time to review the situation.

It was not a pleasant situation. Close to two hundred Luftwaffe planes had been shot down in the last four days, but although the German losses far outstripped those of the British, Fighter Command ended up even worse off. Dowding had lost the use of most of his frontline airfields, many of his most experienced pilots, and several of his all-important radar stations. By Göring's orders, the radar stations were low-priority targets, but they had been constructed in such a rushed and harried manner that little effort had been put into camouflaging or protecting them. It had been all Dowding could do to get them ready in time; now he bitterly regretted the time wasted arguing with the Air Ministry over their necessity, the time and money wasted on Lindemann's silly schemes, simply to pacify Churchill.

But he threw such thoughts behind him. One of the comforts of not having enough time to do what is necessary is that one doesn't waste time on unprofitable regrets. As Dr. Johnson noted, the imminence of death concentrates the mind wonderfully. So what was it that he could do?

Getting together with Keith Park, he emphasized that they must reorganize in line with his original plans. In particular, No. 12 Group had been wasted in the preceding weeks. That afternoon, Park issued a new directive to his Controllers: "If all our squadrons around London are off the ground engaging enemy mass attacks, ask No. 12 Group or Command Controller to provide squadrons to patrol [our] aerodromes."

Dowding made sure that the message was passed on to Leigh-Mallory, who immediately informed all his squadron commanders to be ready, they were finally about to be called into the fight. Douglas Bader told him in turn that when he was called on by 11 Group, he wasn't going to send off two or three of his men to combat twenty or thirty Messerschmitts. He would take his whole squadron with him.

All he needed was sufficient warning, and then they'd see what a massed force could do.

Leigh-Mallory didn't remind him that so far it hadn't worked, that there wasn't sufficient warning time. To him, as to Bader, it was simply up to 11 Group to give them enough time. Simple problems demand simple solutions—to a simple mind.

For the moment, though, all was quiet, damp with rain. All problems were hidden by the lovely clouds that finally came to hide the cruel sun of that bright summer. From Monday through Friday, August 19 through 24, each day dawned darkly; each day the worn-out pilots opened one eye and looked lovingly at the drizzle, then closed it, rolled over, and went back to sleep.

Occasionally the sun broke through over England, and a few bombers would slip through the clouds and drop a few bombs, but hardly anyone noticed. In Germany the mood was not quite so sanguine, as Göring summoned his group leaders and lambasted them furiously. Why had Fighter Command not yet been destroyed? He called them cowards and incompetents and fired half of them. He promoted a group of young Turks, fighter pilots who had distinguished themselves in the action, to take their place. Chief among these was a heavily moustached veteran of the Spanish Civil War, Adolf Galland, who became the youngest general in the German armed forces. Göring set them loose, telling them to choose their own targets, bomb whatever they liked—except for London. Hitler reserved the right to make that decision himself.

It was hard to understand Hitler. At the beginning of the war, the British had feared that London would be the first target, the "fat cow," in Churchill's phrase, sitting there helplessly to "attract birds of prey." London's children had been evacuated to the country to avoid the bombs, which didn't fall. Day after day, the bombers came, but they came to the coastal towns and the aerodromes, to Birmingham and Coventry, to villages such as Brize Norton and Harwell, to Rochester and Church Fenton. Not a solitary bomb was dropped on London, and no one understood why.

It was said that Hitler had a respect for great cities, due to his architectural background, or that he still hoped England would surrender and didn't want to stir up animosity by bombing their capital, but neither of these makes sense. To be sure, nothing about a sociopath makes sense if one looks at him as at a sane man. For whatever reason, London remained inviolate, safe.

Every morning, Göring looked out the window, cursing the clouds, reading the weather reports and throwing them to the floor. He had promised Hitler victory over Fighter Command within a few days, and now the days were stretching out to weeks. Further delays were unthinkable, for the autumn was fast approaching. Where was the *verdammte* sun? What was keeping it hidden?

At Bentley Priory, Dowding knew the answer. God was holding the sun in His hands, granting Fighter Command the respite it needed. He had prayed for radar, he had worked to provide modern fighters and concrete airfields and underground phone lines, but all that, in the end, was nothing without the benevolence and active, personal intervention of God. "I pay my homage to those dear boys, those gallant boys, who gave their all that our nation might live," he would later write. "I pay my tribute to their leaders and commanders; but I say with absolute conviction that, but for God's intervention, the Battle of Britain would have been lost."

On Saturday, August 24, God evidently decided enough was enough. The sun came out again.

twenty-six

THE SUN came out, and so did the Luftwaffe. They came swarming out of France like angry hornets whose hive has been attacked. At 8:30 in the morning a hundred bombers and fighters hit Dover, which was not a particularly important target. The reason became clear at ten o'clock, when the bombers turned for home. At that point, a new group of German fighters swept in, hoping to catch the exhausted defenders low on fuel and ammunition. The radar operators were alert, however, and the defenders retired, leaving the Me's wandering over the English countryside free and sassy, but impotent.

The raids resumed shortly after lunch, this time in earnest. Every one of 11 Group's airfields was attacked. Some of the raids were beaten off, but Tangmere, Hornchurch, and Manston were devastated. Every squadron of 11 Group was engaged, and radar picked up still more bombers. In accord with Park's instructions, the Controllers called on 12 Group to protect the North Weald aerodrome, and three minutes later, Bader's 242 Squadron was scrambling. But instead of racing off to North Weald, the first Hurricanes to be airborne turned and circled around, following Bader's orders, while the next section took off. And then both sections circled again while the third section took off.

By the time the entire squadron was scrambled it was too late. They arrived over North Weald to find the skies empty except for a black cloud slowly rising, twisting in the wind, blanketing the burning aerodrome. Bader called the Controllers for instructions: Where were the bloody Huns?

They were gone, sailing safely home, leaving behind battered and burning airfields at Hornchurch and Hawkinge, at Manston and Croydon, at Tangmere and Middle Wallop, at all the fighter airfields ringing London. They left Fighter Command battered and bruised, teetering on its last legs. Another few weeks of such attacks, Dowding realized, and Göring would be right: The invasion could take place unimpeded.

And then the Lord God intervened once again, in a *very* mysterious way. His wonders to perform. That night, the Germans bombed London.

For the moment, nobody understood the significance of that act. Not even Dowding realized that it contained the seeds of England's deliverance and his personal downfall. At the very beginning of the war, London was assumed to be the main target of any enemy. But then, as month followed month and no bombs dropped, it seemed that London was the safest place to be. The evacuees drifted back, and life settled down again.

So now, when the bombs finally fell, the only surprise was that it had taken so long. Nobody understood that the Luftwaffe had just made the biggest mistake of the war, for at the moment nothing of much significance seemed to have happened, and, indeed, the next day the war continued as before.

The airfields at Manston and Warmwell were attacked by three hundred bombers, and although most of them were beaten off, a few scattered bombs fell, by chance severing the telephone lines to both airfields and severely disrupting the incoming radar information. As soon as these raids retired, another hundred came barreling in and the bombs continued to fall.

Day after day they fell, and one by one Dowding's airfields went out of action. Yet as each raid came over, somehow a few more Spitfires rose to meet it, and as each day passed, the date for invasion loomed closer and closer while still remaining indefinably away. Hitler, in consultation with Admiral Erich Raeder, Göring, and their combined meteorological staffs, had scheduled it for September 15 to take advantage of the unusual combination of high tides, calm waters, and a full moon. With the onset of *Adlerangriff,* Göring had promised that not only would the waters be calm by then, but the skies would be free of RAF fighters. But as August turned into September, those "last few Spitfires" somehow continued to appear.

Sometimes they appeared too late, and these instances gave Göring the impression that he was nearly at his goal. But he didn't know what was really going on; he didn't understand the ongoing contretemps between Park and Leigh-Mallory.

Every one of 11 Group's squadrons was scrambled every day, and there wasn't a single day when all their planes returned to base. They came back to the ground smoking and skidding along farmers' meadows or crashing in flames or spinning down with a dead pilot fallen over the controls; they fell into the sea and into country villages and into the streets of Birmingham and Portland. And the next day, each squadron would be able to send up only a dozen planes instead of eighteen, and then only ten planes, eight planes, a half dozen . . .

No. 11 Group could no longer defend their own bases, but when they called on 12 Group for help they got something less than what was needed. Hornchurch and North Weald were attacked again, and again the call went to Bader. But while he was circling over his own base to the northeast, gathering up his forces, Hornchurch and North Weald were destroyed. On the following days, when more bombers came in toward Debden, they called on 12 Group again, and again the large force came too late; Debden was devastated.

Bader argued angrily to Leigh-Mallory that he could do the job if only he were given a decent warning. Leigh-Mallory didn't tell him that no one could give him that warning in time, the radar-communications network was doing all it could, and that's all there was. It took about four minutes for the radar warning to reach the squadron and only six minutes for the Luftwaffe bombers to cross the Channel and approach their targets. But Leigh-Mallory ignored this fact of life and told Bader he was right, to go on doing what he could.

At the end of August, a raid came in against Biggin Hill while all of 11 Group's fighters were already in action against other raids. Again 12 Group failed to respond in time, and while the ground crews were trying to clear the damage, another raid swept in and destroyed the gas and water mains, the electric cables, hangars, depots, and workshops. As the battle raged to a climax, Biggin Hill, the most important of Dowding's airfields, was out of action.

Another raid went at North Weald again, and once more Bader took his squadron around in circles, forming up into strength. As they did, he was thinking how best to organize his attack. But this was the classic mistake: If each squadron leader organized his own attack, Dowding's system was useless. Bader never did realize this. Instead, he was thinking that since it was late afternoon, if the Jerries had any sense they'd circle around and come in from the west, with the sun at their backs.

The Sector Controller, analyzing the radar data, steered him from the ground onto Vector 190, taking them almost due south from their base at Coltishall. Bader ignored him, wheeling his Group out on Vector 260, bringing them around to the west, trying to get up-sun of where he *knew* the Jerries would be.

The Controller told him to maintain fifteen thousand feet altitude. But Bader was always aware of "the Hun in the sun," and he didn't want to be looking up into the glare above to find the enemy. He soared up to twenty thousand feet, where he waited, circling patiently, twenty miles west and five thousand feet above where the Controller had sent him.

And this time he was right. A group of thirty Heinkels with Me 110 escorts, maybe fifty or sixty in all, came in below him. He had positioned his squadron perfectly, and he wheeled over and took his lads down onto the enemy.

It was just as he had always proclaimed. His fighters didn't quite reach them before they dropped their bombs, but they massacred them as they fled, claiming twelve aircraft shot down without loss. "In a few lethal moments all Bader's long-held beliefs had been confirmed," his biographer would later write.

But were they? The enemy attack had wiped out another of Dowding's precious airfields. Bader's argument was that, despite this successful attack, the Luftwaffe couldn't accept such high losses and would soon have to back off. It would have been a good argument—if he had actually shot down twelve of the bombers. But Luftwaffe records found after the war showed that the force had lost only two bombers. Again and again in the next few days, when Bader's Big Wing formation did manage to get into action, this would remain a feature of their claims, for with so many fighters attacking at once, several planes would be aiming at the same target. In the turmoil, no pilot would notice the others, and when the target was shot down, each pilot would quite honestly but mistakenly claim it.

Furthermore, although Bader in his enthusiasm couldn't realize this, the interception had been made in perfect position because Bader had *guessed* the enemy's intentions right, but you can't fight a war on guesses. No one can guess right all the time. The Luftwaffe bombers often came straight and hard at their target, and if they had done that on this day, Bader would have been sitting all alone five thousand feet above and fifteen miles west of where the enemy was, doodling along helplessly as he so often was.

Dowding's defense system relied on radar, but radar information was useless unless it was organized by Controllers who could see where all the raids were going. It was a complex system, and all the parts had to fit together if it was to work. The radar stations would pick up an enemy coming in and would report by land line directly to the Filter Room at Fighter Command headquarters at Bentley Priory. The radar signal would be followed until the bombers' track was established and their target tentatively identified, and then Group HQ and the relevant sector stations were notified. At the same time, or at least as soon as the bombers passed over the coast, ground observers would spot them and send their information on to Observer Corps Centre, and thence to the sector stations and Groups concerned, usually 11 Group. There Keith Park would decide which sectors to activate, the sector commander would decide which aerodrome should be contacted, and each aerodrome commander would decide which squadrons were to be scrambled. Once airborne, the fighters were directed by radio to make the interception.

Most importantly, the system depended on the fighter pilots' following the instructions of the radar-directed Controllers. This enabled the Controllers to direct the entire battle, whereas a fighter pilot could see only what was in front of him. Finally, the Controllers had to know not only where the enemy was but also where their own aircraft were so that they could direct reinforcements where needed. Bader's guesses as to the Luftwaffe's intentions on each raid were the stuff of romantic, dashing heroes; it made good entertainment but very bad strategy. When it worked it looked good, but only because of the overblown claims of enemy destroyed, and usually it didn't work at all.

Leigh-Mallory should have clamped him down, should have explained that Bader's job was not to think, and certainly not to guess, but to follow orders and to fight. It's always hard for the man in the thick of the action to realize that he doesn't have the whole picture in front of him. It's hard for him to obey orders when he thinks he knows better than the fat cats sitting safely on the ground. It's hard, but it's necessary.

And meanwhile the system was being beaten down. Biggin Hill, the pivot of 11 Group's work, was virtually deserted; one squadron still operated from there, but the others had been moved and all the supporting operations were useless. Another five of the most used airfields were out of action, while the six sector stations were barely limping along. The forward airfields at Manston and Lympne had been abandoned. As August spilled over into the first week of September, Dowding's intricate system was crumbling under the onslaught.

Those last few Spitfires, however, were still coming up to continue the fight. Hitler ordered the invasion timetable reset, to give Göring another few days to finish the job. Operation Sea Lion, the invasion of Britain, would commence on September 20.

twenty-seven

AND THEN, in a fit of pique, Hitler lost the war.

Ten days previously—or rather, on the *night* of August 24— German bombers unloaded their explosives and incendiaries on London, and nobody knew why. Actually, nobody knew why they hadn't hit London earlier; that was the first mystery, and one that has never been satisfactorily answered. We know now that Hitler had specifically ordered the sanctity of London, but the reason for this decision is lost in the mists of his mind. The Luftwaffe was free to bomb anywhere else in England: houses, shops, hospitals, factories—he didn't care. Why did he keep London safe?

Later in the war, when the Nazis were forced to evacuate Paris, he gave orders that the French city was to be burned to the ground. Had the German commander followed that order, nothing of military significance would have been gained; Hitler just wanted to destroy the city. So the idea of his respect for a wonderful city is ludicrous, and we have to forget the idea that he spared London for that reason.

Another idea is that he didn't want to make the English so angry that they wouldn't agree to a negotiated peace. This is hard to square with his orders that the English could be bombed anywhere and everywhere else. The most reasonable position is to accept that it's impossible to understand the mind of a dead psychopath and to try instead to understand why London was bombed on August 24 and how this action and the resulting reaction changed the course of the war.

The cold facts are that at ten o'clock on that night, more than a hundred bombers flew up the Thames and unloaded their explosives and incendiaries on East Ham and Stepney, Bethnal Green and Finsbury, and the City. The attacks started seventy-six fires, most of them in the poorest sections of town.

There are three competing theories as to why Hitler's standing order to leave London alone was ignored. The first of these goes back to the Luftwaffe's attacks during the preceding day, in which all the airfields ringing London were attacked. This theory looks on those attacks as the beginning of the assault on London, but that doesn't make sense to me. The night bombers of August were not bothered by fighters, not even remotely. Since the beginning of the war, only one bomber had been shot down by a night fighter, so it would make no sense to begin the night bombing of London by trying to knock out the fighter airfields, especially since all of 11 Group's airfields, not just those close to the city, were in position to defend London. The reason for attacking the airfields ringing London was clearly just a continuation of the attack on all of Fighter Command's fields.

Moreover, a decision by Hitler to finally hit London would leave its mark in the records of the Third Reich, and although extensive searches have been made through all these records, no such operational order exists. On the contrary, it is clear from the German records that the attack was unauthorized.

The second theory takes these records into account and makes sense if we modify it a bit. It states that the bombing was simply a navigational mistake. But while day bombers fly in compact formations, night bombers fly individual routes. How could more than a hundred bombers make the same mistake? This is especially difficult to accept since the Thames River flashes in the moonlight like a neon arrow pointing the way to the heart of London, where it winds back and forth as if signaling, "Here it is!"

Many night raids used the Thames arrow to begin their operations, following it to London and then dispersing to the airfields and towns around it. On the night in question there were clouds drifting over the moon, so it really wouldn't be hard for the bombers to become lost over the blacked-out country. Imagine now that you're in such a bomber, searching for your assigned target, having no luck, trying to find your way, and at the same time, you are desperately trying to avoid the searchlights and antiaircraft fire. Looking out into the darkness in fear of a night fighter, you suddenly see a splash of bombs ahead. All it would have taken was one bomber to panic amid the antiaircraft fire and drop its bombs on the first bit of land it saw when the clouds parted for a moment, and then all the others would think, "Well, there's a target. It might not be mine, but it's something." And as a few bombers dropped their bombs on the first explosions, the fires below would attract the others, as bees to the scent of a flower, or mosquitoes to the scent of my wife.

Josef Knobel was the operations officer with one of the bomber groups that night. He recalled a teleprinter signal from Göring that every unit received early the following morning. As clearly as he recalls, it said: "It is to be reported immediately which crews dropped bombs on London, which is prohibited. The Führer has ordered that the commanders who did this are to be reassigned to the infantry." (There is, however, no official record of any such reassignment.)

The third theory is Dowding's, who starts with the second theory—a navigational mistake—but wonders how the bombers came to make such a mistake. Instead of clouds and panic, he sees in these events the hand of God: "I could hardly believe that the Germans would have made such a mistake. From then on it was gradually borne in upon me that it was a supernatural intervention at that particular time."

Consider what was happening at this particular time. Dowding realized that *Adlerangriff* was succeeding. He was rotating squadrons in and out of the battle, but by now the rate of casualties was so serious that a new squadron brought into the fight would become depleted and exhausted before any of the resting squadrons were ready to come back in to take its place. The training units weren't able to produce enough trained pilots to replace those lost. Every day, Fighter Command was falling behind in pilots and in supporting facilities, as the airfields were knocked out of the fight.

The pilots who were in the fighting recognized this as well. Johnny Johnson, one of the top aces, remembered that "if the airfields had got another heavy thumping, I'm not sure they would have stood it." Added another of the Few, Pilot Officer Pat Hancock, "Had they gone on bombing the airfields, I might have been speaking German today, except I wouldn't still be here."

But they didn't go on bombing the airfields, for as Dowding saw it, God intervened. The bombers got lost, they dropped their bombs on London, and a different set of dominos began to fall.

Whatever caused the bombs to drop on London, they changed the course of the war. Churchill's heart, hardened either by God or by his own natural fury, railed against this savage attack on civilian populations. The attack was nothing new in that sense; the night bombers had been hitting other cities all summer. But attacking London drew forth Churchill's anger and fear, for to be the head of a British government that couldn't defend London was to be the head of nothing. He ordered his own bombers to hit Berlin.

Arthur "Bomber" Harris, the head of Bomber Command, respectfully demurred. His force wasn't ready for such a strike. Berlin was too far away, and his long-range bombers were just beginning to come off the production lines. He had available only a few smaller bombers, which would have to carry so much fuel they wouldn't have much room for bombs. He wanted to continue to use them to strike at specific targets, as he had been doing all summer— a plan that would eventually be proven to be little more than a superstition. The navigation capabilities at this time just weren't good enough for most of his bombers to find even large cities at night, let alone factories or railroad yards. Although he was sending out bombers to hit these targets, most of his bombs didn't even land in the cities in which the targets were located. (The only effective bombing the British were doing was against the invasion barges along the French coast.)

Harris didn't realize this yet, but he argued that to begin a war of reprisals against each other's capital cities would favor the Germans, who had more bombers at their command. Even more important, London was just a few miles inside England, close to the French airfields that housed the German bombers, whereas Berlin was hidden deep in the heart of Germany, far from the British aerodromes, too far for fighter escorts. Bombing Berlin would serve no purpose except to bring even worse retaliation against the English population. London was, Harris reminded Churchill in his own words of twenty years ago, "a fat white cow" tethered to the stake in plain view, while Berlin was hidden far away in the forests of the night.

All this was true—but irrelevant. Hitler had bombed London, and he had to be answered. Actually, when the first bombs fell on the London suburbs of Croydon and Wimbledon a few nights earlier, Churchill had urged retaliation. Now that the city itself had been bombed, there was no holding him back.

He thundered, "Go!" and Bomber Command went. Without fighter escort they couldn't possibly fly over Germany in daylight, but the very next night some eighty twin-engine bombers were sent to Berlin. Most of them didn't make it; it was beyond their powers to navigate such a long distance over a dark continent with no visible landmarks. They dropped their bombs here and there, hither and yon, most of them falling on empty fields and woods. But twenty-nine of the bombers did bomb Berlin, where the havoc they caused was out of all proportion to the actual blast of the bombs. Not a single Berliner was killed, no factory was hit, and there was no military damage at all. But the inviolate skies over Berlin had been violated, and that was insufferable.

"Sie könn' mich Meier heissen," Göring had boasted. "You can call me Meier"—a Jewish name, the worst of all Aryan insults—"if bombs ever fall on the sacred soil of Germany." And here were bombs falling not just on Germany, but on Berlin. Hitler was furious, but no more so than Churchill, who sent his bombers back again a few nights later, and then again and again. Harris complained that his bombers were being wasted, that no real damage was being done, but Churchill was adamant. The bloody Boche had to be shown!

Again and again, night after night, the British bombers circled over Berlin, dropping toilet bowls and wrenches along with a few bombs, until finally Hitler exploded with more vehemence than the British explosives. He ordered the Luftwaffe to attack London in full strength. Not a hundred lost bombers dropping their load at random, but every bomber in the Luftwaffe, hundreds and hundreds of them. And not sneaking in at night like the British cowards, but roaring up the Thames in full daylight. On September 4, he spoke on radio to the whole German nation, furiously raging, promising to "wipe London from the face of the earth."

"If they attack our cities, we will raze *their* cities to the ground! We will stop the murderous activities of these air pirates, so help us God! If the British air force drops three thousand or four thousand kilos of bombs, then we will drop three *hundred* thousand or four *hundred* thousand kilos!"

No more Mr. Nice Guy. Invoking the help of God—*"Gott mit uns!"*—he ordered Göring to destroy London.

And Dowding, in his turn, thanked God.

twenty-eight

H<small>E THANKED</small> G<small>OD</small>, because the attacks on London would give his airfields a desperately needed respite. He knew his chicks could fight the Luftwaffe to a standstill in the skies, but if their bases were destroyed they'd be helpless. A fighter pilot, no matter how brave or how skilled, and no matter what a wonderful machine his Spitfire is, still has to land it when the day's action is done. Coming in at a hundred miles an hour, he needs an aerodrome with long and uncratered runways; he needs repair shops to service his engine after every few flights and to patch the jagged holes blasted by the Messerschmitts' cannon; and he needs food to eat and a bed to sleep in.

By the first week of September, the men of Fighter Command had none of those luxuries. They were at the end of their rope, and Dowding didn't yet know of God's goodness. And then, on September 7, it all changed.

Harold Macmillan (postwar Prime Minister): "Sept 7 is a great day in my memory, for then we were told that the invasion was imminent. The signal *Cromwell* was given, and with this password flying from mouth to mouth and the church bells ringing, the Army came to instant readiness and the Home Guard stood to arms. We waited for the great moment."

The day began quietly, after the horror of the past week. The previous day had been the worst yet, beginning at 8:40 in the morning with a squadron of Hurricanes from Northolt rising to cut off a fleet of bombers and then being bounced themselves by a mass of Me 109s. The squadron lost five planes in fewer minutes.

The attacks continued throughout the long day. By the end, although they had shot down nearly fifty Germans, Fighter Command had lost twenty-five fighters. Dowding was again being forced to send untrained chicks up to fight. In desperation he ordered that squadrons that had lost most of their pilots in the past few weeks should be taken out of action, but not as a unit: They were to give up their remaining experienced pilots to form the nucleus of the newer squadrons that he was forced to bring into the fight. It was a move that had to hurt morale, he understood, since fighter pilots are trained to fight as a team, but he had no choice; bringing in a new squadron without experience would be throwing them to the wolves. Hopefully, the veterans would be able to impart some knowledge.

Hopefully? He had little hope as the next day, September 7, dawned with a bright yellow sun and clear blue skies and, most puzzling, with quiet radar screens. At Bentley Priory, Dowding strode silently back and forth, pausing each time to look out the French windows on the glorious summer day. But what he saw was something quite different from the flowers and trees. He saw his aerodromes and radar stations battered and broken. In another few days of this clear summer weather the Spits would be driven out of the air, the Wehrmacht would cross the Channel, and Hermann Göring would be laughing in this very room.

The past week, Hitler had broadcast his scorn: "In England they are filled with fright and wonder. They keep asking, 'Why doesn't he come?' Be calm. Be calm. *Er kommt! Er kommt!*"

Dowding didn't doubt him. His boys had done their best, but the end was clear and was coming fast. That morning, the Air Ministry had issued to all commands its Invasion Alert No. 1: *Invasion is imminent and may be expected within 24 hours.*

After the war, Göring testified at his Nuremberg trial that although Hitler ordered reprisal raids on London, he (Göring) "as a soldier" objected to such terror bombing. But this was self-serving nonsense. He hadn't objected to the terror bombing of Guernica or Rotterdam, and this testimony was clearly nothing but a last-ditch attempt to save his own life. When the argument was rejected, he committed suicide.

The opinions of his two top Luftwaffe group commanders were split. Hugo Sperrle disagreed with the order, understanding that the attacks on British airfields were slowly but surely destroying Dowding's power to resist. Albert Kesselring, on the other hand, thought that attacking London would be quicker: It was a target Dowding would have to defend, and it would force the RAF to commit its last fighters.

None of these arguments mattered in the least. Hitler had made an emotional and irrevocable decision, just as Churchill had, and on September 7 the war entered a new phase.

That afternoon Göring stood with Kesselring on the French coast, at Cape Blanc Nez. Looking through a telescope, the Reichsmarschall could see the distant cliffs of Dover, and above him he could see hundreds upon hundreds of German warplanes thundering over the waters, *fliegen gegen England.* He announced that he "had taken over personal command of the Luftwaffe in its war against England."

Laughing, chortling, he urged them on. It was rather peculiar that he was in such a good mood, considering what it must have been like explaining to Hitler how he had let bombs fall on Berlin. But he was an irrepressible egomaniac, and the sight of all those planes did make an impressive sight: 625 bombers escorted by even more fighters, fill-ing the sky, blocking the sun, flying against England.

Against London.

Now, finally, the radar screens began to light up. In the Operations Room at Bentley Priory, it was just a few minutes before four o'clock when the first headphoned WAAF moved. Getting up from her stool, she picked up a black counter and placed it on the map table. It was labeled "20+." On the balcony, the senior Controller picked up his telephone and notified Dowding.

That black marker was the first of many; as the German fleets built up over France and headed across the Channel, the map table began to be covered with them. By the time Dowding reached the room, there were more than ever before, and minute by minute, the WAAFs moved around the table, placing new counters beside the old. From every airfield along the French coast the Luftwaffe bombers and fighters came lumbering into the air, and on the squadron readiness boards lining the operations wall, lights began to come on as every squadron in 11 Group was ordered to varying states of readiness.

But where should they be vectored? As usual, the Germans were coming straight across the Channel for London, but always the large formations finally would break apart and scatter for the surrounding airfields, keeping their targets secret until the last moment. Today, the Controllers thought, it didn't matter; they had no alternative but to protect all their airfields as best they could. They sent the Spits and Hurris away from London, patrolling the approaches to the aerodromes.

It was not only a gorgeous summer day, but also a Saturday, and the fields and meadows of the countryside were dotted with people relaxing and trying to forget the war. White-trousered cricket players and parasol-holding ladies with picnic baskets, children rolling hoops and throwing balls, babies crawling and old men stretched out in deck chairs gathered in the sunshine and looked up into the blue sky at the birds flitting—until a far-off rumbling broke in over the chirping birds, drowning out the sounds of children calling, babies crying, bats hitting balls.

The rumbling grew from a sullen thunder into a deafening roar as the black-winged monstrosities took over the sky. Straight up the Thames they came, blocking out the sun, a cloud of death twenty miles wide and forty miles long. It took a full ten minutes for those locusts with black crosses on their wings to pass overhead. Unbelievably, minute after minute, as the lead planes passed over the horizon, more of them came trailing their thunder, covering the cricket patches and meadows with their terrible shadow.

Up the river they roared. Motorists heard their angry sound and pulled off the road to stare up into a suddenly foreign, hostile sky. Families picnicking in the fields gathered up their children in fear, hoping the bombs wouldn't fall out of those bellies onto their heads, wondering where they would fall, wondering where the RAF was, afraid that this might be their last day in a free country.

Underground, far from the sun and sky, deep under the earth of Bentley Priory, Dowding and his Controllers could see no airplanes. They stood silently on the balcony watching nothing but the markers on the map table below, but these were all too real—and too scattered. The red markers signifying the British fighters were far from London, guarding their airfields, as the black Luftwaffe markers were pushed slowly and steadily straight up the Thames toward London.

And still they waited and watched as more counters were placed on the board. There never had been so many. Outside in the bright sunlight, a thousand German aircraft were thundering up the Thames. Clearly now, this was going to be the largest aerial bombing attack in history. Every one of Park's II Group fighters was in the air and too far away, for now it became clear that the bomber formations were not breaking up, scattering toward the aerodromes; they continued on their way, inexorable, straight to London.

Responding late, finally realizing that something new was happening, the Controllers brought their fighters in, taking them away from the airfields and racing them due east to meet the enemy. But they were too few and too late.

The first contact was made by four squadrons that wheeled around a towering cloud and past a bank of haze, and when they broke into the clear, they suddenly faced a sky full of black German planes racing toward them at a combined closing speed of more than four hundred miles an hour. There was no time to think, just barely enough time for instant reaction. They wheeled and dove into them.

The bombers were in the center, but around them and pulled up high above them were swarms of angry Messerschmitts, hundreds of them, filling the sky. The Spits dove into them, but couldn't stop them. The bombers got through, as Baldwin had warned they must; they came through the fighter defenses and others came streaming in behind them, and London town twenty thousand feet below exploded and disappeared into a thick, black pall of smoke.

The British fighters came racing in from where they had been held around their scattered airfields. They came tearing into the bombers as quickly and ferociously as they could, but the 650 Messerschmitts drove them off again and again, and wave after wave of bombers came through the dogfights and dropped their bombs into the roaring inferno that now was London.

Winston Churchill spent the afternoon with Keith Park in 11 Group's Operations Room. "In a little while, all our squadrons were fighting, and some had already begun to return for fuel. All were in the air . . . there was not one squadron left in reserve. At this moment Park spoke to Dowding at Stanmore asking for three squadrons of No 12 Group to be put at his disposal in case of another major attack . . . this was done. . . . I became conscious of the anxiety of the Commander, who now stood still behind his subordinate's chair. Hitherto

I had watched in silence. I now asked: 'What other reserves have we?' 'There are none,' said Air Vice Marshal Park. In an account which he wrote afterwards he said that I 'looked grave.' Well I might . . . the odds were great; our margins small; the stakes infinite."

Dowding sent Park's request for help up to Leigh-Mallory, and Douglas Bader's 242 Squadron was scrambled from its aerodrome at Coltishall, northeast of London. But a few days previously, Leigh-Mallory had told Bader that the next time the Group was called on for help, he was not only to take the three Coltishall squadrons, but also to rendezvous with two more from nearby Duxford and lead them all in one massive wing. He was to take the radar information fed to him by 11 Group, but he was to decide himself how best to use it to set up his attack. He was ordered to ignore any orders from the 11 Group Controllers.

And so as London burned, Bader wheeled his three squadrons around over Coltishall, getting them into battle formation. He then took them over to Duxford and wheeled around again as the two Duxford squadrons joined him. But, being held in readiness every day, they had never had time to practice this move, which proved more difficult than Bader had imagined. As they finally climbed away toward London, he tried to line them up into a mass he could control, but there were too many of them; the formation was too cumbersome for the rapid maneuvering that was necessary. One of the squadrons, No. 303, was composed of Polish survivors of the Warsaw massacre who had found their way to England. They had been kept out of the fighting because they barely understood English, which made it impossible to control them in the air. Now they conveniently forgot the little English they had and ignored Bader's orders, leaving his swirling, half-formed Wing behind, climbing full throttle and alone to find the Germans.

By the time Bader caught up with the enemy, he had lost two more of his squadrons and the Poles had already disappeared into the German swarm—and that swarm had already unloaded its bombs and turned for home. He led his partial Wing into a diving attack, shooting down one bomber and losing two Hurricanes. The other two squadrons of the Wing never arrived in time to do any fighting at all.

London exploded and burned. City homes and apartments, office buildings and docks crumbled and disappeared in the worst inferno since 1660—and that inferno was soon surpassed. Fire spurted into the air and along the streets and even into the Thames when a sugar warehouse poured a stream of burning, liquefied sugar that covered the surface of the river. The oil tanks, the gasworks, the heart of the city, and the suburbs blazed from end to end.

But the fires at the airfields had been put out, and no new ones started on this day. The ground crews were busy at Kenley and Biggin Hill and Tangmere, repairing the damage of the previous weeks without being interrupted by falling bombs. They were filling in the craters and clearing away the rubble at Manston and Ramsgate, they were repairing the telephone lines and the maintenance shops at Croydon and North Weald. The radar stations at Ventnor, Dover, Rye, and Pevesey had been out of the battle for days, but now new generators were installed and new wires were being strung for the aerials.

Fighter Command lost another twenty pilots that day, but they destroyed fifty German planes, and when the Spits returned home they came back to peaceful aerodromes. They didn't have to circle towering black fumes rising from the cratered grass, looking for a safe place to land. Instead they found the fields in better condition than when they had left, they found the mechanics waiting to repair their shot-up kites, and the NAAFI was waiting with a hot mug of tea.

When his bombers returned and reported the fires raging all over London, the sky black with smoke, the city devastated, Göring bounced around in joy. He radioed to Hitler that the invasion could take place as scheduled. The RAF had been defeated and the way lay open.

But the Kriegsmarine waited till that evening, when all the returning planes had been counted, and then pointed out that fifty of them had not come home. Göring laughed them off: He had sent out a thousand planes and had lost only 5 percent. Yes, the admirals replied doubtfully, but still, fifty planes . . . obviously there were at least a few British fighters still around.

All right, all right, *der Dicke* laughed at their concern. He would hit London again.

twenty-nine

WHEN CHURCHILL left 11 Group's Operations Room at the end of the day, he got into his car with General Sir Hastings Ismay, who remembered the moment clearly: "His first words were, 'Don't speak to me. I have never been so moved.' He sat in silence for a while, then leaned forward and whispered, 'Never in the field of human conflict has so much been owed by so many to so few.'"

The German admirals again confronted Göring with their concerns. They told Hitler that they could not guarantee the safety of the invading force unless the sky over the Channel was swept free of the RAF, and despite Göring's blustering, it was clear to them that the RAF was still alive and well.

Hitler nodded, and Göring blushed furiously. He spent the next day gathering his forces together. He called his fighter commanders to Karinhall and presented them with the Gold Pilot Medal, then suddenly began to lambaste them for not fulfilling his predictions of victory. "Are you purposely trying to make me look foolish before the Führer?" he screamed. (Pete Rose once told me that the secret of being a good manager is knowing which players need a pat on the back and which need a kick in the ass. Evidently, Göring's managing strategy was to give his players both.)

General Adolf Galland, the Luftwaffe's top fighter commander, whom Göring had only recently promoted to this position, told his men, with just a bit of tongue in cheek, "The Reichsmarschall let us know quite plainly that he was not satisfied with the fighters." Göring then turned friendly again, asking what he could do to help them. What did they need to destroy the RAF? Galland replied, "I should like a squadron or two of Spitfires."

Göring was not amused. "He stamped off, growling as he went."

Transporting the Wehrmacht across the English Channel would necessitate a series of preparations, such as the laying of a minefield to keep the Royal Navy at bay. The Kriegsmarine needed ten days to do this, so if the invasion was to take place on September 20, they had to begin by September 11. On September 9, Göring announced he was ready to storm the British skies yet again, to finish the job, to wipe out those "last few Spitfires." Hitler nodded without comment; he would wait for the results of this day's fighting before issuing the order to begin the mine laying.

The first reports were good. The Messerschmitt pilots came back and reported they had destroyed thirty British fighters. But then came second thoughts. Göring had thought there weren't that many Spitfires left; if the German fighters had destroyed thirty, how many were there in the air this day? And then came the reports of the bomber squadrons: They had lost nearly forty.

It was perplexing. Clearly the RAF was stronger than Göring had thought. Actually the score would have been even worse had Bader's Big Wing proved as effective as he had thought. After circling around to get his planes in formation, he had finally found a group of Dorniers and dove in to attack, claiming nineteen of them shot down. But no Dornier wrecks were found on the ground, and the German records show that all those planes returned to base. Two of Bader's pilots collided in the overcrowded sky; both were killed.

Hitler postponed Operation Sea Lion once more. The invasion barges would have to cross the Channel under cover of darkness, but with a full moon so they could find their way. They would have to reach the beaches at dawn, and the landing had to be made on an ebb tide so the landing craft could be securely beached. Putting all this together meant that the invasion night would have to match a full moon with an ebb tide coincident with the following dawn. The week of September 19–26 would have these conditions, but this would be the last time before the winter rains and snow would come. Postponement beyond that date would be impossible. Hitler decided on one last delay: Invasion was scheduled for September 24, with the final order to go or to cancel to be given on the fourteenth.

At the beginning of the summer, when Hitler first decided to invade England, Göring had promised to destroy the RAF "within a few days." That was precisely what he now had left.

Weather was bad on September 10, but on the eleventh, the Luftwaffe rose again to the attack, and again those last few Spitfires doused Göring's jollity. The losses were more than forty aircraft for each side. All right, Göring thought, the RAF did have more fighters than he had expected, but they had just lost another forty. They couldn't have many more; the job was nearly finished. One more massive raid—*once more into the breach, my band of brothers,* he thought, quoting Shakespeare, whom the Germans loved just as the British loved Beethoven. Once more into the breach, and the victory is ours!

Hit them with everything, he thought. Break their spirits, break their backs, throw everything in, hold nothing back. He gathered his forces together on the twelfth and thirteenth, and then on the fourteenth, the weather deteriorated. He sent out a few raids to hit the radar stations in preparation for a massive assault on the following day. Just in case Dowding had any fighters left—and just in case their radar worked—he wanted it out of order. On Sunday, September 15, he would hit them with everything he had. He would overwhelm them, crush them. His fighters were rested, his bombers loaded and ready to go. He promised Hitler that the invasion could proceed as planned.

Hitler glowered. Göring had been promising to destroy the British since before Dunkirk. When he left, Hitler informed his general staff that he had decided to postpone once again, and for the last time, his decision on Sea Lion. He would wait until Göring's supreme effort was over, and then he would evaluate the situation. He would make a final decision on September 17. No further postponements would be possible.

As September 15 dawned over England, the stars disappeared and a bright blue clarity spread over the heavens. The sun rose strong and hot, burning away the morning mists that tried to cling to the damp grass of the aerodromes. The British pilots finished their breakfasts and came wandering out to the flight line. They sat down at card tables to play pontoon or stretched out in the traditional deck chairs to catch a few rays. Three days before, they had been harried, exhausted, bleary-eyed. But they were young and healthy, and with the past few days off, were once again "the gayest band that ever flew."

That is, most of them were. Others were throwing up their breakfasts behind the operations shacks, while still others were suffering the "shits" in the latrine. The Poles were glowering at the sky, trying to force it to unveil the Germans: They wanted nothing but to kill Germans. The Americans—there were a half dozen of them, one of whom would survive—were chatting. The French were dreaming of Paris. The Czechs and Belgians were solemn, waiting.

At ten minutes before eleven o'clock, the radar station at Rye reported an echo. Twenty-plus forming up ten miles below Boulogne. Two squadrons of No. 11 Group were ordered to readiness. Quickly, more plots began to come in. Ten-plus, twenty-plus, thirty-plus. It was going to be a big day, which was no surprise.

The invasion barges had been piling up along the French coast, and every night Bomber Command had gone out to sink them, and every night they reported more and more of them. In addition, the Ultra decoding experts at Bletchley Park had just intercepted an order setting up a unit to organize quick turnarounds for supply and troop-carrying aircraft. The purpose of this was clear: These planes would be carrying paratroopers and supplies across the Channel and, upon completing the round-trip, would be quickly reloaded and sent back. Finally, the coming autumnal weather was no secret on either side of the Channel; everyone in England knew the invasion had to come soon or not at all.

Today would be the day, Dowding decided. All summer he had hoarded his fighters, sending them up a few at a time into overwhelming odds so that he might have another few ready for tomorrow. But today, with an exquisite sense of timing, he realized there would be no more tomorrows. He would meet them today with everything he had. He would stake it all on this last throw of the dice.

As the first radar reports came in, Park ordered all his squadrons to readiness, but didn't scramble them. There was something strange about the radar reports: The blips had always moved quickly across the Channel toward London, but today they were stationary. Or, rather, they seemed to be moving in circles, gaining height...

Of course. They were doing what Bader did with his silly Big Wing. Instead of moving into the attack, the first planes were circling over their bases, building up their formations and climbing together to altitude. As Park watched, he saw the fighter blips forming over the bombers. Göring must be worried that they hadn't been coordinating properly, so today they were forming up before they started across the water—never realizing that they were being watched by radar. They were giving Fighter Command what it needed most: time.

Park ordered the information sent immediately to 12 Group. For once, Bader might be able to do a bit of good.

The first raid was attacked by twenty Spits of No. 11 Group as it crossed the coast, and within minutes, four full squadrons joined them. As London slid up over the horizon, four squadrons of Hurricanes came diving out of the noonday sun in a wild head-on attack. The bombers tried to turn away, but now Bader's Duxford Wing came thundering in; he had put the extra minutes of warning to good use, and now he brought five whole squadrons of fresh fighters blasting their way through the escorting Messerschmitts before they could react, sweeping like a scythe through the bomber formation.

The bomber formation broke apart under that fire. They dropped their bombs where they were and turned and ran back to France, harried and hassled by a sky suddenly full of British fighters; they returned to find the fat Reichsmarschall trembling with rage. How dare they tell him they couldn't vanquish the British! He ordered them to refill their bomb bays, to refill their tanks, and never mind their stomachs. They were going right back to catch the British on the ground and unprepared.

But Dowding was quite prepared. The Spits and Hurris were rearmed and refueled almost before their wheels stopped turning. The pilots were plied with tea and biscuits, dropping them on the grass when the calls came through: twenty-plus and thirty-plus, building up all over northeastern France. By two o'clock, the Luftwaffe was back again, hundreds of them sweeping in once more, heading straight for London.

A few Hurricanes met them as they crossed the coast, but the escorting Me's beat them off. A squadron of Spitfires joined in, but were still too few to break through. To the bomber crews, Göring finally appeared to be right: There were just a few fighters left . . .

And then another squadron of Spits came sailing around the clouds, and another of Hurris came under them. Squadron after squadron came flying into the fray as Park followed Dowding's orders and sent up everything he had, and the bombers began to fall flaming from the sky.

And then, just as they reached London, Bader's Duxford Wing came out of nowhere. The radar stations had seen the enemy early enough to give sufficient warning, and there was no need to guess at which target the enemy was heading for. Finally today, his idea worked. The five-squadron Wing came diving out of the sun, pouring through the escorting fighters and crashing through the bomber formation, scattering them, burning them, destroying them. In an instant, the black-crossed sky was fluttering with black smoke from burning Heinkels and white-parasoled parachutes.

The Messerschmitts were left turning and twisting in the wind, trying to herd the bombers back together, and failing that impossible task, the German fighters now realized they had better try to save themselves as the Spitfires flashed around them. Even No. 10 Group got into the action as two of its squadrons came diving out of the sun. And the Me's whirled around and, at each turn, they saw more fighters, more British roundels on the wings, more bright red flashes of machine guns. Where were all these British fighters coming from?

At Bentley Priory, the radar reports showed no further buildups over France, and Dowding knew that this was the height of the battle, this was the climax of the summer. He called Park and Leigh-Mallory: Send in everything, hold nothing back.

The Messerschmitt and Heinkel crews had been told there were no more fighters left in Britain, and now six more squadrons of 11 Group dropped onto them from the seemingly infinite sky. The bombers turned and fled for home. The Messerschmitts tried to protect them but they had been fighting too many Spitfires for too long, and now in each of their cockpits, a small red light began to wink.

Their fuel was nearly gone, and they still had fifty miles of England and another twenty miles of cold, wet Channel waters to cross. One by one, they began to dive away for home, with Spitfires spitting tracers at their tails and with Hurricanes turning their attention to the bombers they left behind.

Winston Churchill left 11 Group headquarters after the afternoon's battle and returned to Chequers, where he went directly to bed for his afternoon nap. When he woke, his private secretary was ready with the day's news. It was a typical day in the summer of 1940: problems, troubles, delays, ships sunk, vessels lost, cities bombed. However, said the private secretary, none of that matters. "All is redeemed by the air. We have shot down a hundred and eighty-five for a loss of under forty."

#

INTERCEPTED RADIO MESSAGE (ENCODED)

FROM: Generalfeldmarschall A. Kesselring, Commanding Officer, Luftflotte 2, Headquarters, Cap Blanc

TO: Reichsmarschall H. Göring, Headquarters, Okerkommandoluftwaffe

MESSAGE READS: We cannot keep it up....

#

thirty

THE RAF hadn't shot down 185 airplanes; the true Luftwaffe loss was 59. It didn't matter. What did matter was that they had beaten off the onslaught, and they were still in existence. More than that, they felt stronger than ever; they smelled the blood of their enemies. They were victorious!

They awoke the next day, Monday, September 16, full of confidence. They had their tea, and they waited for the Luftwaffe to come back. They bloody well dared the Luftwaffe to come back!

The sun rose into another clear blue summer's sky, but nothing else rose into that sky. The day's radar operators were up at dawn, staring at their screens, seeing nothing. The radar transmitters sent continuous radio waves across the Channel, and none of them bounced back. At the German aerodromes, all was quiet. At the British aerodromes, patched now and in full operation, the Spitfire engines turned over, their full-throated rumbling caressing the grass. For the rest of their lives, the fighter pilots would swear there was no sound in the world as lovely as a Spitfire engine. Today they were lulled to sleep by the sound, they dozed in the sun or chewed their nails, and some of them vomited whenever the telephone rang, but it was nothing except a message that the morning tea was late or someone had forgotten his flying boots.

In France, Göring was holding another meeting with his senior commanders, a bewildered and beaten group. He asked for suggestions, but they had none. Galland thought better of asking again for Spitfires. He had seen enough of them already. Behind every cloud, they all said, coming out of the sun, climbing from below, south of London, east of London, everywhere they looked, there was always another squadron of Spitfires coming at them.

Göring tried to rally them. They had met the last of the British fighters, he exhorted them. All that was needed was one more effort. No one answered. He stared at them. They looked away, they looked at the walls, they looked out the window at the sky. Over Spain, over Poland, over France, that sky had belonged to them.

It was no longer theirs.

On Tuesday, September 17, the day of Hitler's final invasion decision, the British wireless service intercepted two signals from the German General Staff. They sent the messages to Bletchley Park, where the staff of decoders got to work on them, using their Enigma machine. The decoded messages were sent, marked *Ultra, For Your Eyes Only,* to Churchill.

The first message was to the officer in charge of the invasion barges that had been piling up along the coast of France and that had been the target of Bomber Command every night. He was ordered to begin dispersing them, sending them back upriver to their home ports.

The other message was to the German officer in Holland who

was in charge of the unit responsible for the quick turnarounds to be organized for the paratroopers and supplies scheduled to be ferried across the Channel when the invasion began. Today's message informed him that his equipment was to be dismantled and that he was to report back to headquarters for reassignment.

The Battle of Britain was over.

part four

Autumn Leaves

During the winter of 1940–1941, British airplane production increased dramatically, so that by the following spring, when the waters of the Channel had calmed again, Hitler turned away from that damned little island. His string of easy victories was over. Instead he invaded Russia, leaving England behind as a massive aircraft carrier from which British and American bombers began to destroy the German industrial capacity, beginning finally his long decline.

But the ordeal of the British people was far from over. Hitler couldn't gain aerial superiority over the island nation, he couldn't invade it, but he could pound and blast it from the air at night, when the cowl of darkness rendered all things invisible. The Battle of Britain was over, but the Blitz had just begun.

Throughout the summer of 1940 the Luftwaffe had been bombing nightly, in what was more than a nuisance but less than anything meaningful. The bombers came to Coventry and Birmingham, to Liverpool and Manchester; they came singly, unescorted by fighters, unseen and invincible. For hours on end, they would drift about above their blacked-out targets, dropping one bomb here, another there. They couldn't see where their bombs would fall, and they didn't do any significant damage. (That estimate would be disputed by the families of the several hundred civilians killed that summer by the German bombs, but England never was in danger of losing the war because of this nighttime harassment.)

Then came September 7, and the Hun hordes were loosed on London. After the day's battle the night bombers came over, and the damage they did was severe. The Thames shone brightly in the dim moonlight, leading them like a fluorescent arrow to the heart of London. They stole along in the dark, and when they reached the big bend in the river they dropped their bombs, turned, and headed home again, and the RAF was helpless to stop them.

The next night they came again, and again on the following night. On September 15 the Luftwaffe was defeated in the daylight sky, but the night raids continued. When the daylight bombing came to a halt, all the bombers were assigned to night duty, and now they came over in force. London was bombed every single night for fifty-seven consecutive nights, and when the Luftwaffe developed radio navigation aids Coventry was destroyed and every other major city was hit hard. The sirens were so ubiquitous that many people routinely went to sleep under their dining room tables instead of in their beds. In London they trooped en masse to the tube stations, despite being warned by the police that it was illegal to bunk down on the platforms overnight.

Churchill turned angrily to Dowding, demanding relief, but Dowding had no help to offer. At least, not quite yet. The answer, he told Churchill, was once again in radar. The scientific wizards were hard at work designing a portable radar set that could be carried in a new fighter with a two-man crew. The fighter, the Bristol Beaufighter, was already coming off the production lines and would be ready for service in a few months. The radar, named AI for Airborne Interception, was not yet ready but progress was being made.

"Progress is being made?!" Churchill roared. Not good enough, not damned good enough by half! Had he no other help to offer? Dowding shook his head no. There was nothing else. The pilots of the Hurricanes and Spitfires couldn't see at night; there was nothing they could do. Churchill glowered and cursed and with vehemence overrode Dowding's decision, ordering that at least one squadron of Hurricanes be detached for night-fighting duties.

To no avail. All that was accomplished was the death of several Hurricane pilots as they tried to land their high-spirited charges in the dark. Not a single bomber was brought down by these planes. Dowding was correct in his helplessness: There was nothing to be done until the Beaufighters and AI were ready.

Dowding was as aware of the problem and as impatient as Churchill; he was simply more realistic. Even before the Blitz had started, a Night Interception Committee—which soon morphed into the Night Air Defence Committee—had been set up to organize plans for bomber defense, and a Fighter Interceptor Unit (FIU) was organized to carry out in practice what ideas the committee came up with. They came up with many ideas, but only one eventually bore fruit: the concept of an airborne radar set that would enable the fighters to see in the dark.

The basic concept of radar-controlled night fighters was quite different from the day fighting scheme, due to the nature of the beast. By day, the bombers came over in large formations, all too visible, surrounded by a shield of fighters. Ground-based radar brought the fighters into visual contact, and then they were on their own. By night, the bombers slunk in one by one, invisible and alone. To combat them was a totally different proposition, and one more difficult to implement. The idea was to have night fighters patrolling a specified area rather than waiting to be scrambled. When a bomber intruded into his airspace, the pilot would be directed by ground radar to fly as near to the bomber as could be accomplished, at which point the fighter's own radar would take over and guide him in close. Finally, visual contact would be made, and the bomber would be shot down.

Easy enough to say, but infinitely hard to accomplish. The problems were many:

1. Producing a radar set small enough to be carried aloft. Remember, the Chain Home radars used transmitters on towers hundreds of feet high.
2. Directing the night fighter from the ground in close to the bomber. Any bomber pilot worth his salt would not be flying straight and level, but would be squirreling around up there.
3. Operating the airborne radar and flying the plane so as to get close enough for visual contact.
4. Finally, actually shooting down the bomber.

In the spring of 1940 a young Welshman named Taffy Bowen had produced a radar set that was sort of workable, and he prepared to demonstrate it to Dowding. The aircraft he had been working with was a Fairey Battle, a single-engine two-seater originally designed as a light bomber (the type that had been demolished in France, now relegated to noncombat duties). To fit both himself and Stuffy into the backseat, they had to dispense with parachutes, but they did manage, and the demonstration was a success—as far as it went. Another Battle flew straight ahead while Bowen, his head under a black hood along with Dowding, directed their plane to intercept successfully.

This was progress, but it was a far cry from having mass-produced sets that worked consistently and were simple enough to be operated by RAF crew rather than by an expert like Taffy Bowen. The test was also a far cry from intercepting a bomber that was taking evasive action instead of toodling along on a prearranged and steady course. When they landed, Dowding took Bowen aside for a two-hour detailed discussion of the problems over continuous cups of coffee. He pointed out the problems as he saw them: Since the night fighter would have to be on standing patrol for many hours at a time, it would have to be a different sort of fighter than the single-engine day types, which carried fuel for only an hour or two. Additionally, it was imperative that visual identification of the bomber be made; for a night fighter to shoot down a British bomber returning from a mission would be disastrous for morale. This meant that the pilot's eyes had to be adapted to the dark night sky, which in turn meant that he couldn't be looking into the comparatively bright radar scope. Putting these together meant that a twin-engine, two-man aircraft was needed.

Bowen would later write, "This was the first time I had heard the argument for a two-engined two-man aircraft advanced with such certainty and with such authority." The people at the Air Ministry were always advocating a single-seat, single-engine machine, not really understanding the difference between shooting down a bomber at night and in the daytime.

Finally, Dowding pointed out that once the night fighter opened fire, the bomber would take quick evasive action and would be lost in the darkness; therefore, the fighter had to have overwhelming armament, capable of destroying the bomber in the first burst. No such airplane yet existed, but the Beaufighter would soon be ready with both cannon and machine guns.

Bowen was impressed: "I had never heard such a clear and definite analysis of the fundamentals of night fighting." He was not as impressed with Professor Lindemann, who also received a demonstration of the system, but who was "quite worried about a dinner appointment in London that evening which he did not want to miss . . . and seemed to be in his usual mood of finding fault with everything and did not have a single positive suggestion to make. . . .

When he got back to London he gave us a poor report. Of all the distinguished people to whom we demonstrated airborne radar, Lindemann was the only one who was unimpressed."

The reason was that Lindemann had his own ideas and couldn't bear the thought that anyone else's might work. After his infrared scheme he came up with another disaster, code-named "Mutton," that involved dropping bombs in front of oncoming bombers, as he explained to Churchill . . .

thirty-two

LINDEMANN STARTED off by saying he would use outmoded bombers, planes the RAF didn't have any use for, which Churchill thought was brilliant. These Harrow bombers would carry 150 small bombs, or, as he called them, aerial mines, weighing just one pound apiece, each of which was attached to a large parachute by a 2,000-foot piano wire. At the other end of the wire was another smaller and furled parachute, with the bomb somewhere in the middle. A squadron of these Harrows would climb up higher than the incoming bomber formations and would cruise along in front of them. They'd then release their bombs at 200-foot intervals, and these would float down by the large parachute in front of the fleet of bombers, providing what was essentially an aerial minefield six miles long and 2,000 feet high.

When the wing of a bomber hit the wire, the impact would trigger the unfurling of the smaller parachute. The drag of the two parachutes might slow the bomber suddenly to below its flying speed, in which case it would stall and crash. If it kept flying, the bomb would slide down the wire and, upon hitting the wing, would explode—and Bob's your uncle, Lindemann explained.

Churchill loved the idea. Lindemann then pounced with his simplified mathematical analysis. The bombs would be accurately laid at 200-foot intervals, and each German bomber has a wingspan of approximately 30 feet, so one could confidently expect that at least—*at least,* he emphasized—10 percent of the bombers would be destroyed. The others, of course, would be panicked; the formation would break up, their bombs could not be accurately dropped, and in essence the entire night-bombing campaign would be brought to its knees.

Churchill chortled appreciatively. This is what he wanted, some new ideas! He turned to Dowding and told him to implement the concept immediately.

Dowding said no. The idea was ludicrous. First of all, he said, the whole concept was based on the idea that the German bombers would be flying in a massive formation, like the day bombers. But night bombers did not attack like that; it would be impossible to stay in formation at night, so instead they rambled about individually. Then how could these aerial mines be laid down accurately in front of them? You'd have to use the entire squadron of Harrows to attack a single night bomber.

Next, the entire difficulty in combating the night attacks was that the bombers couldn't be found at night, and if Dowding's fast fighters couldn't find them, how could the slow Harrow bombers? They wouldn't know where to drop their "aerial mines." Finally, the mines that missed the bombers would continue to fall to earth as normal bombs: We'd be bombing England ourselves! The entire idea made no sense at all, Dowding concluded.

This was not the attitude Churchill wanted to see in his officers. He reminded Dowding of the tank, which had also been thought to be unworkable until he, Churchill, had pushed it through. It had won the war for them. Was he now to face the same stubborn resistance to new ideas? No, by God! Work on Lindemann's Long Aerial Mine was to begin immediately, code-named "Mutton" for secrecy.

And so it did, and nothing ever came of it. One squadron eventually became operational in December 1940. They had no success until March 13, 1941, when bombers attacked Liverpool, Glasgow, and Hull. To avoid the Harrows' bombing England themselves, the RAF had decided to use the technique only over open water, and because of the lack of large German night bomber formations, single Harrows would attack single bombers—making Lindemann's original idea of an aerial minefield impossible. On this night, radar was able to place a Harrow four miles in front of, and several thousand feet above, one of the bombers a few miles off the coast near Swanage. The Harrow dropped its mines, which, radar showed, missed the bomber by several miles. But there were other Germans in the area, and the pilot of the Harrow *thought* he saw a small explosion, followed by a larger one, and then he felt a concussion. He interpreted this as the small bomb going off and then the bomber crashing into the sea, producing the concussion that jarred his airplane.

But he couldn't have felt any concussion, because he was at seventeen thousand feet, much too high to feel any concussion when the bomber hit the sea. There was no other evidence of a kill, but he was given credit for a probable. The postwar German records show no bomber lost over Swanage that night.

No other Harrow came even that close to success, and by the following fall the squadron was reassigned to other duties. "Mutton" was forgotten, after the expenditure of "millions of pounds and tens of millions of man hours."

Lindemann had other ideas, some of which were better but still wrong. He thought the air force could link its searchlights to radar beams, so that when the radar caught a bomber, the searchlight would automatically turn on and follow the bomber wherever it went, until a night fighter or antiaircraft shell would bring it down. This was an intelligent concept, recognizing that both radar and light were forms of electromagnetic radiation and could be coupled, but it showed a complete lack of knowledge of the technical intricacies involved. Once caught in the searchlight beam, the bomber would naturally take violent evasive action, and the current state of radar technology was not capable of following such maneuvers. It would take computer control to manage this, and computers of that degree of sophistication had not yet even been thought of.

Recognizing the difficulty of shooting down an airplane from the ground, he came up with another way to use radar. To hit a small, moving target like an airplane that is traveling hundreds of miles an hour and is several miles high necessitates finding its exact position, estimating correctly its future position by knowing its exact speed and direction, and knowing its exact altitude. Even if you could do that—which you couldn't in 1940—you would then have to know the exact wind conditions at all altitudes from the ground up to the target. All this is impossible, even in daylight. In 1940 the antiaircraft guns did more harm to people on the ground, when the shrapnel fell back down, as it must, than the weapons did to the enemy airplanes. The guns were fired only as a morale booster, to show the population that something was being done to stop the bombers.

Lindemann thought of including a small radar system in each antiaircraft shell, to send out a radar beam that would be reflected by the target. The shell would compare the frequency of the outgoing waves to the incoming waves to determine how close it was getting to the target. Because of the Doppler effect, the incoming waves would increase in frequency as the target was approached, and would begin to decrease as the shell sped past the target. At the moment of the switch from increasing frequency to decreasing, the shell would be at its closest possible position, and would automatically detonate.

This was a brilliant idea, but again not technically feasible in the summer of 1940. Later in the war, a combined British and American team was able to get it working in time to be put into action against the Japanese kamikaze attacks in the Pacific, but it was years too late for the Battle of Britain.

Other ideas from other people bombarded Churchill and, through him, Dowding. The death ray wouldn't go away. Liquid nitrogen was also a favorite, with suggestions ranging from freezing the Channel and thus trapping the German invasion barges (which would have allowed the Wehrmacht to step out and walk across the ice) to freezing clouds into solid bases on which antiaircraft guns could be mounted. These ideas were summarily dismissed, but some were not so obviously silly and had to be tried out. One such idea was the Turbinlite.

This concept started by noting that the basic problem was that you couldn't see the bombers at night, then went on to note that the Hurricanes Churchill had insisted on sending up were trying to avoid this problem by attacking bombers that were caught in search-light beams. This scheme didn't work because the Hurricanes and the searchlights weren't integrated and couldn't possibly be. Consequently, when a bomber was caught in the beam it would immediately take evasive action and be lost again in the darkness before the Hurri could turn on to it, aim, and fire. The suggested solution was to have the searchlights and Hurris acting as a team, and this was to be done by using Havocs.

The Douglas Havoc was a twin-engine bomber the RAF had bought from America. It was designed as a tactical bomber, acting, like the German Stuka, in support of ground troops. The problem was that the British had no ground troops in action, and so no one knew quite what to do with these Havocs.

A few of them had been converted into night fighters, but they were not fast enough to catch the Luftwaffe bombers, and the machine guns they were fitted with weren't powerful enough to shoot them down in a short burst. So the suggestion was to remove the Havocs' noses and replace them with powerful searchlights. These Turbinlite Havocs would fly together with two Hurricanes, and when radar brought them close to an enemy bomber, the Havoc would turn on its searchlight and the Hurris would shoot the thing down.

Again, Churchill was enthusiastic. Again, Dowding pointed out the obvious difficulty. The Havoc would have to hold the bomber in its searchlight beam for at least several seconds while the Hurris attacked. If it could do that, it could shoot the bomber down itself. The problem was that it couldn't do that; it wasn't fast enough or maneuverable enough. As soon as the light was turned on, the bomber would twist away and vanish.

And again Churchill growled, and Dowding shrugged, and the Turbinlite Havocs were outfitted and took to the air. Not a single bomber was brought down.

Churchill's growl died down to an ominous rumble. He explained with brooding impatience to Dowding that he, Dowding, was the head of Fighter Command. As such he was responsible for the defense of the kingdom, which was being bombed every damned night with impudent imperviousness. Had he, Dowding, nothing to suggest? Were the British helpless against the Hun?

Dowding could only repeat that yes, at the moment they were helpless. They had the solution in mind, but not yet in hand. The work on airborne radar was progressing as rapidly as possible, as was the production of the fast, heavily armed Beaufighter. A not-quite-perfect radar had been fitted into a not-quite-suitable night fighter, the Bristol Blenheim, and one success had been obtained.

It happened on the night of July 22. A Dornier was tracked by ground radar and the Fighter Interceptor Unit sent up one of its Blenheims. Ground control directed it toward the Dornier until radar contact was reported by the Blenheim's operator, who then brought the plane closer and closer, until suddenly the pilot caught a glimpse of it just overhead, silhouetted against the moon. He lifted his nose and opened fire. For some reason the Dornier continued flying straight and level (perhaps the pilot was killed with the first burst) and the Blenheim was able to pour a full ten-second burst of bullets into it. Just when he thought nothing was happening, the Dornier's fuel tank exploded and it crashed in flames.

Dowding explained that this showed the system was sound and ultimately would prove to be the answer Churchill was seeking. What the RAF needed was a mass-produced AI radar that would work consistently and a fighter with proper armament. Both were nearly ready by the end of the summer. Flight Lieutenant G. Ashfield, who had shot down the Dornier in July, was given FIU's first Beaufighter, and on the night of September 5, he took off on its first operational interception. As before, ground control found a bomber for him and brought him in close enough for his own operator to take over. Tracking him on the airborne set, he closed in—and the radar screen went blank. The equipment had failed.

And that was the situation, Dowding explained. They were almost there: The Beaufighters were now coming off the production line and the airborne radar sets were being improved daily. In another few months—

"Months?" Churchill's low rumble burst forth into a full-throated roar.

Dowding shrugged. There was nothing else he—or Churchill or Lindemann or anyone else—could do. The night-bombing problem would be solved, but not just yet. They would have to be patient.

But Churchill was not a patient man, not when the bombs continued to fall every night. As Sir John Slessor explained, "Mr. Churchill's boundless imagination and romantic spirit often soared above the dusty levels of practical reality." To him every problem must of necessity have a solution, and he wanted the solution right away. "All I wanted," he later remarked when in a more mellow mood, "was a reasonable discussion [of the problem], followed by compliance with my wishes."

At the time, when the bombs were actually falling, he was not at all in a mellow mood. By the following spring Dowding's solution was in effect; airborne radar was working, the Beaufighters were flying, and the bombers began to fall. By the summer of 1941 the Blitz was over. But Dowding's refusal to acquiesce to Churchill's demands for immediate help in the autumn of 1940, Dowding's willingness to admit his helplessness when indeed he was helpless, left a rankling bitterness in Churchill's heart.

And so it was that the Luftwaffe's mistaken bombing of London led to Churchill's revenge bombing against Berlin, which in turn led to Hitler ordering the Luftwaffe to switch its attacks from Dowding's airfields to London, which saved England but precipitated Dowding's downfall.

thirty-three

CHURCHILL had been Dowding's staunchest supporter despite—
or perhaps because of—Dowding's refusal to bend quietly to his
will. Most people were afraid of Churchill, and when he blustered
and ranted they were all too quick to give in to him, whether he was
right or wrong. What Churchill really admired was the man who
could argue with him, who was capable of disagreeing with him, but
who would do that by mustering facts and basing his arguments on
those facts.

When Dowding butted heads with him over the issue of sending
fighters to France, Churchill had been angry. But only at first.
Dowding had been right, and Churchill was thankful to him for saving England from the Luftwaffe with the fighters he had saved from
France. When the Secretary of State for Air wanted to fire Dowding,
Churchill had turned on him, telling him bluntly that Dowding was
the best man he had and was not to be dismissed.

But that was when Dowding had been right. Now, Churchill felt,
he was wrong. When Lindemann's ideas were actually tested, they
failed, but in September of 1940 those tests were in the future. What
was happening in the present was the Blitz, and Dowding was standing there saying there was nothing to be done about it. That was
unacceptable.

There were other problems brewing for Dowding. Intrigues, deep and sinister, brewing unseen in stations unknown. It began with Douglas Bader, that incredibly brave man of action but not of intellect. To give you an idea, first, of the spirit of the man:

Later in the war he was shot down over France. He baled out, breaking off one of his prosthetic legs and leaving it behind as he struggled out of the burning Spitfire, and was imprisoned by the Germans. His captors, impressed by his reputation and obvious valor, searched the wreckage and found his leg. It was bent out of shape, but they repaired it, cleaned and polished it, and brought it to him. He strapped it on, it fit, and he thanked them profusely, shaking hands with great smiles all around. That same night, as soon as all lights were out, he tied his bed sheets together into a makeshift rope, crawled out a window, climbed down, and escaped.

Upon being recaptured, he tried to talk the Germans, pilot to pilot, into letting him try out one of their Me 109s, promising just to make one circuit around the field and land. They laughed, showing that some Germans do have a sense of humor.

But all this was in the future. In the autumn of 1940, he was trying to inveigle himself past—not the Germans—but his air officer commanding, Stuffy Dowding. It happened that the adjutant of Bader's squadron, Flight Leader Peter Macdonald, was a Member of Parliament. He took Bader's cause to Harold Balfour, the Undersecretary of State for Air, who replied that it was quite wrong for a squadron adjutant to interfere in what was, after all, a matter of strategy decided by the commander in chief. Macdonald then used his parliamentary prerogative to seek an audience with Churchill.

There is no record of Churchill's response to Macdonald's plea that Dowding's strategy was wrong and was costing unnecessary casualties, but the Flight Leader's plea came at the same time that Churchill was becoming increasingly disillusioned with the way Dowding was handling the night bombing. (There is also no record of whether Macdonald took this unprecedented step on the urging of Bader or Leigh-Mallory or if he went on his own, fueled only by the persistent complaints that Bader was making in the mess.)

At any rate, what happened next was a special meeting called by Cyril Newall, Dowding's old friendly enemy and now Chief of the Air Staff, "to discuss major tactics by fighter formations, and to hear a report on the progress of night interception." The meeting was held in Newall's office, but when Newall called in sick at the last minute the chair was taken by the Deputy Chief, Sholto Douglas. (Whether Newall truly was sick or whether he wanted to disassociate himself from what was going to be a lynching is not clear.)

Do you remember Sholto Douglas? He was serving under Dowding just after the First World War, when the Air Ministry decided to court-martial him. Dowding refused to convene the court-martial, at a time when he himself was balancing on the razor edge of being fired, thus putting himself at risk but saving Douglas's career.

So here we go on October 17, 1940. Dowding showed up at the meeting expecting to hold the floor and give the Air Ministry a summary of his strategy in the battle—which, remember, he had just won—and to discuss the progress being made by the radar wizards for night interceptions. Imagine his shock when he entered the room to find, among the dozen assembled Air Marshals and Air Vice-Marshals, one lowly Squadron Leader: Douglas Bader.

Leigh-Mallory explained that he had brought him along so they could hear the views of someone who was actually doing the fighting. That may sound reasonable, but there were many other people also doing the fighting, and all present knew that Bader's view was only one side. For example, Al Deere, a wing commander and one of the highest scorers in the battle, said, "From a fighter pilot's point of view, I hold that Bader's wing concept was wrong. I know that most wing leaders agree with me, and certainly those who had the benefit of later experience." It would have been quite easy to send for Deere, or anyone else "who was actually doing the fighting," to present this point of view, but Douglas did not see fit to do so.

Instead of calling a recess to do this, or even just turning the floor over to Dowding, Sholto Douglas took the floor himself and asked the meeting to consider why enemy formations should not be met with sufficient numbers to overwhelm them. He then went on for quite some time on this proposition, essentially presenting Bader's and Leigh-Mallory's views as the prime idea and asking why it should not have been the proper cause of action. In Keith Park's words, "He asked why [Park and Dowding] had not, throughout the Battle of Britain, adopted the big wing formations which had been used so successfully by Leigh-Mallory." That is, Dowding was presented with an accusation and with the necessity to prove himself innocent of it, instead of being asked to present his own views as the focus of discussion.

Douglas then called on Bader, who repeated the false stories of the Big Wing's successes. (Keep in mind that he thought the stories were true, since the claims of enemy destroyed by the Wing were indeed impressive; it was the actuality that was not.) He pointed out the simple fact that it was better to face the enemy with equal or greater numbers, rather than with the penny-packets sent up by Dowding. He ignored, as did Leigh-Mallory, the equally simple facts that the radar warnings did not give sufficient time to assemble the Wing and get it to where it was needed, and that to have committed all of Fighter Command's resources in large, pitched battles was exactly what the Luftwaffe wanted.

Keith Park tried to answer, pointing out that most of the squadrons were equipped only with high-frequency (HF) radio instead of very-high-frequency (VHF) radio, and HF was inefficient, fading in and out, making coordinated attacks difficult if not impossible to achieve. For whatever reason or combination of reasons, he argued, the Big Wing attacks that had been carried out so far had not been successful at all. But no one seemed to be listening. Leigh-Mallory then took the floor and said he could get the Big Wing into the air and on its way in six minutes. No one asked him why, during the past summer, it had always taken more than a quarter of an hour to do so, resulting in the Wing being always too late to engage the bombers before they reached their targets. Instead, he repeated Bader's lecture on the simple values of overwhelming force, and the assembled audience very nearly broke into hearty applause.

In essence, the room was stacked, and Dowding was bushwhacked. When the minutes were circulated, they were one-sided, with all criticism of the Big Wing omitted. Park sent a correction memo to Douglas, asking that it be included in the final copy of the minutes. Douglas refused, saying that such criticisms were "inappropriate."

The official stance of the Air Ministry was, therefore, that the Battle of Britain had been mishandled. Dowding was, in Park's words, "condemned" by the meeting, and the "Wings controversy was used as a pretext for dismissing Dowding."

The meeting continued in the afternoon with a discussion of night-fighting tactics. Just three nights previously, Coventry had been demolished by a night bombing attack in which not a single bomber was brought down. This brought home in violent fashion the inadequacy of the night air defenses, which Sholto Douglas pronounced shameful. Dowding presented his view that there was nothing to be done until airborne radar and the Beaufighter were ready, and this would take another few months. Douglas replied that he could see no reason not to take action immediately with what they had. He advocated sending up Hurricanes with pilots trained to see as best they could in the dark, and waxed eloquent on the Turbinlite Havocs.

It is hard to imagine how any trained pilot could think the Turbinlite system would work. If the Havoc could track and catch a bomber, why not simply shoot it down instead of illuminating it? After all, if the Havoc shot and missed, the bomber wouldn't know anything about it, and so the Havoc could keep on trying. But as soon as the Havoc turned on the searchlight, the bomber would immediately take evasive action. The pilot of the Havoc would at the same time be blinded by the sudden light, would lose his night vision, and would never be able to find the bomber again. It was the silliest scheme imaginable.

Sending up single-seater Hurricanes was not as silly, but turned out even worse. Not only did they never shoot down a single bomber, but several pilots were killed trying to land in the dark.

Dowding had often wondered "why some senior officers in the Services show all the symptoms of mental paralysis after the age of forty-five or so." It was the sort of comment that accounted for the hostility of the Air Staff. But never mind, the two schemes were endorsed by Douglas and everyone else at the meeting. Dowding was ordered by the Air Staff to immediately implement them.

No improvement in night defense followed, and three weeks later, Dowding was fired.

In the aftermath of the greatest British victory since Waterloo, Dowding was dismissed as head of Fighter Command. In his recollections he claimed that out of the blue he received a phone call from Sir Archibald Sinclair, the Secretary of State for Air, telling him that he "was to relinquish Command immediately." Asking what was meant by "immediately," he was told "within twenty-four hours." Dowding replied that it was "absurd" to be fired like that "unless it was thought I had committed some major crime," but he was told that the decision had been taken, and that was that.

But memories are often faulty, and that is not what happened. A few months earlier, as we have seen, he was told that his retirement would take place on October 31. Nothing had been said about it since then, until he was called to a meeting with Sinclair at the Air Ministry on November 13. There he was told—in person, not by a phone call—that he was to relinquish his command, not within twenty-four hours, but within the quite reasonable time of a couple of weeks. Dowding protested, but Sinclair said only that he "had come to the conclusion that it was right to make the change." Dowding replied that he wished to talk to Churchill about it, and he did so; Churchill concurred with Sinclair.

The reasons for his dismissal have long been debated. Certainly the Big Wing and night-bombing controversies were part of it, but there were other reasons not terribly hard to discern. Why, for example, did Sholto Douglas slant the October meeting so drastically against Dowding? With the best will in the world, one might say that he honestly believed Dowding was wrong, but who was it who personally benefited when Dowding was dismissed? Meet Sholto Douglas, the new Commander in Chief of Fighter Command. (He immediately sent up Hurricanes and Turbinlite Havocs to combat the night bombers, but met with no success until airborne radar and the Beaufighter were ready the following spring.)

And why were the members of the Air Ministry so hostile to Dowding? Just look back on his history with them. He fought them every step of the way since taking over Fighter Command—for bulletproof glass in the Spitfires, for concrete runways, for underground telephone lines, for radar instead of Lindemann's infrared, for an adequate fighter defense that involved building fighters instead of bombers—and being right was no defense. He had already antagonized most of them even earlier in his career, and they were simply waiting, seething, for the excuse that Bader, Leigh-Mallory, and Coventry gave them.

Bader progressed no further in the RAF; he was a fighter pilot, not a strategist, not the stuff of air marshals. But Leigh-Mallory got his reward. When Park was fired along with Dowding, Leigh-Mallory took Park's place, later becoming head of the combined invasion air forces in 1944. His appointment, however, was not a success, and four months after D-day he was transferred to command the Allied air forces in Southeast Asia. On the flight out, his plane flew into a mountain; both he and his wife were killed.

Although Dowding had brilliantly won the Battle of Britain and saved the country from invasion, there is a word to be said for the opposition, for his removal at this time. He was, after all, past the age for retirement, the date of which had been settled before the battle began, and as one of his personal assistants remembered, "he was almost blind with fatigue; he obviously needed a long rest, he was burnt out." And although his strategy was perfect for the battle, perhaps now it was time for a change. Fighter Command was about to go on the offensive, and as it began to fight over France instead of over England, the Big Wings were the proper formations. Since Dowding's outstanding characteristic, so far as the Air Staff were concerned, was his stubbornness, one can understand how they might well have distrusted his ability to shift gears and embrace the concept he had forsworn. And although his stance on night-fighter interceptions was proved correct by future events, at the time it was certainly frustrating to be told there was nothing to be done.

Finally, there was the increasing chance of embarrassment as Dowding talked more and more openly of his rather peculiar ideas. To be sure, there were plenty of people in every country who called upon their God for help and who thought they saw evidence of divine intervention in their affairs, but when he talked of Shakespeare being the only man in the kingdom who could operate a gun, when he mentioned his conversations with his dead wife and his dead pilots—which he was beginning to do in private conversations, though not yet in public—it doesn't seem wrong to suppose that people might begin to get worried.

And so, "they just got rid of me," as he plaintively said. He left Bentley Priory as he had arrived, without brass bands, without fanfare. Sholto Douglas was shown into his office to take over the reins of Fighter Command and found Dowding working at his desk. Without looking up, Stuffy finished the letter he was writing to his chicks:

My dear Fighter Boys,

In sending you this my last message, I wish I could say all that is in my heart. I cannot hope to surpass the simple eloquence of the

Prime Minister's words, "Never before has so much been owed by so many to so few." The debt remains and will increase.

In saying goodbye to you I want you to know how continually you have been in my thoughts, and that, though our direct connection may be severed, I may yet be able to help you in your gallant fight.

Goodbye to you and God bless you all.

Air Chief Marshal Hugh Dowding November 24th 1940

When he finished, he stood up, said "Good morning" to Douglas, put on his hat, walked out of the office from which he had guided the free world to its first victory over Hitler, and faded away as old soldiers often do. He was sent on a public-relations mission to the United States and succeeded only in antagonizing the Americans by insisting that their bombers would be useless without fighter escort. When he returned, he met with Churchill, who told him that "he had never heard of my retirement until he saw it in the papers. I was so astonished that I said 'Do you mean to say that you were really never told about my retirement?' He said 'I knew nothing about it till I saw it in the papers.'"

Dowding was right to be astonished, for Churchill's claim was unbelievable. As Lord Balfour, then Under-Secretary for the Air Ministry, said, "This is pure nonsense. . . . Any Service Secretary of State would not have made a vital high command change without reference to, and prior agreement with, the Minister of Defence [i.e., Churchill]. In Sinclair's case I know that he would not have changed the AOC of an important fighter group, much less the Commander-in-Chief, without superior approval. . . . I would wager any sum that Churchill knew and had approved the change, and also the name of Dowding's successor."

In 1942 Dowding retired officially from the Royal Air Force, receiving a pension of thirteen hundred pounds yearly. The Air

Ministry refused to honor him by promotion to Marshal of the Royal Air Force, but Churchill saw to it that he was elevated to the peerage as Lord Dowding of Bentley Priory. He was asked to write an official report on the Battle of Britain, which they then never published. Instead the Ministry wrote its own history, without even mentioning his name. Churchill was infuriated by this. He wrote to Sinclair: "The jealousies and cliquism which have led to the committing of this offence are a discredit to the Air Ministry, and I do not think any other Service Department would have been guilty of such a piece of work. What would have been said if . . . the Admiralty had told the tale of Trafalgar and left Lord Nelson out of it?"

After the war, when Churchill wrote his own history of the struggle, he seems to have forgotten to ask himself that same question. In his tale of the Battle of France, he ignores Dowding's insistence on sending no more Hurricanes across the Channel, writing only that "I decided to ask . . . for the despatch of six more [Hurricane squadrons] . . . and that was the final limit." If Churchill had had his way, the valiant Few who won the Battle of Britain would have been the futile Too Few who would have lost it. (Dowding later commented only that "you couldn't expect the man to admit that he nearly lost us the Battle of Britain before it began.")

Many years later, at the premiere of the movie *The Battle of Britain*, Dowding—crippled by arthritis—was wheeled into the theater, and the audience stood up and cheered. At the following Royal Performance there was no such reaction. The reason was that at the first showing the audience was made up of the former pilots, his chicks; at the second, the audience was composed of the high muckety-mucks who had gotten rid of him.

And so Dowding finally retired—to begin what he considered the most important mission in his life.

thirty-four

ON THE EVENING of May 21, 1944, a British Lancaster bomber piloted by a young man named Max Whiting did not return from a mission over Germany. His wife, Muriel, received the standard telegram telling her that her husband was "missing in action." The months passed by, and neither she nor Max's father could get any further information.

She woke early one morning to find a "tall, thin man in grey flannel trousers and a bluish shirt . . . [with] greyish hair and very blue eyes. I knew him at once . . . he was someone I loved dearly. . . . I laughed with happiness and called to him, 'Hugh' . . ."

And then he faded away. Muriel had no idea who this man was until several weeks later, when she spotted in a Sunday paper an article written by Dowding, along with his picture. It seemed to be the same man, but she "dismissed the entire incident as too fantastic for words."

By this time Dowding had published a book, *Many Mansions,* in which he spoke of matters spiritual. He wrote, for example, that "the Earth is the centre of a series of hollow spheres each bigger than the last. . . . Each of these spheres represents a state of spiritual development a little in advance of that below." But of more interest to

Muriel and her father-in-law was Dowding's witness to life after death, as in the tale of a Polish pilot who was shot down:

"Yes, I am shot down and out. I have survived many fights, but not this one . . . I cannot control the aircraft . . . I fall quite consciously. I get up without any pain . . . I wander about, I feel well . . . my leg is healed. I go to the French peasants and ask for help, but they do not see me . . . I see colours everywhere . . . I pray for help and it comes to me. Someone looking very strange and yet quite like ourselves comes to me, he tells me not to mind the change, it is best for all."

Mr. Whiting urged Muriel to write to Dowding, to ask if he could find out anything about Max's fate, either through official channels or by his contacts with the other world. She received "a kindly reply," and then several months passed with no further word. Finally another letter came from Dowding, inviting her to come to lunch at his club, the United Services Club in Pall Mall, and to meet his medium.

They had lunch with the medium, and after she left, Dowding invited Muriel to stay for tea. She looked at him and, in that moment, "I knew." He was the man who used to appear in her dreams when she was a little girl, calming her nightmares and promising to marry her. He was the man with "greyish hair and very blue eyes," who had appeared to wake her with laughter after Max disappeared. She gasped, "Hugh!" and he smiled kindly.

Three days later he wrote again, setting up an appointment for a séance with the medium, at which time Max's death was "confirmed." Sometime later, after many meetings, old Stuffy told her he loved her dearly, and though he was old enough to be her father, he hoped she would marry him. And so she did.

Years later they were talking about his reputation for communicating with the dead and how it had led many widows, or wives of missing airmen, to write to him asking for help. Muriel asked if he had made a practice of inviting them all to lunch, as he had her.

"Only you," he said. "Because your husband asked me to."

He explained that he had written to invite her because Max had contacted him through a medium, and had told him to ask her out to lunch. "You will like her," he had promised.

Secure now in a loving marriage, Dowding set out to bring to the world the promise of goodness and fulfillment that his knowledge of the universal truth proclaimed. "The facts which I do know, I know with that complete certainty of personal conviction which nothing can shake. Among these are the facts that I am in constant personal communication with my wife and other relations and friends who have gone ahead of me into the next stage of life."

Even before this he had made several attempts to spread the word. In 1943 he published a series of articles in the *Sunday Pictorial* telling of the messages he received from the beyond, and in October 1942 he talked openly to a gathering of the Few. It was at a dinner party at the Savoy Hotel, given by a group of American fliers. They had invited the veterans of the Battle of Britain, and Dowding was the guest of honor. Although he had previously spoken of his beliefs to several of his chicks in personal conversations, this was the first time anyone remembers hearing him speak out in public. As one of them, Hugh Dundas, remembers, "All of us in that room felt the greatest respect and affection for our old chief, but his totally unexpected revelations, when he told us over the port that he was in regular communication with many of our friends who had been killed in action and that they were all in good shape and quite happy, had a macabre effect on the company. I am afraid that the reaction of most of us at that time was that 'the old boy had gone round the bend.' . . . The thought of our former colleagues lurking mysteriously around us in that room at the Savoy, waiting for us to get in touch with them, tended to charge the atmosphere and quicken our thirsts. Thus it was a collection of fighter pilots in an advanced state of alcoholic hilarity which was discharged at a late hour upon the night clubs of London."

Dowding wrote books, pamphlets, and newspaper articles, striving to bring his visions to the people. When he entered the House of Lords, he was greeted warmly by his old antagonist, Boom Trenchard, who had been the first—and, until Dowding made his appearance—the only RAF man to become a peer of the realm. "We need you, Stuffy," he said. "At last we've got another voice here in the Lords to support the RAF."

He was wrong. Dowding never spoke in defense of the air force, never pushed a proposal for its expansion. He dropped the air force as completely as they had dropped him, the only difference being that he didn't do it out of spite or for personal advantage. He had more important issues to push, and his only connection with the RAF now was in helping dead pilots find their way to eternity and comforting with the Truth those left behind. His only concern now was to spread the Word. He made ardent speeches in the House of Lords, but they were for vegetarianism or against vivisection, explaining that all lives are holy and eternal.

He explained that death is a gradual process, during which time the astral body leaves the etheric double, "floating near the latter till the 'silver cord' (which is a very real thing) is broken . . . and the etheric double is discarded with the physical body" while the true being goes on to the astral world. He taught that "the most improbable thing about fairies and gnomes is that they are so exactly like our conceptions . . . formless little blobs of light when they are about their work of tending or nourishing the plants; but they have little minds and the power of clothing their thought-forms in etheric material." He had no doubt that flying saucers were real and extraterrestrial.

He received messages from Sir Gerald Lock, a wealthy Guards subaltern who died a hundred years ago and who was upset because his descendants didn't treat the Irish as lovingly as he had done.

Dowding's wife Muriel shared in all these beliefs and didn't quibble when Hugh spent loving time with his first (dead) wife.

He discovered the secret of perpetual motion and testified to the goodness of God, though not to conventional religion. He talked to people from Atlantis, "the home of the Fourth Root race . . . [whose] evil caused volcanic catastrophes in 10,000 B.C. The survivors fled to Egypt and built the pyramids." He advocated magnetic healing rays to cure gout and arthritis.

All to little avail. No one was interested. In 1943, he wrote plaintively to a friend that "5 publishers have now refused my book." Eventually, his books were published by the Psychic Press or other small publishers, but he was preaching to the choir. He became a hero to the psychic community, but was regarded as a nut by everyone else. With his quiet sense of humor, he himself liked to tell the story of two Americans who heard him give a spiritualism lecture. One of them asked his neighbor, "Is this Lord Dowding any relation to Sir Hugh Dowding who fought the Battle of Britain?" His friend replied, "He must be his father. In England the son of a Lord is a Sir." The first man added, "Gee, I wonder what a smart guy like him would think of his old man going off the rails that way."

He knew this was the majority opinion, but it didn't matter; he never wavered. Together with his living wife, Muriel, he fought against cruelty to animals and vivisection experiments, founding with her the charity Beauty Without Cruelty to advocate cosmetics production without animal experiments. With his dead wife, Clarice, he comforted and guided the dead through the astral plane to their peace.

In 1970, at the age of eighty-eight and with all the controversies that surrounded him unresolved, he left this life to join the spirit world he so loved and where—according to all the séances at which he has since materialized and the mediums throughout the world who still adore him—he continues to live happily ever after.

Epilogue

If England had lost the Battle of Britain, the subsequent history of World War II and indeed the second half of the twentieth century would have been drastically different. That battle was directed by Hugh Dowding from before its beginning—with the development of the RAF's first monoplane eight-gunned fighters and radar, together with their supporting components—through the Battle of France and his stand against Churchill, all the way to its victorious conclusion. Yet he has received little thanks.

Aside from one or two gracious comments, such as acknowledging his defeat of the Scandinavian German bombers with the comment "genius in the art of war," Churchill in his histories largely ignored Dowding's contributions. One should note that these histories, although admired by much of the world, were not admired so universally by the military professionals. A staff member of the Imperial Defence College wrote to General Sir Hastings Ismay: "I've been reading Winston's book. Of course, he doesn't *really* understand modern war."

Which may have been slightly unfair since Churchill didn't write much of whatever he signed his name to. In particular, his history of the battle was largely ghostwritten: Ismay, writing to Air Marshal Sir John Slessor, said: "The Battle of Britain figures in his next volume.

So far as I remember, he got the story written for him at piece rates by an ex-airman Don, recommended to me before I left for India, but whose name I have forgotten."

You might reflect that since he took credit—and the Nobel Prize—for these books, he should also take the blame for their inaccuracies. At any rate, despite lambasting the Air Ministry for neglecting Dowding in its official account of the battle, he himself diminished Dowding's contributions, particularly when acknowledging them would have necessitated diminishing his own. And such is Churchill's reputation that many authors who followed him have accepted his lead.

William Manchester's massive Churchill biography doesn't mention the contretemps about depleting Fighter Command by sending Hurricanes to France. In another recent history of that battle, Ernest May's *Strange Victory*, Dowding's name is not even mentioned. When the Marquess of Londonderry wrote a history of the development of the RAF up through the Battle of Britain (*Wings of Destiny*), he mentioned Dowding in only two sentences. Another story, *Battles over Britain*, by Guy de la Bedoyère, doesn't mention Dowding at all, and barely mentions radar.

It is in the reminiscences of the fighter pilots themselves that Dowding stands tall today. Again and again their trust, gratitude, and—yes, even affection for old Stuffy—come through loud and clear.

Flying Officer Chris Foxley-Norris: "He was a father figure. You felt that as long as his hand was on the tiller all was going to be well."

Squadron Leader Sandy Johnston: "Great names would later arise ... and great battles won. ... But they were all courtesy of Stuffy Dowding. None of those people would even have been heard of if Stuffy hadn't been there, if he hadn't won the Battle of Britain."

Squadron Leader George Darley: "Dowding was too nice a chap and he came up against a gang of thugs. Leigh-Mallory was very jealous of him. . . ."

Nor was it only the pilots. Elizabeth Quayle, a WAAF Operations Room plotter at Bentley Priory, recalled: "We all admired our Stuffy enormously. We had great loyalty to him. I think you might call it affection. . . ."

There stand today two sculptures of Dowding in London. One is a full statue erected in 1958 in front of the Church of St. Clement Dane, the "official" church of the Royal Air Force, in the Strand. It was commissioned not by the British government but by private sub-scription of the Battle of Britain pilots. The other sculpture is in the Belgrave Square lobby of the Spiritualist Association of Great Britain.

When World War II came to America, my father became an air-raid warden in Philadelphia. He would put on his white armband and take up his flashlight and go off into the neighborhood to make sure no lights were slipping out of un-blacked-out windows to help guide German bombers to their destination. I, being a smart-ass kid at the time, laughed.

"Hitler doesn't have any aircraft carriers," I told him, "and there are no German bombers with enough range to cross the Atlantic, let alone get back home again. There's no way we can be bombed."

He told me about the newspapers reporting Roosevelt's warning that German bombers could reach us from Africa, and I, with the assurance of youth, replied that Roosevelt didn't know what he was talking about.

I was a snot-nosed, impertinent kid, but I was right. Roosevelt—or the newspapers—were only trying to scare us into taking the war seriously. There was no way Philadelphia could be bombed from the air in 1942.

But in the spring of 1941, Willy Messerschmitt had been awarded a contract for a four-engine bomber capable of carrying four thou-sand pounds of bombs over a distance of nine thousand miles; that is, the bomber would be capable of bombing America and returning to Berlin. Its official designation was the *Amerikabomber*.

The Amerikabomber first flew a year later, but failed to achieve its specified range and airspeed. Design work continued. On May 16, 1942, Hermann Göring called a conference at Luftwaffe headquarters to plan a new series of aircraft capable of bombing American cities, with New York as the primary target. These included jet bombers and flying wing designs, far in advance of anything the United States had.

In the spring of 1944, American and British bombers, flying from bases in England, destroyed the Amerikabomber prototypes and the factory set up for its production. The more advanced designs by the firms of Focke-Wulf, Fokker, and Horten were similarly wrecked by the Allied bombing.

Without Britain as a base, there would have been no such bombing of Germany, and the Amerikabombers would have been in full production. Without the bombing of Germany from bases in England, the full strength of the Luftwaffe would have been available for the Eastern Front, and Russia would have been defeated. (When asked by Russian captors after the war which was the turning point, Stalingrad or Moscow, General von Runstedt shook his head. "The Battle of Britain," he replied.)

If the Luftwaffe had prevailed over England, by 1945 the Amerikabombers would have been flying across the Atlantic, competing with Werner von Braun's V-10 rocket in the destruction of American cities.

So, thank you, Stuffy. Wherever you are.

* * *

If he had been only the man who pushed through the development of the eight-gun monoplane fighters that won the battle . . . If he had been only the first military man to understand the promise of radar, and who had the faith to base his defense on it . . . If he had been only the man who fought to implement the supporting facilities—the Ops Rooms, Controllers, WAAFs, and complex underground telephone system—that made it possible for radar to work . . . If he had been, finally, only the man who understood what was at stake in the battle—as his adversary, Hermann Göring, did not—and who thus set in place the strategy that won . . .

If he had been any one of these men he would take his place among the heroes of the Second World War. But he did it all.

* * *

The peace and happiness of thousands of millions unborn, through countless generations to come, depended directly on his decisions.

—C. S. Forester

* * *

To him, the people of Britain and of the free world owe largely the way of life and the liberties they enjoy today.

—Inscription on Dowding's tomb
in Westminster Abbey

* * *

Acknowledgments

This book began a long incubation more than twenty years ago in Edinburgh when I happened to pick up a copy of Richard Hillary's *Last Enemy*, and then, browsing through the library stacks in Miami, stumbled into the weird world of Dowding's *Lychgate*.

Although there has been no biography of Lord Dowding for the past thirty-five years, a vast compendium of journal articles, histories, biographies, and autobiographies covers the Battles of France and Britain from every conceivable point of view. The best of these are listed in the Bibliography. Unfortunately, most of them are either out of print or unpublished in the United States. A good university library is mandatory, and I would like to thank the staffs at the University of Miami, Southern Illinois University, and Rice University, as well as those at the Snow Library, Orleans, Massachusetts. I also thank the Trustees and staffs at the Liddell Hart Centre for Military Archives at Kings College, London, and the Royal Air Force Museum at Hendon. Dowding's personal quotes are from his books, unpublished correspondence, and the two biographies listed in the Bibliography. Personal recollections from Gerald Pollinger, Johnny Kent, Denis Robinson, Mrs. "Skip" Wilkins, and Taffy Bowen were enormously valuable, as was the help of the staffs at Bentley Priory, Bawdsey Manor Hall, RAF Coltishall, and the Imperial War

Museum at Duxford aerodrome. I am also grateful that Her Majesty's Government did not totally dismantle Kenley aerodrome before I was able to visit it. (Hawkinge and many of the others are now cornfields or estate housing developments.)

While the military facts of the summer of 1940 are now well-known, their interpretation remains ambiguous—as can be seen from even a quick perusal of the bibliographic sources—and they are sometimes conveniently and selectively forgotten. The story told here is, I believe, correct, but one should bear in mind the classic description first applied to cosmologists but equally pertinent to historians: often in error, seldom in doubt.

My wife, Leila L., was, as always, an anchor in a swirling morass of mud.

Bibliography

DOWDING BIOGRAPHIES

Collier, Basil. *Leader of the Few.* London: Jarrolds, 1957.

Wright, Robert. *The Man Who Won the Battle of Britain.* New York: Scribners, 1969.

AUTOBIOGRAPHIES

Bader, Douglas. *Fight for the Sky.* New York: Doubleday, 1973.

Balfour, Harold. *Wings over Westminster.* London: Hutchinson, 1973.

Bowen, E. G. *Radar Days.* Bristol: Adam Hilger, 1987.

Douglas, Sholto. *Years of Combat.* London: Collins, 1963.

———. *Years of Command.* London: Collins, 1966.

Dowding, Lady Muriel. *The Psychic Life of Muriel.* Wheaton, IL: Theosophical Publishing House, 1980.

Dundas, Hugh. *Flying Start.* London: Stanley Paul, 1988.

Grinnell-Milne, Duncan. *Wind in the Wires.* London: Hurst and Blackett, 1933.

Hillary, Richard. *The Last Enemy.* London: Pan, 1969. Also published in the United States as *Falling Through Space.*

Ismay, Hastings. *The Memoirs of General the Lord Ismay.* London: Heinemann, 1960.

Jones, R. V. *The Wizard War*. New York: Coward, McCann & Geoghegan, 1978.

Macmillan, Harold. *The Blast of War, 1939–1945*. London: Macmillan, 1967.

Slessor, Sir John. *The Central Blue*. London: Cassell, 1956.

Radar

Buderi, Robert. *The Invention That Changed the World*. Boston: Little, Brown, 1997.

Fisher, David E. *A Race on the Edge of Time*. New York: McGraw-Hill, 1987.

Kinsey, Gordon. *Orfordness*. Lavenham, Suffolk: Terence Dalton, 1981.

———. *Bawdsey*. Lavenham, Suffolk: Terence Dalton, 1983.

Rowe, E. P. *One Story of Radar*. London: Cambridge University Press, 1948.

Watson-Watt, Robert. *Three Steps to Radar*. New York: Dial Press, 1959.

Biographies

Birkenhead, Earl of. *The Prof in Two Worlds*. New York: Collins, 1961.

Clark, Ronald W. *The Rise of the Boffins*. London: Phoenix House, 1962.

Fort, Adrian. *Prof: The Life of Frederick Lindemann*. London: Jonathan Cape, 2003.

Orange, Vincent. *Sir Keith Park*. London: Methuen, 1984.

Saward, Dudley. *Bomber Harris*. New York: Doubleday, 1985.

Churchillania

Churchill, Winston. *The Second World War*. Vol. 2, *Their Finest Hour*. London: Ebenezer Baylis and Sons, 1949.

Colville, John Rupert. *Footprints in Time*. London: Collins, 1976.

———. *Winston Churchill and His Inner Circle*. New York: Wyndham Books, 1981.

———. *The Fringes of Power: 10 Downing Street Diaries, 1939–1955*. New York: Norton, 1985.

Gilbert, Martin. *Winston Churchill: The Wilderness Years.* London: Macmillan, 1981.

Jenkins, Roy. *Churchill.* New York: Farrar Straus and Giroux, 2001.

Lewin, Ronald. *Churchill as Warlord.* Newcastle: Batsford, 1973.

Taylor, A. J. P., et al. *Churchill Revised: A Critical Assessment.* New York: Dial Press, 1969.

RAF HISTORIES

Addison, Paul, and Jeremy Crang, eds. *The Burning Blue.* London: Pimlico, 2000.

Bungay, Stephen. *The Most Dangerous Enemy.* London: Aurum, 2000.

Dean, Maurice. *The Royal Air Force and Two World Wars.* London: Cassell, 1979.

Fuller, J. F. C. *Towards Armageddon.* London: Lovat Dickson, 1937.

Gelb, N. *Scramble.* London: Michael Joseph, 1986.

Jacobs, Paul, and Robert Lightsey. *Battle of Britain Illustrated.* New York: McGraw-Hill, 2003.

Johnson, J. E. "Johnny." *Glorious Summer.* London: Stanley Paul, 1990.

Johnson, J. E. "Johnny," and Laddie Lucas. *Winged Victory.* London: Stanley Paul, 1995.

Mason, Francis K. *Battle over Britain.* London: McWhirter Twins, 1969.

Price, Alfred. *Blitz on Britain, 1939–1945.* London: Ian Allen, 1977.

Ray, John. *The Battle of Britain.* London: Cassell, 1994.

Richards, Denis. *Royal Air Force, 1939–45.* Vol. 1, *The Fight at Odds.* London: Her Majesty's Stationery Office, 1953.

Terraine, John. *The Right of the Line.* London: Hodder & Stoughton, 1985.

Townsend, Peter. *Duel of Eagles.* London: Weidenfeld and Nicolson, 1970.

Willis, John. *Churchill's Few.* London: Michael Joseph, 1985.

Wood, Derek, and Derek Dempster. *The Narrow Margin.* London: Tri-Service Press, 1990.

Wykeham, Peter. *Fighter Command.* New York: Arno, 1980.

Luftwaffe Histories

Bekker, Cajus. *Angriffshöhe 4000.* Hamburg: G. Stalling, 1964.

Herwig, Dieter, and Heinz Rode. *Luftwaffe Secret Projects, Strategic Bombers, 1935–1945.* Leicester: Midland Publishing, 2000.

Spiritualism

Dowding, Hugh. *Twelve Legions of Angels.* London: Jarrolds, 1946.

———. *Lychgate.* London: Rider, 1945.

———. *Many Mansions.* London: Psychic Book Club, 1950.

———. *The Dark Star.* London: Museum Press, 1951.

Stein, Gordon. *The Sorcerer of Kings.* Buffalo: Prometheus, 1993.

Miscellany

Dahl, Roald. *Over to You.* Middlesex: Penguin, 1973.

Inwood, Stephen. *A History of London.* New York: Carroll and Graf, 1998.

Sassoon, Siegfried. "Base Details." In *Counter-Attack and Other Poems.* New York: E. P. Dutton & Company, 1918.

Snow, C. P. *Science and Government.* Cambridge, MA: Harvard University Press, 1961.

Journals

Groopman, A. L. "The Battle of Britain and the Principles of War." *Aerospace Historian* (September 1971): 138–144.

Haslam, E. B. "How Lord Dowding Came to Leave Fighter Command." *Journal of Strategic Studies* 4, no. 2 (1981): 175–186.

Unpublished Sources

Swords, Sean S. "A Technical History of the Beginnings of Radar." Paper, Trinity College, Dublin, 1983.

Liddell Hart Archives for Military History, King's College, Strand Campus, London

Eadon, Nicholas P.: Correspondence.

Ismay, General Sir Hastings: ISMAY 2/3/105–106.

Liddell Hart Correspondence: LH 1/245/1–2, LH 1/245/12, LH 1/245/25.

Royal Air Force Museum, Hendon: Papers of 1st Baron Dowding of Bentley Priory

AC71/17/1–3: AOC Trans-Jordan and Palestine, 1929–1930.

AC71/17/4–25: AOC Fighter Command, 1936–1940.

AC71/17/26: Reports on Night Interception Trials, 1940.

AC71/17/27: British Air Commission, Washington, 1940–1941.

AC71/17/28–50: Retirement Correspondence, 1942–1970.

AC95/124/1: Photocopied Correspondence.

MF10086/1–10: Microfilmed Documents.

Index